Maid Maren's Memories

Maren Dancer

Contents

Page Left Blank Intentionally

Chapter 1
Family Origins And Influence

I'm guessing that the reason I initially started writing this book was more to vent my feelings and find an escape than actually to publish it. At this time in my life, I had a lot of problems going on, and I could not, for the life of me, cope with all of them without becoming a bundle of nerves. Given all this, plus a growing desire to write was the real impetus for this book.

However, by now, it has grown well beyond that starting point. When I initially decided to write about my life, I began, chronologically, to pick out stories that jumped out of my memory. This orderly progression shifted to a more haphazard one as I got into things - more by related topics. Now, a few years later, I'm revamping the entire book according to phases of my life and the threads that have run throughout.

"Family Influence..."

The strength of my family's influence has shown up, both consciously and unconsciously, throughout my life...so "family" seems an appropriate starting place in my story to give you a good idea where I have come from.

The people in my family, who have inspired me, go back to my grandparents' generation, including my mother's stepfather. My father's parents were both born in Ireland and moved to Canada after they were married - and they were both gone by the time I was born. My Dad was the only one in his family who moved out west. In summers as a youngster, we did spend a bit of time on the two Saskatchewan farms of Dad's sister who married a local farmer, and his brother who had taken over the family homestead…and much less time in California with a 2nd sister who married an American businessman. Therefore, the influence of my dad's family was more from a distance.

Whereas, my mother's family was very available to me as I grew up, so they had much more of an impact on my life than did my father's family. My Grandmother was born in England, and her husband was killed in the war when the two girls were young. My Mom was the elder of the two, and the younger one was Aunt Lil. After a year or so on their own, my Grandmother (upon her brother's invitation to accompany him and his wife), took my Mom and Aunt Lil to Canada to the Canadian prairies. That turned out to be the beginning of a new life - Grandma married a Canadian farmer, and she and my mom and aunt settled with their new dad on his farm in Saskatchewan. Four more children were born.

Meanwhile, my mother became a teacher. In the first township that she was posted, she met my Dad, who was back home from university. It was the Great Depression of the 1920s, and there was no work in his field of expertise even though he had obtained three degrees: B.A., B.Sc., B.Com., leaning heavily towards Economics. So, he had decided to help out his brother on the family homestead for a while.

When my mother arrived at Dad's Saskatchewan town to teach, they instantly fell in love, and within the year, Mom had said "yes" to Dad's proposal. Because Dad didn't ultimately want to settle down as a farmer, he decided to move, alone, to Vancouver to find work. Then he planned to send for his beloved, marry her and settle down in the city - where his degrees had prepared him to work. And he did. For his first couple of years, he and my mom ran a corner store that he bought. Next, he sold cars, and I think he sold life insurance too. But it was his next job as a bookkeeper for a drug company that got him closer to his goal of becoming a Chartered Accountant.

Within a few years, his dream job opened up - a Chartered Accountancy firm offered to take Dad on to article with them (like an apprenticeship), and he was on his way. When he finished his articling and his exams to become a Chartered Accountant, he prepared to open up his own firm. He did that within a year, with the help of his new partner - the gold medalist of that year! He was now settled in the career that satisfied him for his working lifetime!

They weren't long in Vancouver before Mom's sister, Aunt Lil, followed her sister. She had been a clerk in a department store, and at her workplace, she met and fell in love with a fellow worker. They both moved to Vancouver to be married - with her sister and brother-in-law standing up for them. What drew my uncle to Vancouver was the same reason as my father's - Vancouver was the place to be to get into his dream career of becoming a machinist (his dream also lasted for a lifetime, like my father's did). Of course, the plus was to live near Aunt Lil's sister and their brother-in-law. I dearly loved spending time with my aunt, uncle, and three cousins, who were my sister's and my frequent playmates. As for my four Saskatchewan aunts and uncles, they were a great source of inspiration for me too - all were hard workers, following their dreams. Mom's older brother was in the Air Force, traveled a lot, and was constantly back and forth between France and Ottawa - so we rarely saw him.

Both sisters were in Vancouver for a short time…but one soon fell in love with an American Aeronautical Engineer and moved with him to the States. Her other sister was a secretary, and one of her jobs took her to a small town on Vancouver Island where she met and married the company's accountant - and of course, settled down there. She only moved back to Vancouver with my uncle once they were retired. Therefore, we rarely saw either of them…but particularly my American aunt.

My Mom's youngest brother had agreed to take over and run the family farm allowing his father to retire. However, my uncle did not stick to his profession (unlike his father/my grandfather). That was because, for him, farming was a tough job physically - working for long hours in all weather…from scorching sun to freezing rain to snowstorms. It was also tough emotionally - often facing the loss of livestock and crops with very little money to show for it.

Farming, in the end, did not turn out to be his idea of an ideal lifestyle. He had sold the farm by the time I had finished high school, and he and his family moved to Vancouver to live near the rest of his family (siblings and parents). He soon opened up his own barbershop - and later joined the nearby school board's janitorial staff. He was a living example for me of a person whose first dream didn't work out, and who just kept going. His ultimate dream was to support his family to live their dreams…and this kept him moving strongly and cheerfully forward.

My grandma and grandpa were the constant driving force that insisted on regular family gatherings. The family members who lived locally would get together for special holidays such as Thanksgiving, Christmas, and Easter egg hunts, plus special family occasions such as birthdays and summer picnics.

In addition to these regular gatherings, ever since I was a young girl, we used to have an annual reunion on my mother's side of the family when the two siblings who lived far to the east in Canada and in the mid-USA plus the

Saskatchewan contingency would also come (in the early days until first my grandparents and then my uncle with his wife and children moved here). It used to take place in my hometown of Vancouver - we had our favorite park that we always went to for our reunion. There were huge trees, a small swimming pool, trapeze bars, and rings and barbeque pits - it was perfect! And even more perfect was that one of my uncles was a fishing hobbyist, and he always supplied the fish for the annually expanding park barbeque. For the non-fish lovers, there were usually some hamburgers and hotdogs (mostly for the kids).

These family reunions helped all of us maintain contact, along with the added benefit of being able to connect with every one of the younger additions to the family since the previous gathering. I remember going to these reunions when I was quite young…and we were still going there when I was seventy, although, that year may have been our last reunion because we were losing too many of my Mom's siblings and spouses or they were not able to make their annual flight from Ottawa or the States.

Along with being so amazing and inspiring, my grandparents and their family also lived to outstandingly ripe ages. The first to pass away was not my mother, even though she was the eldest, but actually was her younger brother. Towards the end, he was bound to a wheelchair and died in his 60s, so one can call him the weak link. Maybe it was due to stress, or maybe it was due merely to the expiration date on his human body (a date that we all seem to have…but often live like we don't). The youngest of the four siblings is still alive at this writing. My aunt has just recently turned 90 - her husband, 92. Except for the younger brother, the other siblings were all in their 90s when they passed away.

All these people inspired me, even more now, as my own age feels very close to theirs. Once I became older, I found myself spending more time with them. I now know that I was among the more fortunate to have inherited the family that I did! Negative family dynamics such as feuds and quarrels were foreign to the family model that I grew up in. We all love one another dearly, and it reflects in our caring attitude towards each other.

Even if there was an instance where one of us thought unkindly of another family member, we kept it to ourselves. My sister and I would often argue with each other - like normal siblings - but always just petty issues that were not carried forward past the end of the day…and besides, our parents did not let us get very far with that kind of thing! That influence, alone, has often stood me in good stead in my adult life. I am slow to get riled up about things - and especially with people. Just as important, I am quick to clean it up - and this training I received threefold: from my family's principles and example, for sure - but additionally, from my churches' teaching for a quarter of a century and also from my personal development courses' training.

Another area of influence that I grew up experiencing, first-hand, was that having a vision, a dream, a "raison d'etre" is a guiding light, making people strong, giving them direction in adversity, helping them to never let anything bring them down – and to always keep going…no matter what. In the olden days, people didn't have access to the sophisticated knowledge on "vision' and "dreams" that you and I do… having grown up in an era where these are encouraged as a "must" in order to be in control of our lives - and not be victims. These words, "vision" and "dreams" are almost household words today, in the 20th century. There have even been famous movies made such as "The Secret" and "Field of Dreams" and Coach Carter…about the importance of "vision"! However, my family lived according to these principles in the early to mid-19th century!

"My Only Sibling, My Sister…"

Before closing this chapter, I wish to acknowledge my only sibling, my sister, who was another major influence in my life. We were both strong people with a large circle of influence…just in very different ways - so different, in fact, that I didn't realize until well along in my adulthood that I was also strong and intelligent and influential. I thought it was only her - and I did much personal development over the years regarding my blindness in this area!

She had a strong sense of good money management and was great at planning and saving her money - all of which allowed her to achieve financial goals and dreams all along in her life.

She made a strong and daring career choice and became a doctor - at a time when female doctors were not yet accepted as equals. She met a Ph.D. doctor in genetics (which was also the field she was on the medical side). They lived together for a couple of years before they were married, long before this was an acceptable practice. She pioneered amniocentesis (a prenatal test to help discover birth defects while in the embryo stage of pregnancy) and spoke about that all over the world. She retired at 51 because she had brilliantly realized - and persuaded her husband - that they could live on his salary and invest hers. Also, they renovated each home they lived in, so their home would increase in value - to name only a couple of ways they leveraged their money. It is solely due to her help in my late forty's - when she strongly suggested some changes in my investment approach (or lack thereof) - that I was able to retire as well as I have.

If I had continued on my path, I would still be working - as many seniors are, and I am not, thanks to her! I am particularly grateful for all she has taught me about making, and following, budgets and making (and keeping updated) a Will, as well as creating a Living Will to help my family and doctors in the event that they are faced with difficult choices at the end of my life.

The most special connection my sister and I have shared is our love of music. We both learned to play the piano...excelled in fact...which showed up in our adult years. One of our earlier teachers, God bless her, had introduced us to the world of playing duets, which well into our adult years, became instead, largely two piano duos. In our forties, we each purchased a second piano, and no matter who visited who, we would play our beloved two-piano works. I remember one memorable holiday when she came to visit me in Vancouver. For a whole week, we spoke very little to each other except from our piano benches…for a piano break!

Chapter 2
Commitment To My Health

As you have read through the chapters, it might seem that I am always concerned about my health. The reason being that throughout my life, I have faced many illnesses and even a few major health conditions. For many years - say between ages eight and twenty-five - my health seemed stable, but the ten-year period between 25 and 35 was the worst period for my health.

When I came out of this, I was stable again for the next 40 years. Allergies - or sensitivities - still seemed to be the main source of my health problems. Of course, allergies are a symptom of deeper issues and are always challenging to deal with because they are invisible. Mostly, in desperation, I ended up dealing with them at the surface level, i.e., coughs, earaches, sinus infections, headaches, rashes, and other secondary symptoms.

Now, in my 70's, I know that it takes money for a good treatment, plus attentiveness to diet and lifestyle, in order to get the most out of food and to prevent an allergic reaction. At that point, at 29, I knew next to nothing about the relationship between the food I ate and my health…I had no idea that the chemicals that cause an allergic reaction could be found in foods.

A Turning Point (With the Help of a Doctor in Santa Barbara)

The fall of '66 became the beginning of a downward turn in my health when we moved to Santa Barbara for my husband's four years of master's and doctoral studies. Our oldest child was three years old, while our youngest child was only six months. It was then that I found the stress of being away from family to be considerable. For the first year, I played and led a choir until it became too much for me. My health was getting worse, and I had lost the verve with which I was used to enjoying my life.

After a simple day's work of looking after my children and my home, I was left feeling tired. Exertion seemed to lead to my developing rashes and feeling dizzy and moody much of the time. It seemed like most of my days were spent in bed, and I was constantly dealing with either a cold or the flu. Like all students, we were financially stretched. Unlike most students, we had two children to take care of. I was transcribing tapes at night after the children were in bed (my husband had picked up the job and I did the work). Then for the next couple of years, I was typing and proofing my husband's thesis. The sheer stress of it all led to a downward spiral of my health over the 4-year period.

I will go back to when I was 29 years old. It was about a year after we had moved to Santa Barbara for my husband's doctoral studies.

That was the year that our doctor diagnosed me with hypoglycemia. A way to describe this condition is that I would eat something, after which my energy would soon spike, and then shortly after, I would feel my energy plummet. The result was that I was very moody and frustrated a lot. I did not have much resistance to colds and often experienced flu-like symptoms, which put me in bed a lot of the time.

That year, I followed my doctor's recommended program, which mainly was some medicine (to prevent diabetes - which I never did understand because I had hypoglycemia, another name for low blood sugar, whereas diabetes is about high blood sugar). He recommended a high protein diet and no stimulants (medicine or alcohol).

Vegetables and fruit (only dietetically sweetened) were okay but not a necessity in the diet (later, I was appalled by the ignorance about health that the diet displayed - but not at that time. This made me feel much better, at least for a while (apparently most new diets, even if not the best for the condition, will make a person feel better initially) …but not for long. Within a year, I began experiencing dizzy spells and moodiness again. I asked my doctor for a retest.

I was scared of what he'd find. As it turned out, I was right…my glycemic index was seriously high again. I was not totally surprised, since I'd had an inkling of this, but still, this was a blow. I remember the sinking feeling inside me when the doctor confirmed my suspicions. I was not sure which way to turn for help because I had only ever known western medicine and was not aware, at that time, of the many other kinds of health approaches and practitioners that were available.

However, 'When one door closes, another opens.' On the way home from the doctor's office, I stopped at a supermarket to buy some dietetically sweetened fruit that was allowed on my diet. At that time, the store was out of it, but the store clerk suggested that I should go to the health food store next door. So, I went…and ended up spending a couple of hours there. I saw foods that I had never seen before (or not in this form or color) such as seedy raisins on twigs, black Mission figs, jumbo Medjool dates, and dark brown apricots. This was fascinating for me, so I asked the clerk all kinds of questions…and I got so much out of that interaction - including an invaluable friend over the following year.

I asked her about the high protein powder that I had seen advertised, and she asked me if I had hypoglycemia. I think she had guessed from all my questions. She told me that she also had had it long ago and she had gotten over it…all she had done was change her diet. That experience changed my life direction, and by the end of that year, with the guidance and encouragement of this woman, my new friend, I had largely turned my health around.

A major shift occurred in my life. Out of my disillusionment and disappointment with the North American healthcare system had come a new realization that I could be responsible for my own health and choose my own healing actions. Prior to this, I only knew about a drug approach…I had known nothing about a healthy eating approach to health. This realization marked the beginning of a new phase in my life. This was the year 1969 (I was 30 years old) when I discovered my way back to health. It was at that time that I took my health into my own hands for the first time in my life. From this time forward, I continued to follow health practitioners - but only as my guides, rather than the only and final option.

We were in California for one more year, so we had that year to become strong with our new-found knowledge and practical applications for the recovery of our health. My husband and both our children had been bothered by health problems too. Though our daughter suffered mostly from tonsillitis, my husband's condition was serious and bothersome with an attack of hepatitis as well as a fungal outbreak in his feet and throat. Undoubtedly, they were all due to his stress.

For the previous three years, he had been a full-time student as well as completely responsible for his family in a foreign country. Along with this, he was working on his thesis and had a wife, me, whom he had not been able to count on due to constant, sudden bouts of illness. Therefore, he often, without notice, had to take care of the household.

That was a particularly messy three-year period. With only one year to do it in (before moving back to Canada), we had a lot to overcome and breakthrough. However, with our determination, plus the continuing health mentorship of our new friend from the health food store, we did it. At the end of that year, when my husband had almost completed his doctoral thesis, he landed his first job, and we returned back home to Vancouver - or rather, the border town of White Rock, to live in the basement suite of my parent's home.

We had begun to feel like we were winning with our health...but that feeling was short-lived. My health scared me that first year back home in Canada - I hardly got out of my dressing gown for five months. I seemed to set back that winter with what felt to me like a terrible bronchial condition, although I did not go to see a doctor to find out what they would call it.

I was afraid that I was seriously sick, but I didn't want to go to a "regular" doctor. In addition, I was faced with the enormous stress of cleaning up my husband's thesis to produce a final thesis document within one year ending June 30th, 1971 (this was the requirement set by his bosses in order to keep his job with the Faculty of Medicine, UBC.).

While on one hand, we were glad to be home; on the other hand, that first year back home in Canada was tough for us. Even though we had been successful in making many changes to our health, yet the stress was taking a toll and slowing down my health gains. Looking back, however, I realize that although it felt like a setback, it was probably, instead, a year or more of cleansing and purification. That process is always difficult - not only physically, but also emotionally. On the bright side, after I gradually came out of it over the following couple of years, I experienced better health than I had known for a very long time.

That first year back home, my husband was in and out of health food stores in our "hometown", Vancouver, BC, (in which, during our final year in California, we had become very comfortable). During these "visits," he would share our/my health struggles and bring home their words of wisdom and encouragement. Many of our health mentors tried to reassure us by saying things like, "sometimes it might look like a setback when really it is a cleansing crisis." Then they would go on to teach us (or me, at least) how to slow down the cleansing if it became too much, as well as how to eliminate the toxicity more effectively. Some were suggesting that I was probably making too many changes all at once. Others pointed to my stress level and encouraged me to balance things in order not to slow down my recovery.

These helpful "hints" were my only health support in those days. I was determined to be in control of my health choices, and I had not yet found any health practitioner(s) to replace the allopathic medical system of the western world that I had grown up with. In time (over the next forty years of my life), I did discover many very helpful alternative health practices (and practitioners). But for that moment in time - my early thirties - eating differently, the way my California friend had shown me - mostly a vegetarian diet of raw, organic fruit and vegetables - was all that I used to help me climb the ladder back to health. Sometimes I still smile when I remember my mother telling her friends, "Maren ate her way to health!" and that was the truth!

I next learned that there's more to health than the food we eat. Food was just my starting place - and a very important piece that has always been the baseline of my health puzzle. Some begin with the mind, others with stress-relieving techniques, and still others are drawn to physical exercise and outdoor activities - I believe we are each drawn to what's best for us. I have used other supportive health practices, but never have I replaced "food" by another practice…rather, I have added on. I have experimented with many different ways of healthy eating - and am currently on a major new diet experiment (which is going very well). I continue to be amazed at what unbelievable changes in my health can be created by different ways of eating, alone.

Over the years, when I did get sick, which still happened but less and less frequently, that was the time when I would try out different types of alternate health approaches. Gradually, over time, I built up an arsenal to choose from (both alternative medical practices as well as diets), for the time when I felt the need for either outside help and guidance or a different way of eating for my best health.

I learned that there is a lot of controversy, stigma, and lack of recognition surrounding all forms of alternate health disciplines (to some degree or other). A lot of this is reflected in the repayment support (or lack thereof) by the government. For most of the "health" services, there is no support - a person is pretty much on their own to afford alternate health services. However, lack of endorsement (financial or otherwise) has never been part of my criterion for following and believing, or disbelieving, in anything…so that did not faze me. I let my health improvement be the judge of the worth of the practice that I was following. Usually, a friend had recommended the particular practice - or I had read or heard about it and intuitively felt it was right for me for whatever I was struggling unsuccessfully with, according to the allopathic system.

For a list of the main alternative health practices, see Appendix 1; and for healthy diets, see Appendix II following the end of this book. You will soon get the idea of the immensity of the field of alternative medicine and health services that I was stepping into - with a wealth of supportive, healthy diets. My starting place on my journey to health was food. Over the past 50 years, I have experienced many different ways of eating - some out of casual interest - but usually out of an alert from a friend, or from something I had read - and usually because of some health struggle I was experiencing at the time.

When I first began my health journey, I was so involved with the day-to-day ups and downs that my new diet and way of thinking brought…that it was a few years before I felt or needed any support other than my health food store owners' and clerks' advice. I just wasn't ready yet for any alternate practitioners' input. When I was, then my husband (he was the researcher amongst the two of us) began researching the different practices and practitioners that our friends were telling us about, and about which we were becoming curious. Our first interest was our diet. Exploring and experimenting was time-consuming - and our main delight. We began with a vegetarian diet (including eggs - although I rarely ate them). It was largely fresh and raw…no meat and no milk or milk-related products like cheese and yogurt. In those days (our final year in California, 1969), I was only following my new friend's advice. After my trip to see my doctor - and the receipt of his confirmation that I was still hypoglycemic - I never returned to him.

Wise or not (according to the allopathic world, I was surrounded by and accustomed to), I was now following my new friend's advice for each step towards my new state of health. To most, it was considered a leap from the frying pan into the fire. For me, it was rather an obvious choice…to be led by someone who had "been there" rather than by someone, albeit learned, who had not (and moreover, whose advice hadn't worked)! I won't pretend it was easy. I wasn't used to doing my own thinking in this area of my life. The allopathic system, for the most part, encourages a total reliance on one's doctor. Therefore, it wasn't easy for me to trust only my own experience and my friend's.

Also, I still tested as hypoglycemic and wasn't well yet. Therefore, I had a lot of symptoms to deal with and often didn't feel good - including feeling moody and insecure much of the time. However, I had my friend to coach and encourage me, and my husband was backing me up - no matter what choices I made, or what different food I put in front of him that he wasn't used to.

In addition, he was used to taking over and looking after the household and family needs when I wasn't up to it! I can't remember exactly how long it took for me to feel the upswing of my health - but I do remember that there were gradually more and more days in between when I was doing better - and we were all getting the hang of the new way of eating and shopping and preparing food.

We didn't know the implication at the time, but my friend taught my husband and I how to grow alfalfa sprouts (as a mainstay of our meals). Plus, she taught us how to make a sweet food bar for our children. She felt they would need to have a healthy "sweet" to help them cope with the sweet "junk" food they were surrounded by in their school lunchrooms (our son in Grade One, our daughter in Pre-school). Our friend taught us many things, but those two things turned out to be momentous - the reason why would show up within a year!

Chapter 3
Isolation Is Stressful –
And My parents Were Wise

The other thing that was contributing to my stress and of feeling "under the weather" still was my isolation. Isolation is something that can hollow you from the inside out. It can make you feel depressed and lose your motivation to get out of bed…and even feel like you have nothing to look forward to.

When we returned from California, we settled into a basement suite in my parents' home, which was an hour outside Vancouver. They had been gone for the winter, and when they returned in the spring, they knew me so well that after one look, they knew something was wrong.

After catching up on the news - which included that we had begun a sprout business in their laundry room that winter - their brains went into gear. High on their list for finding a solution was for our family to move into Vancouver on our own and find a place to live in Vancouver so that we could be near my husband's work. This would end his long commute and give us all more family time. That was something that I, for one, was in dire need of. Having company can have marvelous effects on your health, both mental and physical - particularly when I am with my spouse, and the children with their dad.

During the previous winter, we had launched a small-scale health food manufacturing business. This was later to become a natural food manufacturing and education business. My father, who was both a chartered accountant and a businessman, showed us how we could use our new business to pay off student debts. He taught us to use our business income to pay a mortgage so that we could move into our own home in Vancouver.

It was a brilliant idea on our parents' part, and it did help me get better significantly faster. They had astutely guessed the primary stress that was causing my bronchial problems. All my life, when there was stress or troubles, my chest and ears were always the ones to break down. It was a horrible feeling, and no matter how many times I went through that, it would always be a terrible experience. The thing about parents is that they live so long with their children's health problems that they just know how to deal with them. Over their lifetime, they often have had to diagnose the problems themselves, and my parents correctly sensed the major source of my ailments.

"The Beginning of a New Life…"

Within a few months, by the summer of 1971, with my parents' help, we found a house in Vancouver to move into. A major criterion was to find a house that had the capability of developing a home business in it. I particularly needed the house to already have a finished basement for the business. I needed this so that we could separate our family life from our business life. I had learned a bit more about myself by that point. I knew that some things just should not be mixed, and it is just good sense to keep a boundary between our personal and professional lives.

My Dad had a vision of this business paying for our mortgage, paying off our student debts, and eventually, providing us with income for holidays, renovating the house, and much more. It was a brilliant plan on my father's part. Furthermore, it gave me something to do every day, and that kept my mind off of my health, which inadvertently improved it. This move brought a totally new way of life.

I was not prepared for the wonderful changes that came about by us moving into Vancouver, as well as from my improved health. I had lived with poor health for most of my life…and so it was a totally new experience for me to realize that being healthy could bring about changes that alone made my life feel so much more worth living. I would wake up every day, looking forward to what it entailed, knowing that I could take on the challenges that would present themselves.

In contrast to my previous isolation and depression, this was a welcome change. Poor health is bound to take a person over so that it becomes an all-consuming focus. This state of health produces a response from the brain. One cannot depend on their own body to perform and do physical activities with their loved ones. Consequently, I had developed a habit of always 'under planning,' which is a disempowering way to live and think.

Once I recognized this, I was gradually able to reprogram my thinking. This radically changed my life. I was in my mid-thirties, the prime of my life, which just kept changing, developing, and getting better and better. My health was beginning to quickly strengthen – as well as the health of our whole family. Being able to be together more as a family because of being close to my husband's work, plus having his thesis behind him (and me), all contributed to my decreased stress and increased health. I began to realize what a constant cloud and damper that his incomplete thesis had become for us. Once it was behind us, we could begin creating a new life for ourselves and our family, and moreover, we had a new home to do it in.

"Passionate Students of Health – And Many Surprises…"

Added to these factors was the fact that I was learning on an on-going basis. Your brain is much more powerful than you give it credit for. The power your thought process has on your way of life is astounding and can affect your life, for better or for worse. I was giving all my time to learn countless new facts about health, and I began taking many new actions to promote better health for myself and my family.

My husband was a much more avid researcher than I was and so he was in constant communication with health food store owners. These people were very much like us…and we gradually came to know them (a few even became friends).

Their stories were much like ours, and it was heartening to hear what they had gone through and radically improved their health and life as a result. Moreover, we were able to move ahead in our own journey much faster, having met these people. They had gone through so much, and we were able to apply what we learned from their experience…it was eye-opening. I also give credit to them for their willingness to help push my health to a better place.

Another of these 'wonderful changes' was to be a homeowner versus a renter. It unleashed our creativity that we had not felt free to exercise in our previously rented homes. We designed, built, and developed our business, and renovated our home to make it more suitable for our lifestyle.

The freedom to do so was something that had an effect on our minds as well. Being free to do as we wished, at the place we lived, gave us energy that was unfound in previous homes. As we renovated our surroundings, at the same time, our health re-shaped itself. Having had a hand in the creation of our space and what we surrounded ourselves by, we saw an unexpectedly positive effect on both our health and thought processes. Once we began growing our sprouts in our space that we had newly created, it felt exciting and enlivening. With my new-found energy, my newest hobby was gardening. At first, it was mostly cleaning it up and discovering what was there...but really, it was an outlet for my health and peace of mind. That was what first got me out there, and my family followed along. Soon, our lives were humming along, busily and happily.

While caring for my family, running the business, and gardening, I was busy almost all the time, and that was what I needed. Being busy helps promote your health along with a sense of self-importance that cannot be felt if you are feeling listless or aimless all the time. That gives way to thinking that there is nothing going on in life for you, and that it would be useless to pursue any interest. That is not a healthy mind-set.

During this period, my new-found, improved health, allowed me to consider many different avenues. For one thing, I was now able to manage many aspects of our healthy food manufacturing proprietorship that my father had helped us establish. I now had energy, interest, and enthusiasm, whereas before, I had had some interest but little energy or enthusiasm to follow through with any of my ideas.

"Our Life Became Both the Subject and Object of Our Children's Education…"

Our children's education turned out to be another new dimension in our lives. Within a year of arriving in town, we were all enrolled in an alternate city school. I say 'we' because our children were under-age for that particular school. However, the staff said they would accept them if one of us agreed to always be present, and I was elected. I was happy about it, as I still found time to spare and could fit that in quite well.

It worked quite well until February, when I was beginning to feel like I was falling behind my business needs. At that point, I asked the school staff if it might work for them if I were to be absent more often, and they agreed because they were feeling comfortable with the way the children had fit into the school by then.

The next schooling crossroad occurred the following fall. By then, with summer holidays in between, we were all involved in either the gardening experience or our business. Both were all-consuming and fascinating in different ways for all of us. We realized we did not want to break our continuity and time together. So off we went to the school board again, and this time we opted for homeschooling.

At first, it did not change anything, though it did give our life a different context altogether. That turned out to be the ultimately most interesting (and often exciting) aspect of our 'new' lives. With the flip of a switch, Robert's and my life and lifestyle became both the subject and object of our children's education. Two of the most major aspects of our life that involved us all were our garden and our health food manufacturing business. They were of equal importance and involvement for all of us (with the exception of my husband, who was also a professor at the University of British Columbia. However, his hours were very flexible because he didn't do much classroom teaching. Mostly, he was writing a book as well as researching different projects on various sites.

"Synergy…"

This is where I would like to talk about my marriage and how it was affected by my health. The synergy of my husband's and my partnership, in the early years of our marriage, was challenged because of my health. It probably was not very noticeable to others, but it was always evident to me, at least when I did not have the health or energy to follow through on our ideas. We were thinkers and action-takers. We had constant reactions to the status quo, the norm, whatever society at large was giving credence to. However, we did not focus on all that. Rather, we noted it, found it not to our liking, and quickly developed new directions of our own making.

While in California, we began learning and practicing whatever we could do to be easier on the environment. The people we were involved with were focused on practices that householders could easily cope with, such as a simple thing like putting a brick in our toilet tank in order to not use so much water.

After those four years, we returned home to British Columbia, where we put into action whatever environmental measures that we had begun learning. California was far ahead of BC in these things, and in many alternate health practices and ideas such as organic food markets. During these four years, while my husband was attending graduate studies in California, we left the church and became vegetarians.

We were synergistic, meaning, we moved as one being to bring each other's visions into being…it didn't matter who started it initially. The Pacific Deaf (and Hearing-Impaired) Fellowship was one of our earlier projects that demonstrated this - probably Robert began developing the idea - but in our usual style, I was a split second behind him, demonstrating the willingness of us both to learn of a need and quickly "step up to the plate." As I continued to grapple with my health, Robert began to work in Vancouver, and we began a whole new way of life there. I was beginning to have more energy and our synergy had us taking on some extremely exciting, interesting, and satisfying projects. Right to the end, we were synergistic – our synergy did not diminish at all (even when our marital union did).

We never knew which of us produced the ideas because the other of us also shot off immediately. I do have a strong sense, though, that it was not always just the same one of us doing the originating…or the following. Moreover, it did not matter from whose brain it came because we shot off as one person, putting the idea into action, as if on a single mission… hence, our synergy.

"We Were Pioneers..."

All books on business teach you how to be better by comparing yourself to a competitor. However, most of our ideas were ahead of their time, so there was no model to follow. It was all new territory, and it was sort of a good thing and bad as well. We had no experience running a business, plus there was nothing to compare ourselves to. Nothing that we could imitate. My father said he was willing to help us with the business side - particularly with business plans and our accounting. This freed us up to focus on developing our ideas.

We had a lot of ideas, but the following were our most important and successful ones. We turned our city property into a mini farm. On that property, we also began a family health food manufacturing business. In our home business, even though we were manufacturing other health products, we were largely growing alfalfa and a mixture of other sprouts. We later moved our manufacturing to a rural property outside of Vancouver.

Because of our inclination to education, we interested some local well-known food stores such as Safeway and

Woodward's to let us demonstrate how to grow alfalfa sprouts.

In addition, we encouraged and assisted local school boards in taking junk-food out of their schools in the communities around us, replacing it with healthy alternatives.

We became importers of exotic fruits like mangoes, papayas, avocados, lychee nuts, and others - this was long before these foods were present in supermarkets as they are today.

Out of our discontent with the health care system, we often directed our passion and innovation towards the field of health. My husband was working full time as a medical sociologist. Here he met and partnered with a colleague, Dr. Roger Rogers. Together, they developed a new course, and later a Department called 'Preventive Medicine' within the Department of Medicine at the University of British Columbia. Dr. Rogers then privately partnered with my husband and me to form a preventive medical center called Therah Wellness Centre in Vancouver.

We were also discontented with the school system, which led us to home-school our two older children and send our third child to an alternate school.

Lastly, after we moved rurally onto a Gulf Island near Vancouver on the mainland, we formed an intentional community on the Gulf Island called Galiano Island. The community is still operating, which is amazing to me, given some of the challenges and struggles that seemed, at times, insurmountable and likely to take it down. Years ago, I sold my share in the community, but both my older children are still part of it - each of them owning a share in the corporation that runs it, and both are landholders. Though neither lives on the Island full time, as is also the case with a good number of the other members, they often entertain the thought of settling there, eventually.

There were other projects – but those were the most significant of them.

"Our Health Food Manufacturing Business - Both A School and Playground..."

From the spring of 1971, for about the next five years, we were in business. Our business gave me an unlimited outlet for my creative abilities. There were advertising flyers and recipes to be created and ideas to put onto paper. I found that there was always something new to create...and endless action possibilities. Moreover, our particular business was like a giant kitchen and school for me (and our children). I had never been part of a business or manufactured anything. I had been a teacher and a musician, and while it did help me in some ways, it was mostly useless knowledge when it came to a business.

"An Added Interest...Hearing-Impaired People..."

We employed people who were hearing-impaired...or "deaf," as they all call themselves. This was due to my husband's background of having deaf parents. We were ahead of the times with our per capita employment of handicapped people in our business – although they are not handicapped if the people around them know their language, as in our case, we did.

For me, employing deaf persons was an added element to our business that made it much more interesting for me (as well as more demanding). I am a people person, and very good in human relations. Although our business was on a very small scale, yet being hearing-impaired, they still had a much greater need for one-on-one instruction and support. Sometimes I needed to call upon Robert to help with the interpretation because of sign language being his first language. However, most of the time, I was able to handle things. My sign language ability really jumped ahead with this much more intense use of sign language than I had ever had.

"Alfalfa Sprouts and Health Food Chocolate Bar…"

Our products were sprouts (mostly alfalfa) and 'Sweet Munchy' bars (alternative food bars). At first, we started out with just one kind of food bar, but then progressed to five different ones, along with 'trail mixes.' The healthy 'candy' was made from six ingredients (approximately equal amounts). A large tub was filled with peanut butter, to which we added carob powder and honey. Then we stirred sunflower and sesame seeds into this gooey mass, plus lightly toasted wheat flakes.

This combo turned into a chocolate bar replacement (a forerunner to meal-replacement food bars) and was named the 'Sweet Munchy' bar. At first, we were selling it by the pound. Robert had his routes to all the health food stores. There were five routes that differed each day of the workweek and then started all over again the next week. At first, he was only delivering pails of sprouts. The word got out about our Sweet Munchy 'candy.' So then, he would arrive at a health food store with his usual sprouts, plus a sixty-pound pail of bulk, Sweet Munchy mixture. They would scoop out the amount they wanted onto a scale. After that, they would sell it in bulk over their counter. Then the Health Department stepped in, insisting that it be put in sealed packaging. They were against selling home-made things in the stores because they had no way to inspect and therefore control the safety and health standard. We bought a heat sealer, and my mother devised a way to press the 'dough' into an edged cookie sheet and then lay a marked wax paper (the sheet had markings the size of the bars; thirty per cookie sheet). We bought small cello bags (about one and a half inches by four inches) into which we dropped each Sweet Munchy bar and sealed it. It was not long before dad enrolled my machinist and mechanically minded uncle to design and build us a candy forming machine to mold the Sweet Munchy dough into bars. Within a year or so, all this progress helped us expand from one Sweet Munchy bar to five bars. The final step was to get the bags printed with all the details that the government insisted must be on them.

"Scary...Demonstrating Our Sprouts in Food Stores..."

My husband was the enthusiastic promoter of our products and health ideas. He was always out talking to people and drumming up new possibilities for us in our business. One of these was for us to demonstrate our sprouts in food stores. His efforts came into fruition, and he had stores like the old Woodward and Safeway stores very interested in the idea of us demonstrating how to grow and use sprouts. Since my husband was busy with his job, I ended up being the one to give the demos in the stores. At first, I was very nervous, but once I was in the demonstration, I was fine. My genuine enthusiasm and easy way with people seemed to be a good combination. Bags of sprouts and alfalfa seeds went out of the store like crazy, and so the management was happy.

As an aside, lots of people thought we were foolish to be teaching others to grow the sprouts. Their rationale was that we were pushing ourselves out of business. Our rationale was that after we, ourselves, had been taught to grow sprouts, we became their best customers. This was because we had become dependent on sprouts for our daily fare and because batches sometimes died on us. Or we would have weeks where we ourselves were too busy to grow them and would have to rush out to the health food store and buy ourselves a large bag of sprouts.

When talking amongst ourselves, our family and our health-minded friends, as well as out in the health food arena, ideas abounded. Shortly, we began speaking to school boards, parent groups, and colleges to encourage and assist them in getting junk food out of the school vending machines and from children's lunches. At times, it was difficult to remain focused and very easy to get lost in the endless ideas and possibilities.

Chapter 4
Gardening

A Gardener Waiting for A Garden to Happen

That was my situation. The whole concept of gardening is basically to understand and appreciate the delicacy of nature. Gardening has a way of changing people and making them better. Maybe it has something to do with being patient when waiting for results. When gardening, you have to wait to see the beauty of your work come to fruition. The patience that it takes is mind-boggling, and the best part is that you cannot really do anything to speed up the process.

This inculcates self-restraint that a person gets to use in all parts of his or her life. Usually, people are so hasty… hasty to achieve success, hasty to get into a relationship, and then hasty to get out. Gardening teaches one that the fruit that is left to ripen over a long period of time is so much sweeter than one that people impatiently eat too early. Have you ever gardened? If you have not, consider doing it – at least for a season – in order to have a chance to learn more about yourself. The time spent alone in the garden, plucking, sowing, fertilizing, and the labor associated with it, everything is so calming that you really get a chance to understand yourself.

At first, I did not realize how much of a gardener I was, 'waiting to happen.' I could not wait to get at it - it was as if that was what was missing from my life. That was part of the reason that brought me out of my bad health. The best part? My family was right behind me! While watching my family, with our varied interests and ages, doing something together, I learned that there is most likely a place for everyone in the realm of gardening. The only thing that is required is the tiniest amount of patience, the patience to explore it, and find their niche for themselves.

When there were four of us, I noticed that we never got frustrated or wanted to give up. If anyone was irritated or had a bad day, then that was just a chance for one of us to lend a shoulder. That is an advantage I feel a family has over a single person having to hold it all together at every turn of events and swing of moods. So, if you are a novice and single – rather than giving up and not gardening, consider rounding up a couple of neighbors or friends to join you. Community gardens are particularly great for singles that have no backyards because they provide a place to get advice, share ideas and find someone to partner with.

"Cleaning Up Is Necessary, But…"

Initially, our family's gardening experience was all about getting our yard cleaned up. It was absolutely necessary and satisfying to get the yard looking cared for - but we did not find it to be an inspiring activity. However, we stuck with it because it was the 'clean look' of the yard that got our creative juices flowing before long. I know that it sounds a bit like advice, but if you want to achieve anything, the first step that you have to take is to get organized. That is of absolute essence. You see, there is a part of human psychology that just finds it so appealing to look at something that is organized and clean.

You may have often heard your parents asking you to make your bed the first thing in the morning. That is simple yet deep advice. The thing is that when you make your bed in the morning, it is the smallest task that you can accomplish. That small task once accomplished becomes a precursor for bigger tasks getting accomplished later in the day. It is the question of finding the motivation to get through your day. Then when you come back home, even if you have had a bad day, then at least you are coming home to a bed that is made. This ideology was given, for one, by an ex-Navy Seal, Admiral, William McRaven.

Though making your bed has nothing to do with gardening, the same ideology still applies. When we worked together as a family, our kids loved doing that initially. However, as is the case with all kids, their pleasure dimmed as time passed. In the beginning, it was hard work, when all we were doing were boring garden activities - mostly pulling weeds out. None of us had any idea that we would come to love gardening as much as we did. At first it just seemed like too much work, so at that stage of our 'gardening life,' we could not know of our future love for it. However, as it turned out, it was the Morning Glories that led us to places we had not dreamt of as a family.

"The Famous Morning Glory Blanket…"

'Morning Glories,' you wonder? When we moved into this house, it was summer, 1971 - school had just vacated. The house that we moved into had been empty for a while prior to our moving in; therefore, we inherited a back yard that had gone wild and was just a horrendous sight to behold. Nightmarish, really! We could not see any of the bushes because of the blanket of Morning Glories that had run itself over all of the border gardens and their bushes.

We all attacked the 'blanket' and had fun exposing our hidden treasures. For quite a while, we just worked on the obvious. It was quite a large lot, so there seemed no end to the wildness and disorder that we were dealing with. However, with all four of us yanking on Morning Glories, unraveling them out of all our bushes and plants along the borders and against the house, we soon began to make progress.

"Weeds...and the Seven Year Rule..."

My biggest life lessons in this garden came from weeds. I had no idea there was so much to know about them. There is a saying about weeds, "One year's seeds become seven years' weeds," meaning that if you miss one weed and leave it there to mature and go to seed, you will be dealing with the plants from that weed for (at least) the next seven years. Another possible lesson from this is that life is unfair. Take one step towards organizing your life, and life may pull you back seven steps. Though on the other hand, you must also understand that there is nothing in life that one cannot handle. Everything can be managed by you, and gardening is just one example of that. When you decide to put in the effort to get results, you most probably will have to be prepared to double your effort to get to the next step.

This saying about weeds became more evident over the years as I gardened on that property. There were about three or four weeds that were the most tenacious. I remember that I knew them all by name at that time, but I seem to have forgotten some of them by now. Three of the hardest to eradicate were Pigweed and Morning Glory - and one we called "section grass." In the case of the Morning Glory, it multiplied rapidly because of unbelievably well-developed root systems that seemed to stretch for miles when I pulled them up. However, it almost always broke off, deeper down than I had gone, and then I would have to deal with it once more when it got going again - and I could count on that it would get going again.

Another lesson that is to be learned here is that you can start to get your life in order by pulling out the "weeds" that are toxic and harmful. When you start "pulling out" the toxic people and the bad habits that have engulfed you for the better part of your life, you realize that they went so much deeper than you had thought or imagined. Change is never easy, but it is certainly worth it because then, you will have a "garden" that is beautiful to look at. In other words, you will have a life that makes you happy to get out of bed and face the day.

When you do, however, you will have to be prepared to face the same set of challenges again…the difference this time being that you will be in a different place, and hopefully, ready to face them this time. When you look in the mirror, you will be happy to see yourself, unlike many people who do not behold a sight that they find appealing and believe in.

One of my biggest lessons about weeds was that a quick fix, such as weeding a whole patch by hoeing it, is very short-sighted. That method works for simple weeds with small roots, but it does not work for any of the three I named above, and a few more whose names I do not remember but which have the same complex, underground root system for multiplying like the Morning Glory.

After gardening a while, I got better at dealing with these types by pouncing on them as soon as I saw the beginning of one showing its head. But it took me a few years to permanently eradicate them from my garden – almost seven (as the saying goes) – just about the time that we moved on.

Of course, there are chemical 'quick fixes,' which I was completely against - being an advocate for natural organic methods. I was glad not to be a commercial organic gardener who has to make choices that balance 'natural' with financial solvency. That is another subject and not one that I will pursue in this book. Choosing 'organic' over 'chemical' was usually a labor-intensive choice, but I was a purist, and my choice was clear to me…organic every time!

"'Real' Gardening…"

Meanwhile, back to our beginning phase…I began to realize that I did not want to continue this kind of gardening forever – weeding and maintaining a garden of flowering plants and shrubs. The yard was really large, both back and front…and I began to think about starting a vegetable garden. All winter, the thoughts had been stirring inside of me as I had read and studied gardening books and seed catalogs.

The desire to move on to bigger and better things is one that can be found in the hearts of all people. Our human tendency is to never be satisfied with our current position, and it is never enough. As an aside, usually, it is not good to give into this restlessness - but in this case, it was! That was something that was beginning to engulf me. In my case, I wanted a vegetable garden. For you, it could be something else. The desire to get a promotion, a raise, settling down, raising a family, going abroad to see the world, or losing weight, and getting in shape.

All these aspirations are things that can be achieved, but do you realize that in order to achieve them, you have to put in the work? You cannot expect to be given a handout to achieve your dreams. In order to achieve your goal, you have to put in the work, and that is often not easy. The work that you put in can be strenuous and laborious, but the fruits or vegetables you eventually get at harvest-time are worth it. You need to have a clear goal!

And for some reason, all your hard work just does not seem that much when you look back at it after having attained the reward. That is just a part of the human psyche...It tends to forget the hard parts and remembers only the good ones. This is why so many people keep working hard for their goal because once they have tasted the reward from hard work, they never want to give up on that feeling.

During my early years, my mother had maintained a sizeable vegetable garden, plus a row of raspberry bushes against the back fence. My sister and I helped my mom with it every summer, though at that point in my life, not always happily. However, now, the pleasurable memories that remained were the strongest. When I broached him on the subject, my husband jumped at the idea, and soon the project took off in the new direction...rolling back the sod first in the back yard, and then in the front yard the following year by digging out all the bushes and plants; so much for our new-found 'treasures!'

"Interest First...Health Second..."

I mentioned earlier that I had adopted gardening for my mental health. It was not that clearly thought out really. Rather, it was instinctive. Deep inside me, I knew that it was high time to introduce change into my life. I did know that something had to be done so that I could improve my health and outlook…and this was the one that drew me.

Perhaps it was because my mother had a garden so that it was kind of like going back to my roots. As it turned out, this was the activity that was needed, and it was almost as if I subconsciously knew that this would positively affect my whole life. The lessons I learned while gardening were ones that I'll always remember. One example was that at times, my family life would get too much for me, and I would become upset over something going on that seemed beyond my control, which happened often enough. I would instinctively head for the garden… and my inner turmoil would simply melt away as I became immersed in my gardening project.

Over the weeks and months, I gradually learned what a great solution it was for me to go outside and garden as a way to de-stress. In the past, I had always headed for the piano when my mood was off – but now, gardening had become my new outlet. I was passionate about my health recovery, and now that I had discovered how healthy it was for me to be outside and working with the earth, I became drawn in…bit by bit at first, then in leaps and bounds. The other aspect that was healthy about it was how my life had begun to change from sedentary to active. The rest of the family soon followed my example and vision.

I would usually be the one to create an action plan, and even if there were inevitable changes that would be needed, nevertheless, it was a place to begin. In order to be at peace, you always need to be able to change. The flexibility needed to adapt to change and the ability to make the decisions at the sight of a challenge are both essential in order to have a good mental state. I believe it is the height of a person's mental state when they can adapt to change and make new decisions on the spot. Everybody can find it within themselves to do this. They just need belief in themselves plus practice.

I was willing – and I was the one with the greatest amount of "free" time. Consequently, I was usually the one to announce what the needs of the week were, or the day, or even the hour. We each had different niches, according to our interests and expertise. Our system was not dictatorial, but rather, democratic and by personal choice. I rarely conscripted, but sometimes I had to be extremely aware - and on the ball - in order to not be stuck with the 'dirty work.' I discovered, however, to my delight, that just because I did not like doing a given task, it did not mean that no one else would want to do it either. I was often pleasantly surprised by the offers.

"When it came to Gardening, my Husband was Generous…"

In our family, my husband would do anything that was needed in the garden, particularly things that were too heavy for me. His willing attitude helped me enormously, as even at this point I was unable to do heavy lifting - and some labor-intensive projects - or sometimes I would run out of energy before a job was completed - and the rest of my family would usually jump in, good-naturedly, and finish it for me.

Although I was the leader in the gardening, my husband soon found his place in it and became as avid a gardener as I was. For him, it was a good balance to his work life. He loved the opportunity to be outdoors, exercising and relaxing. The most relaxing activity for him was to water the entire garden, which was becoming bigger by the day.

Slowly but surely, we were finding our niches and seeing the results of our hard work.

This was motivational for the entire family and taught all of us persistence and perseverance…no matter what it took. However, we were fortunate that the more that a person cares about the survival and outcome of their particular project, the more emotionally involved they are, and the easier it is to hang in there till the need is completely handled. This fact helped us all to become good gardeners - young and old.

One of my husband's specialties became flower gardening with our daughter. They both loved flowers; they often planned the flowers together. They built a trellis and planted sweet peas to climb on it and then filled the borders of our front yard with Marguerites. The other things he loved best were big energy things, like filling pails with dirt and hauling them up to our carport roof to make a roof garden.

He also loved rotating the compost, moving it from a full bin to an empty one to become riper, or moving ripe compost out from the 'matured' bin, onto the garden. I, on the other hand, liked anything to do with vegetables, and I specialized in small, detailed jobs like planting, weeding, planning, and record-keeping.

My son became the main gardener…and is still gardening thirty-five years later (larger scale - with tractors) and has a landscape gardening business! He loved the veggies – and was proud of some of the giant specimens that he grew. Of course, at twelve years of age, he needed adult input, and so we got a gardening tutor for him. But it wasn't for long because my son was soon capably doing his own thing - even showing his tutor new stuff.

Our daughter found her niche with flowers, which is still a strong theme in her life.

"Red Wrigglers…"

Composting was my husband's number one favorite garden job. He put in enormous wooden bins against the house and was constantly rotating them. I always looked forward to the day when the compost was mature (we would match it up with the perfect biodynamic cycle on our special garden calendar (as an aside, we followed the bio-dynamic gardening cycle's calendar for the best time frames for all the different garden activities).

On the right day, off would come the front boards in the bins that were ready. We would pitch it by shovelfuls onto the garden. We ate a lot of avocados in those days - in part because we liked avocados a lot, but mostly because we imported them as part of our business. But because sometimes they would get ahead of us and ripen faster than we could sell or eat them…hence, that week, they made us some very 'rich' compost, along with over-ripe mangoes and papayas.

But the avocados were the ones that I loved the most on compost day. They would roll out onto the garden. - I am talking about the perfectly round variety here - with each outer skin looking like it was still intact. I would eagerly and gingerly break it apart, and by now, the brittle shell would crumble to display a perfect ball of wriggling small red worms - Red Wrigglers. What a sight – I still smile at the fond memory.

All the gardening and the hard work that we put in day after day (and year after year) was having a positive effect on us. After each day of work, we could see that the garden looked that much better…and each day's accomplishment helped us in continuing forward, giving us hope to carry on to the next day. However, what helped us the most to keep going every day was that we had big goals and a very large vision, and these helped us on days where our achievements weren't at the optimal level or quite so obvious.

We need to understand that it is extremely important for us to notice and appreciate the accomplishments in our life. However, just a bit of improvement over generally noticing and appreciating, once in a while, would be to acknowledge the result at the end of every day. Only then will you really notice that slowly, but surely, each day is getting easier. Although milestones are important and even exciting, it is the accomplishment, each day…that is what brings you to that milestone, and is therefore equally, if not more, important in improving your life.

Chapter 5
Schooling - Education - Mexico

"No More Ordinary School Experience for Our Children..."

After living in Vancouver for a year, we realized that we didn't wish our children to have an ordinary schooling experience. This was mainly because we didn't have an ordinary lifestyle or beliefs in so many areas of our lives. As a lifestyle, we were all completely invested in our manufacturing business, along with gardening. Until that time, our children had been attending the neighborhood school - our son was in grade two, and our daughter was in kindergarten. The fact of the matter was...after the free-flow possible during the summer when school was closed, we realized we were all enjoying the spontaneous flow of our life. It gave us a chance to improve, both as a family and as individuals, and to have control over our choices.

So, we went off to the school board to talk about our situation. They were more than understanding and suggested that we sign up with a nearby neighborhood school so that we would be eligible for library services and to sign out school textbooks or any other things that schools offer in addition to regular classrooms (which we wanted out of). My husband and I weren't very enthusiastic but agreed because it made the school board very happy to be able to keep track of us and to feel like our children wouldn't be deprived of everything that school systems offer. We kept this connection up in appearance only, and didn't avail ourselves of anything, not because of any belief or position, but simply because we were so happy and productive and following what we wanted to (that includes all of us).

To be really honest, in the very beginning, our son was bored as well as feeling unmotivated to create anything for himself. My husband and I figured that he had been told exactly what to do for long enough that he had forgotten how to think for himself. For the first four or five weeks, he spent his time moaning that there was nothing to do. We just let him moan and didn't suggest much. But once he got over that phase, that was the last time I ever heard about boredom from him again in his life…he soon "got with the program," so to speak, and allowed himself to discover and develop interests. Our daughter was very introspective and artistic and a dreamer, so she had no trouble making up things to do.

After a few months, we went back to the school board for their recommendation of a city school that might be classified as an alternate school. We were given a name, and upon investigating, we learned that our children were under-age for their program, which began at grade four. However, the school decided to give us a bit of leeway in the matter and accepted our children on a trial basis, with the stipulation that I attend school with them. This would be just to look out for their personal needs. My husband and I believed that this could be an easier transition - particularly for our son - than no school, which he had found so difficult. In addition, it was a much better fit for us than regular schools.

For example, this new school was very lenient about attendance - like being late or missing a class - both of which were apt to happen from time to time with some of our family priorities. Also, our children didn't have to take the academic courses but could opt for photography, pottery, and other interesting courses. We just had to comply with the condition that I was to be there with them and attend classes regularly.

"Time out for Mexico..."

That same year, we drove to Mexico. We had just settled into the new school, and barely two months had passed when my husband and I got a strong urge to go on a driving trip to Mexico. Fortunately, our children weren't enrolled in any of the academic subjects. We cleared it with the school and let the school know that we were turning it into an educational trip for our children. We took diaries to write in and maps and travel books of Mexico. We were gone for six weeks from early December of '72 through mid-January of '73.

This was a double holiday…away from our business as well as away from school - the latter being the most important. We had our priorities straight, and we realized that in most cases, the needs of our children superseded ours. In this case, for them to have real-life lessons was worth much more than staying at school and only reading about life in books. We capitalized on the long Christmas holiday and just extended it so that we would have a really good amount of time for the long drive to Mexico and back. Before we could take such a long break, we had to deal with our sprouting business.

Although our family (including my mother and father) was the main workforce, we did have other people helping us as well. There were a few deaf people whom we knew from our Pacific Deaf Fellowship days, which was the whole time my husband attended university. Though we had quite a few people helping us, our business still wasn't organized, developed, or large enough to have all aspects of our business covered by other people - things like taking sprout orders or delivering, and in addition, beginning the whole growing cycle.

After studying the needs of our sprouting business, we concluded that we needed to run our growing cycle down and put our sprouting operation on hold while we were gone. Therefore, just before we left on our trip, we completed the sprout cycle and packaged and delivered them. There were three wholesale distributors - one each for the Woodward's and the Safeway stores who took care of the bulk of our orders... and a third distributor who looked after most of the health food stores.

Last, we individually delivered to a few health-food stores that we always looked after ourselves. There was a variety of reasons why we gave them this special treatment, but mostly, these owners had become our friends, or we regularly did our personal shopping there. The final piece we put in place was that we arranged for a couple of our workers to come to our house near the end of our trip to start up a new growing cycle that would be ready for us to package and deliver immediately upon our return. Our non-perishable items like our food bars and trail mixes were easier to deal with because we could stock everyone up with enough to last while we were gone.

"Off to Mexico - Education for the whole family…"

The trip was an eye-opener for us all, not just our children. Although my husband and I had obviously already experienced quite a bit of the world and life, the trip still taught us many things. The weather was surprising to start with. I thought that by the time we reached California, it would be warm. That, however, did not turn out to be the case - there was a lot of snow in northern through mid-California.

We thought we would do a diagonal through Bakersfield Pass towards Arizona but were surprised at how much it was snowing through the mountain pass as well. When we reached Arizona, the country people had toques - and often were wrapped in blankets as they wandered along desert roads. It was much colder than we had expected. Although we were from the north and found their idea of cold to be funny, still, the cold continued all the way down to Puerto Vallarta before we felt warm, by any standard. Then the heat hit us, cold to the north, and hot to the south. It was almost as if there was a line drawn across the road. Talking about a "line," it seems to me that the heat "line" might have coincided with the Tropic of Cancer or close - just don't quote me on that.

We were traveling in our camper van (a Ford Econoline) that we had outfitted simply - with a customized roof that we could raise to give us height and a wooden platform bed on which all four of us could fit. There was also some storage underneath it, plus a bench table. We didn't get more elaborate than this - that is, no stove or fridge or bathroom. We cooked on our Coleman gas stove outside, used an old-fashioned cooler and headed for the bushes or public toilets.

At home, the van was used for our perishable food business, and therefore it was outfitted with a refrigeration unit. When we first hit the heat, we would turn it on when we were too hot. However, it always seemed a luxury to use it, and anyway, it didn't take us long before we got used to the heat. After that, we drove without the refrigeration most of the time. Though we had gotten used to the climate change from Vancouver to California and onwards, we were staggered by the pollution, particularly by old trucks and buses. We were flabbergasted to see just how many old vehicles were on the roads in Mexico and the clouds of black exhaust that poured out of them as they putt-putted their way along. It was a sign of poverty and also their lack of awareness of environmental issues - they were just eking out their living, as best they could. We were having trouble breathing because the air was so bad, and we realized our good fortune to live in a place that insists on a much higher level of vehicle performance.

This was one of the most prominent things that we learned about our lives while on that trip. Even though we had faced our fair share of challenges, seeing what we saw about the way that these people were living their life, really brought home just how fortunate we were. The main difference between them and us was that we were aware when things got tough. Whereas, these people had seen so much hardship in their lifetime that they had gotten used to it and accepted it as a given. Moreover, they weren't aware that there was a better way to live than what they now had…and most certainly, they had no idea that they could ever have anything different.

For my husband and me, it was of utmost importance that we realize just how fortunate we were and in retrospect, that was the best lesson we could have taught our children and also learned ourselves. If given a choice to learn about life by living it - or learning academically, I would choose learning from life over learning academically. Yes, our children could have come to some of these understandings by themselves, but with us to help by pointing things out that they were too young to notice, they had a chance to learn more about life - and faster than on their own - which would help them throughout their entire life.

One of the biggest lessons that we were helping them to understand is that life is rarely the way it seems. There are twists and turns on even what seemingly looks like a straight road. We helped them to understand that the path that they were on was the consequence of their decisions. Or even if it is not, and even if life has made their decision for them - and already dealt them that hand - it is still up to them to play it wisely. Otherwise, they will end up on a path that doesn't lead to their dreams (or worse). We attempted to help them experience (and therefore understand) that that decision ultimately rests on them - and that they, alone, have that power. Otherwise, they are powerless to create their life and their dreams. This is one of the biggest lessons they had the opportunity to learn - much more so than in a public-school setting.

"Norma Jean Nilsson...and Professor Edmund Bordeaux Szekely..."

Our first major destination was Lake Chapala because our friends, Norma Jean Nilsson and Professor Edmund Bordeaux Szekely, had a home on the lake. As an aside, we had first learned of them through our friend's (Dr. Szekely's) writing. He and his wife had many homes (San Diego in southern California; Mission, BC Canada, about 50 miles from our home in Vancouver, BC; Lake Chapala in Mexico, and more). When my husband and I became interested in the early Essenes (BC) and their lifestyle, and when we turned up Professor's translations of the Essenes from the Dead Sea Scrolls, further research led us to the Szekelys, only an hour from our home.

We went out to meet them, and that meeting led to an invitation to visit them when we were in Mexico. Their home was close to the center of Mexico, and we had tremendous fun along the way, exploring and enjoying the experiences. One such incident was more nerve-wracking than fun, though a great experience, nonetheless. We started along a road in good faith, which shortly turned into a creek bed. We soon discovered that we had to keep going because we couldn't turn around to go back. That was just plain scary. We came out of that experience with a new respect for our van - we had put it in low gear, and it just kept slowly, steadily, climbing over pebbles and even small boulders. When we arrived at the end of this "creek bed road," there was a reward…a small town.

I had learned a little Spanish before going there on the trip, though it was more of a courtesy than useful, because if needed, when an actual situation arose, I was not able to communicate my point. That didn't mean that there weren't other ways, though. In most cases, sign language was sufficient. Because Robert and I knew the sign language of deaf persons, we were used to making up signs and creating understanding "out of thin air." That ability came in a handy way more than did our Spanish dictionary or our beginner's vocabulary. As interesting as it turned out to be, we heaved a big sigh of relief when we came back out on the main road again!

"Wow...living beside a tourist attraction..."

Eventually, we arrived at Lake Chapala, which is south of the major city of Guadalajara and near the small towns of Ajijic and Jocotepec. Our friends, Professor and Norma Bordeaux Szekely had a beautiful home and property on Lake Chapala. A mutual, long-time friend of us all, Eugene Farmer, was already in the vicinity. We met him originally when he and his former wife owned a health food store in North Vancouver, where we sold our alfalfa sprouts. He had driven from Canada to Lake Chapala in his home-made motorhome, arriving there a few days prior to us.

Eugene introduced us to a magnificent resort that was adjacent to our friends' property, and we all decided to stay there together. It had a geyser that erupted regularly on the edge of the property. That held some fascination for most of our little group - particularly our children. In the following week, we all went everywhere together. There were many little towns, and always a market, along the lakeside, so we went from one side of the lake to the other, with Eugene as our guide - and with him along, saw many things we wouldn't have otherwise noticed.

Eventually, after we had seen all we wanted to see, and before we had worn out our welcome with our friends, the Bordeaux-Szekely's, we asked them to point us in the direction of Cuyutlan. This is a tiny town in the state of Colima on the coast, near the city of Manzanillo. We reluctantly said goodbye to our friend, Eugene. Having decided to take a large detour in order to see Mexico City, we soon realized that even though the general pollution and smog in Mexico was bothering us, we had had no idea how much worse it was in Mexico City.

We first got an inkling of their smog problem only when we were getting somewhat close to the city. It was after dark, and as we were coming from the heights above the city, we pulled over to a lookout point. As we looked down into the crater in which Mexico City is built, all we could see was the blanket of smog hanging over it. As we drew closer - the smog was thick enough to cut it with a knife.

"Mexico City - a nightmare for our Canadian driving and anti-pollution mentality..."

We promptly changed our minds about sightseeing in the city and drove rapidly through the nightmare of Mexico City. That was a horrible experience for us: we saw that the air was black and, moreover, we couldn't breathe...so we drove all that night toward the Gulf of Mexico. We arrived early in the morning at the city of Vera Cruz and looked gratefully out our windows at the beach and the Gulf, which seemed all the more beautiful after the smog of the previous day. However, we were soon to discover that Vera Cruz had another kind of problem. We parked, and all of us piled out of the van, only to be shocked by the attack we felt from the wind sandblasting us. Without further ado, we all scrambled back into the van faster than we got out, nursing our sore legs.

This was not something we had bargained for. After a very short family pow-wow, we voted to retrace our steps. Although we were very disappointed, we belatedly realized what a treasure we had with Lake Chapala where we had come from. Having more than satisfied our curiosity about both the Gulf of Mexico and Mexico City, we quickly skirted the basin that it was in and headed out to Cuyutlan, a little town on the western seacoast.

"Cuyutlan Was More Our Cup of Tea…"

Professor Bordeaux-Szekely and his wife, Norma, owned a small plot of land on the beach there at Cuyutlan, and they had invited us to feel free to camp on it with our van. We had to have help finding the lot lines, but a neighbor helped us. That was a happy time as we all loved being on the beach - the expanse and freedom of it, and the great unpolluted air of the ocean!

A major benefit to a slow driving trip across the country was that we had lots of family communication time and a chance to understand each other better. Even more, individually, we had a lot of time for reflection. With all the time and hard work my children and husband and I had put into the garden and our business - even though I was working right alongside them and we had bonded over that as well - we needed some time out…a change of pace. Hence the reason that my husband and I had felt so strongly about taking the kids out of school for a break. Among other things, we needed to teach them about the importance of family and for all of us to have a chance to think about and talk over our priorities. They needed to learn to balance fun along with work. There is no point in working if you can't cash that in for fun. That is a major point of working. If you work and work and keep on working without making time for the important things in life, then what is the point of being successful? Most people tend to equate success with having a thick, fat wallet and a hefty bank account. Let me ask you something, is there any point in having all that money and no one to share it with or time to enjoy it? Everyone needs to realize that money is the means to an end. Not the end, in and of itself.

So even if you do have a lot of money, but you work a hundred plus hours a week and ignore the important things in your life: your family, your friends, your health, your hobbies, your interests, or even just to take time out to do nothing - having the money is questionable. Even doing nothing is important, just sitting around with a "cup of tea," looking out of the window, away from your phone, laptop, or TV.

As an aside, once I had regained my health and energy, I have struggled with this one on and off throughout my life.

I would say that my husband did also, but much less than I did. Also, my oldest...all his life. It showed up early when on his twelfth birthday he wanted to work in our business - and so my mom and dad came in to work with him before we all celebrated his birthday that evening. Another instance that comes to my mind is the time we couldn't get him to stop gardening for the afternoon and go with us all on our bike ride to the lake (or perhaps it was the beach). Our daughter was different - she was the only one of us who wasn't drawn to be always moving and working. By nature, she was a dreamer, an artist, and was much less driven than the rest of us.

You need to realize that if you keep on working without balancing it with relaxing and playful things, eventually you are going to burn out. So why even get to that point? Being focused is a curse and a blessing at the same time...because you may be the best at your job/ or business, but you might have lost sight of your priorities and your dreams. You cannot afford to do that, because without the little things (that bring you happiness), the money will be worth little.

On future trips when we flew into Mexico with no van, having to travel to Cuyutlan by bus, we always had to stay in a hotel - nice enough, but not the freedom and simplicity of living in a van on the beach (my husband and I were hippies at heart - and I think I still am). On our first trip, because we had our van, it didn't matter to us that Cuyutlan had no market (just a boardwalk in front of a row of hotels) because we were able to drive as often as we wished to the nearest town - and once to the larger one of Manzanillo. We loved the Mexican fruit and coconuts. Moreover, we tried to stay away from eating things off the bushes in order to not be ingesting the pesticides and water-borne bacteria that tourists' intestines are susceptible to.

We did pretty well - cooked our veggies…or for things we ate raw like our salad veggies, we washed those things in a tub of water to which we had added a couple of drops of our trusty Shaklee Basic H! On future trips, we relied almost entirely on the hotel - and when we ventured further, we spent a lot of time on a bus, or a lot of money on a taxi. It was hard for us to leave all this warm freedom behind and head for home. Our compromise was to stay longer in order to have maximum time in the warmth and on the beach - and then we did a quick dash for home.

Chapter 6
Back to Reality

When we returned from Mexico in January, life was exactly the same as we left it. We all fell into what we had been doing prior to our trip. The children and I went back to school once again; Robert returned to work at the university; and all of us popped back into our various roles in our business and took care of the aspects that each of us had done previously.

However, within a couple of months, I realized I no longer wanted to go to school. It wasn't that I was tired of going there every day - the repetition was not the issue that I was averse to (in fact, I encourage it; a good schedule allows a person to follow all their activities and responsibilities).

Rather, I had other things I wanted to do with my life now, and now, the original need for me to go to school, seemed handled. The vacation had given me much needed time to dream and think about all sorts of new possibilities, and I had become more aware of how much I wanted (and perhaps "needed") to have something that was mine.

Whatever I had done up until that point was with or for my family. That was just beginning to get redundant. I felt that they were ready to let go of me - at least somewhat.

It was timely because I was beginning to feel the need of wanting to branch out on my own and to accomplish some things that were uniquely mine - not tied into family things as my whole raison d'etre (reason for existence). As an aside, this turned out to be a perhaps lifelong search and on-going source of discontent and restlessness that I would always have to contend with... and another aside, the sense of accomplishment that one gets from doing something that they do all on their own is very effective for one's self-esteem - which I often struggled with - and therefore, could be helpful for me.

"A Nice Surprise..."

For a start, I wanted to be more involved in our business. That wasn't an expression or activity that was solely mine. However, there were needs that I could take on that no one else was looking after, and in addition, I was the one who could take care of these things the best. One example was any designing needed on packaging, or recipes, or production shortfall to fulfill orders of trail packs and food bars. The business was something that managed to give me a sense of accomplishment, and also it never bored me.

While we were gone to Mexico, that was the first time we had ever left other people to look after our business. Although we had closed it down for much of our vacation, there was the first part of the growing cycle that our helpers looked after for us while we were gone on our holiday… and they delivered the crop, right on time as promised. The crop was there, ready to be packaged and delivered on the day following our return, just as we had requested. We had been a bit apprehensive about leaving them to do it, however, they did really well with it all.

That experience gave us the confidence to follow through with our plan to expand the business. We now knew that we could trust our helpers in our absence, which was a huge thing for us, as we mostly had had to do everything by ourselves, up to this point.

"First Things First…The Children's Schooling"
We knew that the expansion would require much more of me than I had been giving, having been spending so much of

my time with the children at school. Once we began the expansion, it would be difficult for me to change my mind… so that now was the time to deeply examine my interest and commitment to take on more tasks and hours in our business before embarking on the expansion. The other issue was whether our children needed me on a daily basis at their school. My husband was a hundred percent behind me, letting go of the school and taking on more, both in our business and other endeavors as well. Anything I would take on in our business would make the expansion more feasible because he personally couldn't take on more than he already had outside of his university job. We both loved our children, but we also felt that my going to school with them was becoming unnecessary.

He urged me to check with the school once more to make sure that they would feel good about me sending the children on their own – and check if the staff thought our children were ready (the staff as well as our children). So I checked first with the school staff, and they said everything was going smoothly - the children were performing up to the expected level of the school…and the staff felt comfortable by now with the children being there on their own…and that it should be fine for me to bow out at this point. Fortunately, I had been right - and the school said yes. They agreed that everything was indeed going smoothly.

Then I checked with the children. I knew that in part, they would be sorry to not have me there any longer. However, I also knew that they would enjoy the increased freedom that they would gain once I was out of the picture. They weren't surprised at my announcement and questions because these ideas had been tossed around by Robert and myself a lot during our trip...and increasingly after we returned. They said they'd be willing to try it out – going by themselves.

I had checked everything that could be checked, but I still had a few lingering doubts (probably guilt-driven), and no one could help me with those. They were always lying there, waiting to pounce on me in a weak moment. However, I knew that there were other things that required my attention – and I was happy to be free to attend to these and to explore other new directions.

Also, it was not as if I was prioritizing my business over my children. I had checked every angle and was pretty sure that they could manage without me - whereas our business could not. I knew that there were things that even now required my attention - and there would quickly be many more once we expanded. However, siding with my "guilt complex"- some people in my life thought that this would be something akin to a sort of desertion and betrayal of my kids.

The flip side of the coin…I had been wondering if my spending that much time in their school could be having a smothering effect on them - or at least not allow them to become independent, which could have an adverse effect. I felt very strongly about raising our children so that they would be well prepared for the world. My withdrawal would most likely be an unexpected but great opportunity for them to learn how to manage without their father and me. However, if I'm remembering correctly, that didn't last long, and a short one and a half semesters later, by their final set of courses for that school year (this school used a trimester system), our children didn't want to go to school. Even more than that, they told us that they felt that they didn't "need" to go to school any longer.

Maybe this was one of the adverse effects of me having been there at all times with them in the beginning - and then not. Maybe they liked having me there to take care of each and every one of their needs rather than having to think for themselves! However, their decision was possibly just the product of having many family discussions about the purpose and pros and cons of schooling. We were a progressive family and paid a lot of attention to the ideas and wishes of our children. They knew that I, their mother, had always been at school with them to take care of each and every one of their needs. Consequently, at this point, they hadn't been as exposed to being on their own, having to fend for themselves, which has upsides as well as downsides.

Thankfully, summer vacation arrived before we had to deal with the lack of enthusiasm and absenteeism…and as it turned out, they didn't return. Summertime began, which meant that our children were free to indulge in following anything that was of interest to them. Initially, they dove into things around our home: they loved making meals and particularly, experimenting with sauces and dressings or even baking with their father (which was a passion of his).

In the garden - being summer and the height of the growing season - there was no end of things to do. Also, shopping. My daughter, particularly, was limited in her likes and vocal with her dislikes around our dinner meals, so we encouraged her to make her own dinner salads, complete with a dressing she would eat.

That included adding her ingredients to the weekly shopping list. This led to the children being agreeable with doing much of the family shopping at the health food store. Their ages were nine and six, which was old enough - at least together - to go out on their own without me worrying about their safety. We didn't have the advantage that the age of cell phones has brought. Then again, our city wasn't as full of perils as it is today - nor traffic - no pun intended.

After they had completed the shopping, they would get a clerk to put their name on the bags and get them stashed out in the back of the store for my husband or me to pick up later. It was a huge saving of time for us, but it was also a great learning experience for them. To this day, they are great shoppers - my daughter stays on top of the best buys and at which stores…my son runs a large produce department and is also aware of the best quality and price at the various wholesalers!

Inside our business, we encouraged them to help in any way that they liked in the endless possibilities. There were the three sides - one, the live growing/sprouting of our different seed crops; the second, the making and packaging of our food bars or packs of trail mixes. The third part was the wholesale import of tropical fruits (that was almost entirely orders, directly in and out of wholesale distributors – and Robert looked after this part of the business).

They loved best working with the food bars, and there always seemed to be trays of bars that had been formed, waiting to be packaged. Whereas, for the sprouts, there were usually only two days (and particular times) when they could work on that side of our business. They seemed to like the variety - which was very helpful for the business needs, but what was great for me was that they wouldn't insist on doing only what they loved best, but rather, they would check with me first to see where they were needed. When one of the sprout packaging days was coming up, we always checked with them to see if we could put their names down on the "staff" list before asking people outside our family (usually deaf persons or my parents) to fill the rest of the needs.

The garden was my son's passion… our daughter, on the other hand, is an artist and at that stage, would decorate anything she could get her hands on – it was almost like living in a madman's painting studio, and things like napkins, notes left on the telephone desk, envelopes, any piece of paper left lying around…all had her impression on them. Also, she loved everything about flowers - drawing and arranging them…and growing them. She was also helpful with other things that were needed – but she was the least practical and most experimental and creative – on paper and in the garden. She was young so we gave her that freedom to follow her heart…it's just that her heart was more creative than practical…whereas her brother was more driven to produce results (their natures have the same inclinations to this day).

With me being a musician, a pianist primarily, I encouraged our children to play a lot of music. They both were learning to play the piano; additionally, my son played the cello, and my daughter was partial towards the violin. I played duets with them on the piano and also accompanied them on each of their stringed instruments - any possible combo that we could manage. Later, with my third child, he learned the piano as well as the trumpet. I didn't know it at the time, but all this musical activity turned out to be a great decision on our part because playing an instrument is believed to expand a child's brain to think in creative ways and become very good at critical thinking. All my children...as witnessed by their current lives...seemed to have benefited greatly from all this musical activity throughout their lives.

This was as much a learning experience as it was a bonding one for the three of us. All of us enjoyed our musical sessions immensely, and I think they helped each of us to relieve a fair bit of the stress that had accumulated from the day's activities. As an aside, I think it is absolutely necessary to have some sort of relief from a day's activities that can help refresh a person's mind so that they can keep getting a new perspective on the tasks that they want to accomplish.

Some people have a very unrealistic view of what they can get away with in respect to their activities and responsibilities. They think that it is manageable for them to do the same thing, without breaks, and still be productive enough to accomplish that same task, with the same level of enthusiasm day after day. That is easier said than done. No matter how good you are or how creative you are, you cannot possibly think of new ideas and new ways to approach the same task with new ideas, indefinitely. Neither will your body stand up to the constant push. Hence, there is a need to relieve stress and refresh in order for your creative processes to continue and also for your body and mind to remain healthy.

For the children, helping us with our business was serving many purposes for themselves. It was educational in a myriad of ways. It gave them real-world exposure, and they learned how practical life actually works. This was a great opportunity for our children. Most people nowadays have completed their education and are certified professionals before they have any real-world exposure in their field. The difficulty with this scenario is that when they come up against a person who has had real-world experience, they will probably not measure up. That is because they have never learned how to handle themselves in real life situations (knowing correct manners, fairness, work ethics...and having experience working with others - to name only a few). Getting hands-on experience in life, is an absolute necessity for a person - as early as possible.

My children also learned the importance of money. We used to pay them for the work they did in our business...which gave them a lot of freedom to buy things they wanted. We didn't always agree with their choices, and they have some bad memories that have stuck with them over the years, of us sometimes stepping in and not honoring their choice (regardless of it being bought with their own money). I would like to point out that I am not proud of those times and could wish that I had been more aware of my mixed messages and inconsistency. They also learned to shop for the family's needs and to research things and bring us back their findings, which, in itself, was a very useful and advanced activity for their ages.

They learned, first-hand, about giving in to their temptations versus beginning by researching their intended purchase. Out of their practice at researching, they became more and more thoughtful about how to spend their money. In the beginning, as is the case with most people, they would think about their desires first, and reasoning came second. However, over time, they learned not to give in to their temptations so easily, and they became more thoughtful on how to spend their money… something that few learn young, and some grownups never, not even the hard way. There are the few fortunate ones who seem to have an innate understanding of money and how to make it grow and leverage it…the Tom Sawyers of the world! And my sister (about whom I already shared in Chapter One).

"Children's Rights - Not to Be Taken Lightly…"

We did our best to be sensitive to their total needs – educational, emotional, and other rights. We knew that they needed teachers and mentors, toys, equipment, playtime with friends, and other necessities, and opportunities – things that could even be considered luxuries but are invaluable in bringing up a child. This was something most parents - in this modern society, where they send their children off to school - do not have the opportunity to do for their children…at least to the extent that we did.

However, we had to be more vigilant than most parents and be careful not to take undue advantage of them in our business - some accused us of "child labor" - we were always under scrutiny. We knew that working in the business must be secondary for our children - that it was absolutely necessary to balance this in favor of exploring new things (both tangible and intangible), including many other needs and wants. The thing is that children need to experience new things and learn about as many different aspects of life as possible for their optimum development. However, our criterion (and aim) wasn't just about academics but rather a completely healthy, all-round system of "life" education that catered to all their needs.

Sometimes my husband and I were able to teach them or point them in the right direction. Other times, we hired a tutor for a specific interest that we were not equipped for - like gymnastics, some English, and Math. We realized that kids need role models to look up to in order to maximize their learning - and therefore, we chose tutors very carefully with that in mind. In addition, parents need to learn about their own limitations. They are apt to think that nobody is equipped to teach their children better than themselves, which is just not true. And even if it were, it could still be desirable to hire a tutor, given the amount of workload that most parents need to manage.

However, that can be tricky because if your children get the idea that you are just not interested in teaching them about a specific thing that they are interested in, then they might lose interest as well. Sometimes, we might have been equipped for it, but overall, it seemed better for our children to have at least some variety and experience from other people. In our case, they often weren't formal tutors - sometimes, they were friends of ours who had specialty areas that they could introduce to our children. The change was good for us because this gave us more time to focus on our own needs - plus, as I mentioned, it was much better for our kids as well. This gave them variety…and in addition, because we had had a break, later when we were with them, they had our undivided attention, and the time spent together was quality rather than forced and a "have to."

"Our Children's Athletic Family…"

A fellow colleague of my husband was a medical doctor and along with her was her scientist husband - both were avid ski and hiking enthusiasts. They took on being our children's "athletic" family, which was very important for our children. We all spent a lot of time outdoors - particularly in our garden…but lacked the physical aspect of nature and wilderness. Children need a substantial amount of exercise for a healthy development of their brain and bodies, so this was a very important add-on for our children's health and education. Our friends took their own two children (five and two years of age) everywhere - and just added ours (nine and six) into the "party." The first place they all went was on a bus trip to Salt Lake City to ski. For years following this very successful initial adventure, during the skiing season, they all went most weekends to Whistler ski resort (two hours' drive from our home). They always stayed in a communal lodge, which made it not just a skiing trip with all its rigor, physically, but also a wonderful experience in how to cooperate with other people.

Another destination with their "athletic family" was the West Coast Trail of Vancouver Island which was much more primitive in those days I've been told. A third trip was to the Purcell Mountains in the southern part of the range that borders between British Columbia and Alberta, just north of the U.S. border. A fourth trip was canoeing on the Bowron Lakes - another rigorous one. Apparently, for that trip, there are two choices: a one-week 72-mile trip, or a shorter, two-day trip. From what I know of our friends, they chose the longer and more difficult of the two canoe trips. All these experiences were of minimal interest to my husband and me as we had the priority of our business and his work life. So our children got to go with people who were actually interested and passionate about this, rather than with us, who would have been ill-equipped in every way or else worried about how our "city farm" (as our garden was affectionately referred to) and our business were doing. These weren't just physical experiences, though, for our children, but rather they got to have fun, be totally stretched in every way, and be involved in what was a socially-building experience for them as well.

The first time my husband and I saw our kids ski was when they were about twelve and fifteen and their new baby brother was about seven months old. Our oldest, Gordon, said he could take baby Colin on his back in the Gerry Carrier. We agreed, with our hearts in our mouths, and off we all set. My husband and I were hopeless - my husband even fell headfirst into a snowdrift. Gordon went flying along, giving his brother his first ride in the snow (later he became a skier too); Shelagh flew by us with speed and grace. Watching our two children skiing, they looked like pros to us, and we were very impressed. That was the only time we saw them ski as we didn't join them on any of their other ski trips (nor their other athletic jaunts). We were thrilled for their sake that they had the chance to have such outstanding outdoor experiences in spite of our not sharing this passion and interest.

"Their Second Travel Family..."

Their other "travel" exposure was during their summer holidays with their aunt and uncle (my sister and brother-in-law), who lived in Toronto. We flew the children to be with them most summers when they were school age. My brother-in-law had children the same age as ours, and they lived very close to us. They always joined ours on these trips and all four flew together to Toronto. Once, they went to a cabin on The Great Lakes where they canoed and did other water sports.

Many trips were spent at my sister's farm, a couple of hours north of Toronto. I don't think that I'm remembering all their trips - but I do remember that they were all great fun. My brother-in-law and sister were particularly great at exposing the children and teaching them a variety of trades and skills needed on a farm - and of course, showing them a good time. We got thinking about a trip destination that all four of us could do together. The thing about all of us going together on a family trip was that even though my husband

and I were minimally interested in our children's athletics, at the same time, we strongly believed that we needed to spend family time with them (and sometimes one-on-one) - and a trip is magical in that it isolates the family and throws them together much more closely than everyday living does at home.

I shared earlier that almost all of my experiences each day were based around time with family, and even though I now felt compelled (even needed) to do something on my own, I still believed that my family came first. Time for my own needs didn't mean to the exclusion of my family's need for me. It just meant that because I had this personal priority, that I needed to be mindful of my family's needs as I began to newly take care of my own emerging ones.

That is how I see life: it is just an endless series of commitments that you take on - or complete. The important thing that I notice is often missing for people in this process is the completion with integrity. Rather, they just quit and move on. I'm suggesting that before taking on a new commitment, you need to quickly review, one by one, your prior commitments and re-choose or give them up with integrity. There's no one way that completion looks, but it's important that the people and groups you leave behind feel taken care of in your completion process. This might mean something as simple as taking time to explain your changing needs, so they understand why you are leaving and not think there is something wrong with them. This might also mean writing up a job description of your position so they can more easily replace you.

To apply these thoughts about completion to my own situation, I needed now to complete my existing way of being with my family without sacrificing their needs in place of my own. This took open, honest communication over a long period of time. Some completions can take place quickly - this one could not. Rather it took place over many months…and had to be reviewed often as all of our needs were constantly changing.

Chapter 7
More About Gardening

That spring I began to garden "in earnest," meaning…I started to grow vegetables…rather than only do prep work. This had gone on for two winters since the days when we first began rolling the sod back just a bit beyond the border gardens and then decided to roll back all the sod on the entire property.

This meant we had created dirt right up to the house - both back and front, making it a challenge to keep the house clean. We weren't living rurally on a farm, but rather, in a sophisticated, largely carpeted, city house. Every time that we would go from house to dirt and back to house – even though we tried to be careful and always left our shoes and overalls at the basement door – we would still bring a lot of dirt inside.

For a solution, my husband decided to lay down wooden planks for walkways (only in the backyard to begin with). He then had a carpenter build about seven or eight raised beds in a long row against the fence running from our house to the lane. Each raised bed had wooden sides (which made them into boxes without bottoms) and planks between each raised bed (or box). The planks eliminated the problem of bringing dirt into the house in the backyard. In the front garden, we covered the ground with leaves in the winter and made cedar mulch walkways between some of the veggies during the summer. In addition, we had garden boots for when the earth was damp or muddy - or summer thongs - which helped. Our gardening was done mainly in the backyard, whereas the front was for crops that we could grow in large quantities or which took a lot of space to grow and didn't need much care - these were corn, cucumbers, potatoes, peas, squash - and so on.

"The Danger Of Becoming A Catalog Gardener..."

I still remember the experience of that first spring, when I had decided the garden, the weather, and I were all ready for planting. All winter (and even the one before that) I had been reading garden catalogs and "how-to" books until my brain was stuffed full of ideas. I was beginning to feel overloaded from the lack of action in the garden itself. I remember having a conversation with one of our tradesmen who was Italian and was working on a brick retaining wall at the front of our property. He had been listening to me for a few weeks and observing my inaction, and one day he asked me how my garden was coming. I told him I felt stuck and was finding it really difficult to take the first step (which he knew, of course, and was why he asked me in the first place). He threw out a couple of ideas and then carried on with his work.

We met the next day, and even though his ideas were good, they weren't exactly what I was looking for. When we met, I told him that I was still stuck, and I didn't think that any number of ideas would help un-stick me - and what I thought I needed was someone to be beside me and show me what to do. I went off to the backyard to think about it some more. Doing gardening alone can be very therapeutic in its own way, however, for me, it no longer seemed like it.

By this time, I had read all the backs of my seed packets many times until I just about had the instructions memorized. I felt overwhelmed for one thing, and secondly, I really didn't know what to do, in actual practice…just like reading about how to drive a car and actually driving a car are very different. You can have theoretical knowledge but doing something on a practical level will have you face so many different types of technicalities that you no longer will be able to relate it back to your book knowledge. That was the problem I was facing.

"My Italian Angel..."

Bless him, if "my" Italian didn't come to the backyard and ask me for the beans he had given me some weeks prior, (from his mother in Italy). I rummaged through my seeds and handed him "his" beans. He said they'd do best against a fence, so we found a stretch of garden that went right up against the fence. He knelt down (I watched his every move), and with his index finger, he drew a line parallel to the fence.

That line was about one and a half inches deep. Then he placed a bean about every two inches apart. He did this until all his beans were in the trench. Using the dirt that he had displaced when he dug his trench, he covered the beans and patted the earth firmly in the row above the beans.

"Next?" He asked.

"Radishes," I said and found the radish packet. He poured a few seeds into his hand as we headed for the first raised bed. He told me that these seeds could be scattered thicker, and I could thin them as they came up. He repeated the procedure, (more or less) – using his finger to make a trough. (This time he made the trough flatter and a bit wider). He took a few seeds at a time from the palm of his hand and scattered them sparsely in the first part of this trough - and patted it firmly. Next, he told me to copy what he had just done…and so I did, until the trough was complete.

We marked names on sticks at the end of each row (I borrowed some popsicle sticks from our family craft supplies). Next was spinach. Then lettuce, carrots, beets. Peas, he said, took more room, and that I should plant only peas in one raised bed. He suggested I soak them overnight and plant them the next day, the same way he had planted the beans.

By the next day, I had completed the first seeding of everything else like broccoli and cabbage and bush beans. It left corn, potatoes, and the soaked peas to plant in the front garden - all of which took more space and needed little care. The tomato plants (which we purchased at a garden shop) were going on the rooftop of the carport, now that my husband was ready to haul the pails of dirt up there. I had just needed a little "hands-on" support - and I was on my way and my husband was waiting patiently for me to be ready to deal with the tomato plants.

"Now There Was No Stopping Us…"

Seeing me making progress, my husband now got in on the act, too. He was great about doing what was needed. He especially liked specific projects such as the tomato one - filling pails with earth, adding one stake in each pail, and then hauling them up onto the flat rooftop of our garage. I mentioned before that he also loved composting.

He had just built three or four large compost bins against the house to replace our little out-of-the-way compost bin that we inherited from the previous owners - for the scale of gardening we were into, we had soon outgrown that tiny bin (although a resident raccoon appreciated the quieter spot that it's "home" had become since the addition of our newest bins)!

As was my husband's way, he would develop what he could, and then he would call upon a couple of men he had found who liked to complete his designs and build them for him. This was for both the garden projects as well as our inside renovations. These helpers had soon built the plank walkways throughout our garden, followed quickly by helping my husband build removable frames to attach to our raised beds to form sides and tops. This turned each raised bed into a mini greenhouse that could be converted seasonally to give more or less warmth to seeds and plants in the raised beds.

In addition, against the garage in the far corner of our backyard, my husband built another compost bin and finally purchased a greenhouse kit. All of us pitched in and helped put it together, using the garage wall for extra strength for one of its sides. That enabled us to get all our seedlings out of our basement. Growing in a greenhouse was a far superior way for them to get ready for transplanting in the main garden.

When both they and the season were ready, their stocks were sturdier, and the plants didn't have to go through the shocking transition from inside to outside. They were used to the daily swings in temperature and light, which they weren't when we started them in our inside growing room (and was one less reason to bring dirt inside). Also, my daughter grew avocado trees in pots - we all had a lot of fun with our many greenhouse experiments.

"We All Found Our Niche…"

In the garden, Robert's role and my role was interchangeable (as they often were in the rest of our lives). Sometimes, I had the vision first that Robert helped me carry out, and other times vice versa. This helped both of us to take on each other's visions in every aspect of our lives. We seamlessly backed each other's visions - but even more, we could input where the other one lacked. Neither of us believed in anything being so…just because society-dictated it, such as marriages being led by the male or females taking on the homemaking and so on.

The downside was that we had to examine the truth of everything we did. We had to make sure we weren't just accepting thoughtlessly what we had grown up hearing and seeing…but rather, that everything was honestly chosen and followed. This is very time and energy-consuming, as opposed to following the societal or religious traditions and roles and inheritance (ideologies we grew up with)!

One marvelous thing we discovered is that there were so many different aspects of gardening that there seemed room for all of us to find things we liked. Of course, there were the ho-hum jobs, too, like weeding - but even then, there always seemed one of us for whom each job spoke, no matter what it was. This was fortunate - it wasn't like housework, where there are some jobs that no one really wants to do like defrosting the fridge or washing the toilet (those are the notorious two)! A small example in the garden is the weeding...most don't like to weed, but it happened to be my love...as composting was my husband's. Our daughter would do most things, but she loved anything to do with flowers!

Our son, Gordon, just loved it all...but the unique needs of each plant became his specialty. Earlier on, we had hired a gardening tutor for him who came a couple of days a week. However, after a few months, the tutor informed us that he was superfluous in that Gordon was beginning to know more than his tutor did and suggested we try him on his own - which turned out to be absolutely correct! By the second year, our garden was quite developed...and by the third, it looked very mature...kind of like we had been doing it forever.

However, we found that there was no end to our education where the garden was concerned. Some things I learned from observing other people's approach; other things I learned from books; still others I learned from experiencing them; and some things I discovered by "accident." My garden gave me so much: a great amount of pleasure, as well as education, health, and relaxation. Being involved with something that had that much variety and breadth to it was amazing because it always gave me something new that I could busy myself with. This proved to be very healthy for me, as well as made me appreciate just how much hard work all of us put into the garden. One year, a Vancouver newspaper sent out a reporter who had fun photographing and writing up our story, titled "A City Farm."

We were just doing what we were led to do, whereas, to others, it seemed ahead of its time, unusual, unique. Unbeknownst to us, farming wasn't that common in the city due to everyone being so busy and compared to a rural farm, having a limited amount of space. However, it wasn't because we were idle that we were led to gardening, but we made time for it because we were so passionately drawn to it. At the start, we didn't know just how fun this would be for us, due to the problems we faced in the very beginning - such as the Morning Glories running all over everything, and so many bushes and not much visible dirt.

The trick was to keep on putting the right foot in front of the left foot, and once we had created a little space and could see the earth, each next step just followed naturally. Then it was the Italian man teaching me a few things, and after that, we were on our way to becoming "farmers." We certainly didn't have the whole vision right from the start. It took beginning it first…and then it became an ever-unfolding activity for us that soon became amazing - certainly for others, but for us as well.

On the other hand, many people in the city didn't appreciate our "farming," and to our immediate neighbors, we were just plain annoying. They thought of us as hippies who were turning our Shaughnessy home and yard into a farm - affecting their bottom line…their property value. However, we couldn't concern ourselves about that. Tying ourselves to societal norms, for any reason - and particularly fear of being thought of as weird - or lowering their property value - wasn't something that we were going to worry about. For us, our garden was turning out perfectly, and we were just making it better and better the longer we were at it!

However, we were beginning to outgrow it - it wasn't big enough to support the level of gardening to which we had grown. We would soon need to move to a rural setting, well beyond the suburbs, and with more land than a city lot offered us - but our "city farm" was a fit for us for about five years altogether.

Chapter 8
A Woman Caught in the
Changing of the Times

It was a wonderful marriage - synergetic, loving, and supportive for the first ten years. However, I found out much later that I had just been going along without paying attention to how things were between us. It was many years later that I learned that relationships and marriages need tending - that they regularly need a bit of analysis and thoughtfully taken actions in order to make improvements, and to continue to deepen and grow (and particularly to grow together). I had thought that whatever was so was so.

The thing about marriage is that when the honeymoon period is over, the spark you once found in each other often is gone. Then the person you loved and trusted, and moreover, saw the stars and moon in your eyes, just becomes another person whom you live with. You lose sight of what made them special, and why you were with them in the first place. It may not happen immediately, not even after an year or so, but almost every marriage goes through a phase where each idiosyncrasy that you once admired, the little things that made you feel butterflies in your stomach when you saw them for the first time, just become a distraction - or even an annoyance - in your busy life. That time is inevitable, which is why you need to constantly be working on your marriage - and yourself.

For some people, it is practically impossible to get up every morning to the same person, live out the same scenario day after day, over and over again and still be madly in love with them. It just is not possible, and when that time comes, it is not just the man's responsibility to work on the marriage, nor is it just up to the woman. It is both their responsibility, and if the level of effort is less from either side, that marriage doesn't stand as much of a chance to work out as when both are committed to putting in the work.

However, I was a woman who was caught in the moods, trends, and changes of the times. In those days, I wasn't very mature in the area of relationship, although I want to be careful in judging and assessing how I was back then. Somehow, we were both a product of the times. I was becoming disillusioned about my life - it seemed too small a life, too limited...unfulfilling...solely as just a mother and wife (and to say this is not in any way to belittle my role of being a wife or a mother. But the healthier I became, the more I wanted and was able to follow through on my goals, wishes, and dreams.

Most people will think that saying that, even thinking it, is a taboo. However, one thing I have learned in all my years is that running away from how you actually feel will just come back to bite you. Being dissatisfied with what you have, while knowing that you can do more with your life… is painful. Knowing in your heart of hearts that you were meant for more than just where you are can lead to feeling caged. I realize, now, that to this day, I have no idea what disillusions my husband was feeling about his life. I'm fairly sure that he mostly was dealing with mine…and how it interfaced with or disrupted his life and path!

Nowadays, people have so many responsibilities thrust on them that it is very hard to find the time to think about what they actually want to be, what they want to do - or even what they don't want to continue doing. Maybe, just maybe, this is the reason that people wake up one morning with the realization that they're stuck in a job they don't want to go to… the worst part being that they can't see how to do anything about it because they have bills to pay, or there's mouths to feed or they are at the top of their company or field with big responsibilities.

They could be making money to fulfill their wildest dreams but don't have the time or freedom to fulfill them. Take the star of Hangover, for example. He had been a doctor, but he actually wanted to be a comedian, and he only pursued that at the wish of his dying wife…and became very successful. The point being that it is okay to be dissatisfied and want more - or different - from your life…and to pursue that!

Perhaps I was feeling housebound and could have benefited from going to work. An obvious choice was to re-apply for a teaching position. But, in looking back and thinking deeply about it, I realized something. It took only the four months of teaching that I did before being married, to know (even way back then) that I no longer wanted to be a teacher…at least not formally in a traditional school. Four months was enough of that for me - too much paperwork and sticking to a predetermined regimen of lesson plans, setting and marking of exams, assessing grades, and so on.

"Hindsight Has 20/20 Vision…"

In hindsight, that would have been a good time for me to change careers and do the appropriate upgrading. Just recently, I ran across my transcripts and cover letter to a California university regarding their Counseling Psychology program - so apparently, at one point, I had been exploring other things. I think Social Work was also a possibility, but it was too government-regulated for my liking and is a profession that I see as overworked and underpaid. However, being a mother of small youngsters, going to California to study was out of the question.

But, for some reason that isn't apparent to me now, I didn't have the foresight to see I was on the right track and just needed to choose a local university or college program. Instead, I carried on with unrelated local activities and personal projects that interested me. Apparently, though, I had had a hunch about something that could interest me much as a future career. However, my timing was off...now I was so involved in family and business projects, I didn't have any desire to develop a career outside of my entrepreneurial life...it was only a mild wish that I dropped and never followed through with.

However, if I had wanted to, if it had been a dream or a strong wish, I could have pursued an alternative way to achieve it. My responsibilities didn't have to stop me…and I am not saying that responsibilities aren't important and that you should just up and abandon your responsibilities on a whim. However, almost always, if there is vision, commitment and willingness, then an opening and even a miracle will occur. In this case, I wasn't there - I had become thrilled by my life by now!

"Our Relationship Went Downhill After the Ten-Year Mark…"

There was a whole lot of change that went on in our relationship around about the ten-year mark – and it was a slow death from then till the twenty-first year. Gradually, our marriage ran aground. We even separated for a couple of weeks once. We did that, in hindsight, with the hopes that both of us would realize something was amiss after being without each other…and maybe it did work for a while.

However, that was not the root of the problem. The bottom line was that I was feeling dissatisfied. We had a good life…we had our business, we had our children, and in practical terms, a really good home life…but sometimes even that is not enough. However, it took eleven years for us to end the marriage after a long, slow - and sometimes painful - ride downhill.

Once, I remember, my parents took my husband and me out for a drive around our neighborhood and talked with us about marriage and what it took…and particularly for a wife. Their take on things was that I needed to take stock and make some changes for things to work. I don't remember what changes, but mostly, it was old thinking, which was that the wife is to obey her husband and follow his lead.

That went over like a lead balloon with me – I didn't think that was the answer to anything (and Robert wasn't into that kind of relationship any more than I was). They meant well – and were doing their best as parents. They loved us both, and it must have been very painful at times for them to watch us struggle and not be able to do anything to help us!

However, the feelings that I had at that time were very complicated: on the one hand, I knew that what I felt was completely alright to feel. I wasn't satisfied, nor would I be even if I were to obey my husband to the letter. On the other hand, that wouldn't change our feelings, nor would it ensure that the marriage would be saved.

We managed to carry on for another ten years before we finally parted. I wasn't unhappy all the time or about everything – it came in waves and was usually sparked by something. We carried on at least two or three years after that before a couple of major events happened. The first is that I had an affair with our business partner. To my way of thinking, it was inevitable, in that Robert and I weren't dealing with any of the issues that existed (and were growing) in our marriage.

In this day and age, I think we might have gone for counseling, but it's impossible to look back now and know what might have improved things or been done differently. I was hungry for something I wasn't getting, and an affair was the outcome. I don't see that as making me a bad person; however, I do think I acted irresponsibly, impulsively, and emotionally.

"A Bad Combination: Our Distraction, A Bad Egg of a Business Manager, And Uncompromising Bank Loan Attitudes…"

The next outcome was that our business bankrupted. This was a horrible time for all of us. My husband, Robert, was so disturbed by me and our business partner's actions that he (and I) lost our focus and didn't give sufficient time or attention to our business. As an aside…some parts of it would make a really funny movie – especially when our business manager, right under our noses, began to use our facility to house his own business products, to use our money to run his own business (by not paying our utility and other critical bills). We had two major bank loans, and one of them "called their loan," the other fell in line, and all our other creditors united against us.

I realize, as I'm writing this, that I still feel bitter towards the bank for their action. Obviously, they were within their legal rights. However, we were doing the best that we had ever done in our business at that time. To add to our misery, our business was far from failing. Therefore, when the banks were upon us and asking for their money, it made no sense to me for the banks to recall the loan.

The auditors were a prestigious firm, and they, too, sided with the two loan corporations' attitudes. Due to that, there was a huge loss of money by all concerned. I still find it hard to imagine why the auditors would suggest that action. Looking at it all now…it seemed both unreasonable - even unscrupulous - to halt the business with outstanding debts when it was doing well enough to have been able to quickly pay them all off.

To my knowledge, the most critical problem was the business manager – there was more than enough money being generated daily to pay all the bills – the business manager just needed to be dethroned, and the money he was siphoning off for his business would soon have paid everything (bills and regular payments to creditors).

Plus, we had growing numbers of orders for all our products. To this day, I don't think the banks acted reasonably or fairly. I believe that if the bankruptcy trustee had chosen, instead, to just preside over us, checking our actions and our books, working alongside us for a few months, the business would soon have paid the unpaid bills and sorted itself out. All the creditors would have been repaid, and there would have been no bankruptcy.

We even had a deal cooking with Saudi Arabia for our sprout manufacturing techniques (like a franchise). Years later, I was going through my file cabinet, and I found that all our correspondence had stopped with them when we bankrupted, but a year or two later, when we were no longer doing the business, they had sent a letter requesting us to move forward on this idea!

Back to my life...We lived a very rich, full, interesting life – it certainly wasn't all difficult or bad. To this day, I marvel at my willingness to give up what I had, in order to discover what I hadn't! I'm not unhappy or regretful about what I chose – it just seems quite a cost, and I have to believe that we were done, and it was time to move on. We had both become different people, and neither of us could give the other what we needed or wanted any longer. Declaring our marriage over was very hard - for me, for my husband, and for our children. However, sometimes, things must run their course, although at the same time, it is good to be actively engaged in this process, rather than be the victim. Therefore, when it is teeter-tottering, it is always better to try every alternative before pulling the plug.

We didn't take our marriage lightly...it was not something that we wanted to just end overnight on a whim... or just because we were feeling exasperated or hopeless...and particularly when our children were involved. We believed that having made a commitment, each of us needed to hold up our end of the commitment. However, some things just aren't meant to last. In the eleven more years that it took for the marriage to completely dissolve, I can say that we tried everything we could think of to salvage our marriage…but we found nothing that worked.

I am not so blind as to think that I was completely in the right. I think my parent's assessment was correct…that the problem lay mostly with me. My husband gave me ultimate freedom, so that wasn't the issue - although he didn't like how often I chose things other than family, and he frequently complained that I was a bad mother. Be that as it may, it was not my husband who was wanting out of the marriage; it was I who was unhappy, even though in the end, it was my husband who asked me to leave because it was too stressful for him to live with my unhappiness. My family was largely taking care of itself…My two older children weren't young kids any longer…and my husband didn't need me; rather, he wanted me to leave him in peace. By that time, I didn't see that I was choosing my own needs over the family or that what I was doing was bad. It was only our youngest son who still had a lot of parental needs - and we agreed to share in his care - about fifty/fifty…but flexibly.

I believe that the outcome was much better than what would have become of us if we had remained together. Put in very simple terms: we were done.

Chapter 9
Life On An Island –
Preamble To Life In Community

This all happened in 1975-76. At the end of '76, I discovered that I was pregnant with our third child. For a couple of years, we had been toying with the idea of moving more rurally to satisfy our urge to "go back to the land" on a larger scale than we could in town. With the recent demise of our business…and now, the news of the imminent birth of our third child…it lit a fire under us, and we decided to do it. As it often happens in life, there are unexpected circumstances that push us to make decisions that we have hitherto found difficult to make until life presented us with a different set of circumstances - as it did for us.

It is, ultimately, those new circumstances which allow us - or even force us - to go in new directions. However, it's a fine line, because the best decisions are not usually made in the heat of the moment; rather, they must be thought through. Therefore, it's a fine line between making a decision too quickly as opposed to taking too long to make the decision…they both have their upsides and their downsides.

In life, as in everything, moderation is the key...you shouldn't be too quick to make a decision, but neither should you be too slow to take the jump. We had been a little bit on the slow side...until some things in our life forced us to deal.

The search for a piece of land, rurally, was fun, and took us a long while to find what we were looking for. We didn't search alone – we found a realtor who spent a lot more time on it than we could. The area in which we had started looking was out in the Fraser Valley because we frequently drove out to visit our American friends who had property in Mission...and initially, we had really liked the area. However, after many months of driving through it, with the stench of cattle manure assailing our nostrils (from the heavy cattle industry in the area), plus the sight of small planes dusting crops with their pesticides, we reluctantly took the Fraser Valley off our list.

One day, the realtor phoned us and said he had found a property that he thought would meet our criteria. However, it was on one of the Gulf Islands. Its saving grace was that it was on the first island stop out from the Mainland – Galiano Island. Even though it wasn't amongst the areas on our list, he wondered if we would consider going to see it with him.

We hoped he was right, and it wasn't totally a wild goose chase - although it sounded like an interesting day trip, at least. Well, he was right. After we arrived on the island, we drove for about ten miles up the island and two miles into the forest on a dirt road. We arrived at an open gate that was the entrance to the property. Inside the gate, there was a fork in the road, and we followed the left one. This took us down a hill and opened out into a thirty-acre valley. That was an unexpected surprise, having traveled all this time through the forest (even the main road that we drove up the island was forested on either side).

The road was built on the crest of a hill, and the land fell away gently on both sides, and then each side leveled out onto a flat valley floor. There were two buildings in the middle of this valley – on the highest piece of land. One was a thirty-foot diameter geodesic dome. At right angles to it was an empty shed (made from beams like railroad ties), closed in on only one end and completely across the back of the shed. It was four bays wide, each wide enough to comfortably house a van like ours (so we kept it in the end bay, which was open on three sides and closed only on the back and roof).

Behind the dome on the opposite side to the shed, was a very old orchard – mostly apples (in time we learned they were good keepers and juicers), and a couple of early apple trees, one crab apple, a couple of prune plum, and a few pear trees. Later, we noticed a small orchard just beyond the shed. It had many fewer trees than the main orchard did – mostly apple, plus a "ginormous" prune plum with a couple more smaller ones (probably self-seeded from the parent tree). Not that day, but eventually (after we owned it), we discovered more trees along the path winding out of the valley and just up a little hill, but before it entered the forest.

There were three of our favorite trees amongst that tiny collection of fruit trees. However, it was not only our favorite but also the residential raccoons' favorite trees – three big, fat, juicy, yellow plum trees. The first time the raccoons beat us to the plums, we couldn't believe that they could (and would) totally clean us out – and boy were we mad…we had been salivating for weeks! From then on, each year after that, the race was on to get them - in their prime, but ahead of the raccoons. After that, we only missed on the rare occasion if we unavoidably had to be gone for a few days and missed the "picking" day. Otherwise, we were up there, every day, checking out the plums (as were the raccoons - every evening, I'm sure).

As you can probably guess, from my detailed description of the fruit trees, I really love fresh, tree-ripened fruit. However, it was the next discovery that settled it for us. The garden wasn't visible from the dome area – but we knew that there was one, from the description we had read on the sales blurb. We decided to follow a pathway that took us to the west side of the valley (whereas the dome, kitchen, and orchards had all been on the east side). Suddenly, the bushes hiding the garden came to an end...and there it was.

"The Garden Was Like Winning the Lottery..."

An enormous garden (a few acres) was surrounded by a combination wood and wire fence and a moat-like ditch – the fence handled the voracious and persistent deer that wandered hungrily by; the ditch handled the high water table and kept the land from returning to a lake (it was a reclaimed lake bed). Speaking of "reclaimed," this garden had already been reclaimed by nature, having been un-tended for at least that summer – the grasses were as tall as I am, and weeds were thriving as well. I remember thinking that that was an extremely good sign of very healthy soil and optimal growing conditions.

It was hard to see any earth with such a thick mat of vegetation (my husband and I were unsuccessfully attempting to scuff it aside). At that moment, our realtor showed up, holding out a shovel. Once Robert started digging…we could hardly believe what we saw: black soil without any rocks. We thought that maybe it was just happening in that spot, so we moved to a different location and dug again…the same result. We were stunned. We just stood there, speechless. We looked at our realtor…he knew we were goners (which must have pleased him immensely)!

We didn't have the money for this purchase (unlike when we first started to look) – because of our bankruptcy in between times, we now had to put our thinking caps on to figure this out. It wasn't very long before my sister and brother-in-law, bless them, stepped forward with a loan for the down payment to get us started. Hence, in the fall of 1976, we were the very happy owners of one hundred and fifteen acres of farm and forest land on Galiano Island.

Chapter 10
Homestead...Then a Community

"First, We Set Up a Homestead...A Few Years Later, A Community..."

The most immediate thing that was needed was for us to clean up the valley (particularly in the two orchards and all the land around the buildings in between the orchards). There was garbage, discarded household items (big and small), broken glass over the entire orchard from target practices, and dysfunctional things at every turn. We went over on the ferry with our van most weekends in the fall, also all winter whenever the weather wasn't icy or snowy, and then in the spring, we went back to our pattern of going most weekends again. We did only two things – and that was to fill our van for a trip to the dump (on our way down the island to our ferry trip back home) - or repair things.

This was important in a whole other way to us. It gave us a chance to relive the time we spent gardening on our urban "farm" - and it achieved exactly what it did then...it gave us relatively simple tasks that we could focus on every day. It was a good past-time, and we were outdoors, which was where we were all happiest.

"The glories of bushwhacking…"

On each trip, after our van was full, and we had reasonably achieved our goals for that trip, we would then spend the remainder of the weekend doing our favorite thing – bushwhacking and exploring. It continued to be our favorite past-time as long as we lived in our island home. Salal bushes grew almost everywhere, and the funniest thing was to lose our balance and disappear beneath the Salal. As an aside…much later that year, after our baby was born - and old enough to be carried on my/our backs in his Gerry carrier - we took him bushwhacking. For me, being small, with my baby behind me, it was even easier to lose my balance and tip over backward into the Salal – he thought that was the most fun – but it often took the whole family to get the two of us back up on my feet again!

The first year, for the longest time, before our baby was born, we just went back and forth for most weekends…and many weekdays, too. Because the children were being home-schooled, it didn't matter which days of the week that we were gone from town. Although he had some constraints, even my husband had a lot of flexibility in that he did not have a nine to five job...was more of a researcher...and had a lot of control over his appointment schedule.

For our work during the week, we were helping the group of people who bought our business from the Bankruptcy Trustee to learn all its ins and outs. I don't think we had to do this, legally, but we felt morally obligated to help the new owners have an easy and productive takeover. Every business has many things in common, but ours had many unique aspects that took them some time to learn.

They only bought the sprouting part of our business - not the Sweet Munchy bars or Trail mixes. There was a local Health Food Wholesaler who bought our new automated bar maker to use for their own bars - but they discontinued our bars and trail mixes - our Sweet Munchy bars were no more after our bankruptcy...we found it hard to believe that our bars were gone. Therefore, we only trained our successors to learn the sprouting operation, the sale having been dependent on our agreeing to train them. We knew some of them because they owned a health food store and restaurant which we had frequented over the years - and because of our friendship, we found it easy and enjoyable to help them learn the business, even though we were still feeling a mixture of sad and mad about the bankruptcy.

"Preparing for family expansion…"

Our third child was to be born at the end of July - and I think that by late spring when it warmed up, and because the successors of our sprout business didn't need much from us any longer, we began spending most of our time in our Galiano home. I would often find myself in a philosophical, dreamy state (which seems very natural for me to have been more introspective at this time of life).

I would picture different scenarios and would mull them over. I had been through the "baby" scenario twice already and now that they were the ages of eleven and fourteen, it seemed to me that the largest part of my parenting of my older two was complete - they were well on their way to being the kind of people they would become…their traits and ways probably wouldn't change much from here on.

It seems such a huge responsibility we have…to give the right and wise mix of unconditional with tough love to our children so they will mature into wise, loving, happy adults.

At this moment, it felt a little daunting, and I wondered how I got through this twice before with my first two children. At the same time, this thought gave me the strength to know that since I had gone through it twice…so I surely would once more.

My births have all been Caesarean, and therefore, by a third one, the doctor just gives a woman a date to show up for her surgery (which is always at least two weeks earlier than her ascertained due date so that there is little chance of going into early labor). Confident that I wouldn't go into labor earlier than my surgery date, I stayed on Galiano as long as I dared before I had to show up at the hospital.

"My Safety Bubble…"

The weather was lovely…we were all happily industrious with our first garden on our land, and I didn't want to leave my "heaven." The swimming was particularly heavenly for me. There was a lake nearby where I went swimming almost daily right up to the last minute before our baby was born. They were all afraid I would drown, so we devised tying an empty four-gallon plastic bottle to my wrist with a couple of feet of rope. If I was out there, alone on the lake (with family or friends far away onshore), and I became tired, I could wrap my arms around the bottle and relax and catch my breath. To whichever one of us devised it, I was grateful...it really worked to give us all peace of mind, and give me my private, portable docking station. Time alone away from the family was particularly good for me, and given that I was pregnant with my third child, I felt that I had a right to that alone time, and my family was great about giving it to me (even if I was only fully alone out in the middle of the lake)!

Chapter 11
Unto Us A Child Was Born

I think we all went into town at that time and my guess is that it was because of the nature of the trip - to welcome a new baby into our family. Otherwise, our children were old enough to stay on their own as they had, previously, many times. Sometimes they stayed at our Vancouver home (which was still available, having not been sold yet by the Bankruptcy Trustee). Other times they also spent time with my parents in White Rock, which was just about an hour by bus.

"Praise Be For Modern Birthing Improvements..."

As for me - I was in the hospital, of course. This time it was a short, easy process for me with just two days in the hospital as opposed to thirteen days for my first hospital birth and eleven days for my second. By the end of the second day, I was doing very well. However, by that time, I'd just about completely had it with the bureaucracy and rigidity. It was a mixed bag because, on the one hand, I was fed up, yet, on the other hand, I was very grateful to be part of a modern,

20th-century hospital for something like a Caesarean birth. Not a whole lot earlier in history (a hundred years earlier, perhaps), I would have died - and often the baby also!

On the third morning, I woke up really early and woke my husband, who was sleeping beside me. I told him that I felt ready for him to go to the front desk and begin processing my release. My husband was as fed up as I was, so he was pleased with what he heard me say - and off he went. However, at the front desk, he found that our doctor, bless him, had already signed me out when he was leaving the day before. It was a weekend, and since he wasn't going to be around, and he knew I was anxious to go home, he signed the necessary papers - bless him! There was no fight, which I must confess I was prepared to go through if needs be.

The doctors wanted me to stay nearby (any hospital) just long enough to ensure that the baby and I were well on our way without any complications needing medical help. A half-hour drive from the hospital, my Mom and Dad had a beach property, so that's where we headed for a few days - and spent most of our time at the beach while we stayed with them. That gave my mom and dad a chance to get acquainted with their third grandchild.

"Water For The Baby - And His Family, Of Course..."

Our first year on our island home had been a mind-blowing change for the city girl that I was - to be on the land, with no well water for almost a year and only wet wood for the stove that first winter! Every week, my husband brought large containers of water back home when he returned from working in town. However, confirmed recycler and environmentalist that I was, it was emotionally difficult to accept that I had to use paper diapers and not cloth ones when we had no water supply. Needless to say, we put in a well, no more than a month after we brought our baby to his new home.

The 30' geodesic dome we lived in was almost two miles off the main road, and there were no neighbors for miles. Since there was no electricity, we used candles and kerosene lamps. We cooked outside in a shed that was open on two sides (we soon put a screen around it to keep the bugs out, although that didn't make it any warmer, of course). We ate a lot of raw food in those days and only used a wood stove for major cooking or a kerosene stove for smaller jobs.

Sleeping was interesting – we closed off an area in the large shed, next to our kitchen, and put up a four-foot high plywood wall with screening beyond that to the ceiling. Next, we set up four simple wooden platform beds with foam for mattresses. Talking about Spartan living – when I think about it now, I would probably have a similar reaction to our parents if any of my children came to me with that news – but at the time, it was exactly how my husband and I wanted to live – and was a classic example of parents not being able to make things easier for their children.

One night an interesting - and scary - thing happened. We had just climbed into bed and snuggled down when we saw a light in the distance, and it seemed like it was coming closer. It was…and came into the orchard that was right beside our outside bedroom. Then a gunshot rang out - and then another… and then silence. My two kids were terrified and whispered to me, asking what it was. In the first place, my husband was in town, and therefore, there was no van to signal the presence of people living there. Our "farm" had been vacant for a long time before we bought it, and therefore it was easy for people to assume it was still empty. I was also feeling terrified and wondered if I should shout

out to the person - but not really having the nerve to do so. Luckily for us, the light began to move into the distance and was soon gone back where they came from. We found out later that it's common for hunters to "pit-lamp," meaning hunt deer at night with lanterns or flashlights. But I'm fairly sure that they wouldn't have done it in our orchard if they had known someone was living there.

"I Am Tireless and I Never Give Up..."

This was a truism about me that showed up frequently throughout my life - and perhaps more so during my Galiano Island days than in any other period of my life. My family had another way of describing this quality in me - "She holds onto things like a fox terrier." I always thought they were being critical of me or annoyed when they said it, and maybe they were, but I was really surprised when I discovered that this (and others) is one of the qualities of a warrior! Moreover, some can be developed but are often ingrained from birth.

But since they are unconventional and most people seem to find them annoying, I found that I generally thought people were right and that I lacked control – or something negative like that. I certainly didn't get the impression that these were positive, desirable qualities to have. I doubt that I am alone in jumping to such a negative conclusion about myself…it is too prevalent that people tend to get taken in by the peer pressure and immediately conclude that they are wrong. I was in my sixties before I figured out that this was actually a good quality. But the thing is, since the quality is ingrained in them, they cannot get rid of it. Sometimes, I wore myself out with it - and everyone around me. But it was a quality that was precious and probably even necessary in order to make it in this somewhat primitive way of life that we were living on our Gulf Island farm.

Our parents – on both sides – couldn't believe we were giving up our town comforts, by choice, for all these experiences that they had grown up with on three separate farms – and would never choose to go back to. However, we had never experienced this way of life – and wanted to. Since we were born in comfort, this was an altogether different adventure for us, where we could face the difficulties that our parents had to go through. However, what was different from our parents, we had a way out if things didn't work, we could always bail and go back to our previous way of life.

I think this knowledge that we could bail took the sting out of the hardship and made it seem not so bad. Whereas my husband's mother thought that to go back to using an outhouse would be the worst thing imaginable for her. They were all incredulous as we would tell them stories of what it was like – and we would laugh and laugh. Whereas it wasn't a laughing matter for any of them – they would just stand and stare at us as if we had gone mad.

"I'm So Glad We Did It, But Now I Don't Know How We Had the Nerve…"

On looking back, it was a very rich experience – full of both tests and lessons learned from the trials and tribulations of our daily life on the farm. However, it wasn't all difficult - there were also extraordinary experiences such as waking up one morning to find our world had turned to hoar frost…with a snowy owl sitting like a statue on our fence post, a stone's throw from our window…and blending in with its white snow-like background

All these things were very new for us, and as such, held great appeal. The saying that people crave what they haven't "tasted" is very true. A person born with a silver spoon in their mouth (which more than not, was the life we had just come from), might crave just going places where he can let loose and not have to act in a certain way. Whereas, the person who was born in the midst of these primitive conditions, they would like nothing more than to be sitting in an amazing hotel where they could get first-class treatment just like the people who had grown up with it.

I even fooled myself – I had thought that I was a soft "city girl," that couldn't survive in "wild" conditions…but not so – I learned what incredible hardships and discomforts I could withstand…and not break under. One very challenging one for me was that every time we left home for about an hour, we would return to find the stove out – we'd see the excessive smoke (or nothing) coming from the chimney… and we'd all groan. You might think this was a small thing – well, I found out that it was big enough to control our decisions. Until you actually get in a situation, you don't know how you will feel or react. Take this dead fire…we certainly got tired of starting up the stove from scratch, because that meant we first had to find enough dry wood to use for kindling. So, before long, we learned to think twice about what each outing was worth! In addition, more importantly, we began to work on building next year's woodpile!

People tend to underestimate themselves a lot when they picture their breaking points. People, all people, are made of much sterner stuff than they think. They can face amazing difficulties and come out perfectly fine. Somehow, when we're in it, everyone finds a way to be okay, even if everything is going wrong in their lives. Anyway, at first, we didn't even have a useable outhouse near the house (there was only one down in the garden – but that was a distance from our dome – and the kids didn't like it because it had no door). Therefore, we'd grab a shovel and head for the woods beside our home. I don't remember how long we put up with this – but for longer than I would have thought possible.

"Babes in The Woods…"

Then there was the garden. That first year or two, we had only hand tools, shovels, hoes, and pails to carry water (from far away) – it was a labor of love – and we didn't have a lot of wins. We discovered that being a reclaimed lake bed with a ditch around the perimeter, plants had to be planted really early so that they had well-established root systems before the heat of the summer came upon them, and the water table went beyond the roots of even the hardiest plants with the longest roots. Plus, there are some plants that just need too much water to be practical in that situation (like celery) and others that turn out woody or bitter (like parsnips - and even most of the carrots). Prior, our family had prided ourselves on being quite experienced gardeners (particularly of vegetables) – but here, we were like babes in the woods.

We learned all about this the hard way…and by our second year, we were starting to get the hang of it, learning from our experience and our failures. However, we all got invaluable advice from a local gardener whom we hired to work along with our two older children, teaching them how to garden in this environment. A big plus was that this fellow loaned us his garden-sized rototiller that second summer. By our third summer, we got our own – and if I remember correctly, by then, our son was doing the largest amount of the gardening – with the odd bit of help from our new gardener friend – and of course, a fair amount still from our daughter who would often work with her brother – and sometimes also with our gardener friend.

My husband and I put less amount of time into the vegetable and fruit garden because there were other things for us to do – there were a lot of general property matters that my husband had to attend to - flooded ditches, a gate that wouldn't close… and I had my hands full with home-making and baby matters. Our daughter loved best to play with her baby brother and keep him happy. In addition, she loved flowers – it became her specialty in the garden while the rest of us favored the vegetables. So here, the same as in our town gardening, we all found our niche – according to our interests and our expertise.

I'm also talking about the needs of the entire property, or the vegetable garden, the family needs (meal planning and prep, shopping, washing clothes, diapers). Then there were critical things like keeping ahead on diapers being washed and dried in time for the next time they were needed…and washing dishes, planning meals (we all took our turn to prepare our special meal that we liked to contribute). If we ran out of things, there was a long wait before they could be refilled. If we ran out of food items, we sometimes got a bit cranky. We learned a lot about ourselves in these times. One thing I learned was that I had assumed we would have a more laid-back and relaxing life (I have no idea where that came from…except from the total ignorance of a city girl's glorified concept of rural farm life.

"What do you do when your husband doesn't come home on the weekend…?"

My husband was working in town and obviously needed a car… so that left me alone with a fourteen-year-old son, an eleven-year-old daughter, and a baby – and no car or phone (it was about three miles to the nearest phone). I wasn't much of a radio person, especially since it had to be run on batteries. Most of the time, having no car didn't bother us… until once when I waited for about three days for my husband to return.

When he didn't come that weekend, by Sunday, the three of us hiked out two miles to the main road and then hitchhiked ten miles down the island with the baby and a few belongings for each of us. There we discovered that the ferries were on strike. It didn't take us long to decide to fly to Vancouver to stay with my husband until the ferries began running again. Naïve us…we had never even considered that possibility – of my husband not coming home when he said he would – and therefore, we had never put anything in place for us to communicate with each other, especially in an emergency. Come to think of it. We were real greenhorns at living in the country. We just got the idea, didn't do much researching or prior planning, and just went and did it!

"I had no idea...!"

Those years were priceless – they have made me appreciate every electric, time-saving device that I now have, every switch that can turn on lights and bring heat in a blink, an electrically run stove – oh yes, and a flush toilet! However, more than the time-savers, there is the comfort that is possible with our modern, western ways. It wasn't as if those years were bad; however, after a certain age, a person does come to appreciate ease and comfort.

I particularly came to appreciate what each flick of a switch represents, the comfort and increased leisure time - because otherwise, it means a highly labor-intensive lifestyle. Moreover, because of these years on Galiano, I am much wiser about what I am made of – both my strengths as well as my weaknesses. Most of us, in our lifetime, don't put ourselves in situations that define us as clearly as this homesteading experience did for me. I often wonder…if I had had 20/20 hindsight, would I still have chosen the often uncomfortable, extremely labor-intensive lifestyle. I might not have…but I bless the universe for its wisdom. We learned so many lessons, it would be impossible to put a price tag on those years. The best word I can think of to describe it is "priceless," really. Some were tangible, physical, real lessons – others were intangible and not even recognized till long after – if ever. Some hitherto intangible ones will no doubt come out along the way.

"No more 'playing house"

We had done what we had previously thought of as serious gardening in the years before we moved to our island home – but it was child's play in comparison. The biggest thing that hit us was that since we were now living on only one income, it was far more important that the vegetables grow through to harvest – because we depended on them for our food. During our town life, we had a lot more available money to replace any lost crops. In our new life, if we lost any crops to bugs, not enough water, weather, or our mistakes – we had to fall back on a lot less varied or questionably nutritious meals (mostly weighted on the carbohydrate side: rice, spaghetti, or potatoes). The other thing was that my husband would have to buy replacement foods in town before coming back home to us.

We were finding that it wasn't the money-saving lifestyle that we had thought it would be…not with all the many unexpected things like the cost of the 400 feet deep well, a rotavator (which is a small machine that you push in front of you, back and forth over the garden - like a small plow that churns up the dirt as it passes over). There were other larger tools that were needed for such large-scale gardening (our town garden was tiny in comparison).

There were also things like the regular ferry trips, a lot more outdoor and gardening clothing and boots, a new stove to heat the dome, and also a new cookstove for our outdoor kitchen…plus a third child's needs. Therefore, there was much more at stake, now, in having our garden succeed…in fact, our whole lifestyle choice was in a constant, delicate balance with possible failure always hanging over us. The weather was often a culprit, such as a long hot, dry spell occurring right after we planted. It didn't happen often, but when it did, it was a really big setback. At those times, the plants would have benefited a lot if they had had some cool or even damp weather.

I remember once there were a whole lot of seedlings that we had carefully tended for weeks. We went to town for a couple of days, and when we returned during a hot, dry spell, we took one look at them and were horrified how limp they looked and how close we were to losing them. On the spot, we decided they had to be planted, not in the morning, but right away. I specifically remember that it was early evening, we were tired – but it was obvious to us all that it was a "now or never" sort of situation. We all scrambled into our work clothes and went out and did the job. It was amazing, really, we wouldn't even think of giving in to our fatigue and leaving the plants to die...and I include our children in this "we" because they are very intelligent and also very caring and were quick to put family needs before their own wishes.

However, sometimes we couldn't see how we could do anything much about it, similar to the classic farmer's plight of a hailstorm, without warning, flattening all the greens and the young cornstalks. Our plight would be to have a rainy spell that just went on and on, right in the middle of strawberry and raspberry season, ensuring that they got moldy. Or when cutworms went to work on our seedlings and a whole row just fell over and died. Think about Murphy's Law in effect: everything that can go wrong, did go wrong. That's where diversification helps, plus a resilient spirit, a good sense of humor (and an ample savings account would have helped)!

"All work and no play makes Jack a dull boy..."

That was a British saying that I grew up with since my mother had a British background. We tried to balance the intense - and often unforgiving - needs with play and relaxation. Biking was a favorite - with baby Colin on one of our backs, or in a bike-seat when older - to explore the many trails around our "farm." Bushwhacking was always a favorite...explore places where there were no visible trails.

Swimming was one of my personal favorites and we had not one, but two, swimming choices - a lake just over one mile away and the ocean about two miles in the other direction. I considered myself very fortunate. Even though I am now in my seventies, to this day, I continue to love swimming. However, I am becoming not so adventurous anymore, and I am definitely not drawn to go into very cold water now…unless the day itself is extremely warm. I also avoid swimming in the spring or fall because that water temperature never suits me anymore. I can remember swimming many May twenty-fourth and Thanksgiving holiday weekends when I was younger. However, by the time I was in my fifties, I had to huddle around the wood fire to get warm again, and into my sixties and seventies, I had become fussy and highly selective of my swimming conditions!

Chapter 12
The Lonely Road
Of An Alternate Health Path

The intensity of the lifestyle was exhausting and added to that was the fact that I wasn't producing enough milk for my baby, which was worrisome. Health professionals had given me several possible reasons for that, one being that I was perhaps not eating the best things for a nursing mother. Raising our third baby (as vegetarians and homesteaders) put us into a steep learning curve! In the earliest days of nursing my third child, I was a fruitarian (ate only fruit, as the name implies).

Most days, one of our family members would look after our baby while I jogged the mile to the lake. But by October, when he was three months old, I had to stop swimming in both the lake and ocean. This was because, by that time of the season, I would return, shivering cold. One morning I even had to walk on the frosty ground to get to the lake, not to mention the temperature of the water! I was regularly "losing my milk," and my baby was beginning to be always hungry. I guess I was using up all my own reserves trying to get and stay warm. On the one hand, I didn't agree with everything the doctor told me about my baby's weight. But on the other hand, even though I wasn't prepared to follow the medical model exactly on how to feed a baby...at the same time, I was becoming worried that I wasn't doing the right thing. At that time my husband began to do a lot of research on the matter because those questions and fears often plagued us as we had chosen such an alternate way of life. Since my experience with hypoglycemia in my late twenties, my husband and I had taken on our own...and our family's...health. This was in the days prior to having computers to research things. However, the lack of a machine to help research something didn't stop us, and so we became researchers the "long-handed" way.

Most strongly, we depended on those who had "been there before." Fortunately, my husband loved to read and find both old and new ways to help us to counteract the issues we were facing. Also, there were health food store owners with whom he could share ideas and ask questions. He had met so many of them in the years that we were living in Vancouver and before we moved to the island...when he was going in and out of health food stores to sell the products we had manufactured. So now he was always coming home from "the big city" with new ideas and answers to our many health questions.

"Changes are a-coming..."

Even though I had my difficult moments, I continued to nurse our baby for about twenty-one months, which raised lots of eyebrows. It wasn't something I planned to do; I just did it. At the twenty-first month mark, two things happened, one right after the other. The first thing was, I quite suddenly felt ready to stop nursing. As usual, my husband was willing to support my needs...and worked out a plan to make the weaning process smooth and easy for both me and our baby, Colin.

Rob planned to wake early, get up and get going...and first off, make some orange juice. Then I would get up and do one of two things, depending on which I had on my mind...either crawl into our van to write for an hour or so; or go to the garden for some quiet weeding time. After I had left the dome, my husband would get our young son up, give him his fresh orange juice, which he loved. He would then dress him, march down to the outhouse that was just beside the garden, call and wave at me from a distance, just so our son knew I was still around, and then leave me alone for a while longer.

I no longer remember what I did on the days he was off to work, but I think we chose a break when he was home for a stretch of ten days to two weeks so we could get the weaning established without emotion or turmoil…my husband was very sensitive and caring about family needs.

The second thing that happened was, we focused on our son's learning to walk. When he was about ten months old, he was "walking" around the furniture, and was so steady that we wondered if he would walk early. However, where we lived was very small, a dome, and we spent most of our time outside. We spent very little time inside except to sleep (when it was too cold to sleep in our outdoor "bedroom"). When it was rainy or too cold to eat at our outdoor picnic table, we would head inside…and also do quiet, leisure activities such as read, write for various projects and play board games.

When we moved to the island, we brought our piano and other instruments and played on them, year-round except we did less "farming" and therefore had more leisure time in the winter. All other activities took place outside the dome, year-round. Wash clothes or clean veggies at the well. Make and store food in a protected area in our barn-like shed. Sleep in another protected area in our shed (mostly year-round). Work in the garden or orchard beyond our dome and shed (less in the winter months but there were things to do there, year-round. Play in the yard and walk in the woods. That pretty well covered our island life.

"Trying not to panic…"

Our son's first year came and went; then thirteen, fourteen, fifteen months also, and still no walking. By twenty months, we took him to a doctor to check him out physically. Nothing was wrong. Therefore, we concluded that he had no incentive to get down off our backs. He had always had the comfort of being carried and the advantage of being "on top of the world." This was all from a position on our backs in a snuggly soft baby carrier when he was really young, and as he grew, he graduated to a more open-style Gerry carrier. He went biking, hiking, and even skiing that way.

Apparently, it was too comfortable and satisfying for him to want to get down and do it all on his own. He could see everything we did – grate the salad, scrub his diapers on a rock, and he even hugged trees as he passed by on a walk in the woods or snatched a sprig of kale to munch on if we were in the garden. Also, there was no risk of skinned knees and hands from the rough and gravely surface that was our yard, or the tree roots and thorny blackberry and wild strawberry runners that ran all over the grassy field beyond. Smart baby!

"He walked, of course…!"

On the Easter weekend, just before he was twenty-one months old, and at the same time, my husband had a break from work, we headed for my parent's home. They were still down south with the other "snowbirds" - and we figured that the two lovely "smooth" patios beside their home with large grassy areas that were mown, short, devoid of sticks and thorns, of course, would be perfect. It almost "killed" the four of us to keep from picking up our young son/brother, but we just knelt down to him, rather than picking him up. However, he walked on the second day! Then, once he had discovered the joys of freedom, it was hard to confine him, even when we had to. After that, until the excitement of his new-found freedom, walking, wore off, we did what seemed like a lot of carrying him in our arms, kicking and screaming to be put down!

"It's now gathering dust..."

That fall, 1979-80, we decided we wanted to write a book...so at the end of November, we flew to Hawaii for seven weeks. Our ages at the time were: Rob (43), Maren (42), Gordon (16), Shelagh (14), and Colin (2). We later called our book: Education Without Schooling. Each of the four of us wrote a section from our point of view, and it was a fabulous experience. Looking back, it was probably a selfish act to keep the book to ourselves. Now I can say that I think it would have been good for us, and I think we would have grown bigger from the experience of publishing.

However, at that time, we didn't care if people would gain a lot from us sharing it with them. In that phase of our life, my husband and I couldn't see a bigger picture. We were afraid of losing our privacy and our individuality, which we had fought hard for. The publisher that was most taken with it warned us what our life might become – a public life, being asked to speak and tour and to advise people on the dilemmas regarding their children's education.

We were very afraid of people knowing too much about us and of having no private life from then on. We were also afraid that touring and public life would take us over, and we wouldn't have any time left to live our dreams, part of which was living a largely country life. More particularly, though, we were afraid of putting our children through things that they didn't wish to be part of - at least at that young stage of their lives.

Therefore, we declined to go any further in publishing the book. Every once in a while, I still find myself having a renewed interest in the idea of the book and wonder whether it could still be published. However, I haven't done anything more about it other than wonder. By now, I suspect that there have been many books on home-schooling written since that time - but it was at least an autobiographical and philosophical thesis of our family...and there it remains.

Chapter 13
Personal Development

Many roads...all lead to Rome

EST, Mastery, Sterling Women's Course, Landmark

Education, Peaks Potentials – and many more.

"Do you know about personal development? I didn't...until I was in it…"

That's what the next phase of my life was all about...personal development. Up to that point, I had just been going along with however my life went and did not know I had anything to do with the creation of my life as it was happening. Moreover, I didn't know I had anything to "develop" or any "growing up" to do. That is the course of life that most people tend to adopt…and I was no different.

They go with the wind, whatever their elders say, whatever seems to be the next step; they take that and think that that is how their life should be spent. Most people do not focus on their personal development as they simply don't know what that means, let alone how that can change their life. Personal development, for me, equates with "gaining confidence," "growing up," actually being able to look yourself in the mirror and be content with the way you are. I didn't know all that, then…but I feel fortunate that I do now. The result is a feeling that can give you a deep satisfaction that nothing else can provide.

In July '81, I took the EST Training and turned a corner in my life - it was my first taste of personal development. EST introduced me to a new way of being that I had not anticipated. I discovered that I was about to turn a corner, regardless of the circumstances. That personal development course helped me and all my family to turn it more gracefully and to consciously choose my (and our) new directions.

"How Did I Find Out About the EST Training (and Begin my Personal Development Journey)?"

That year, in 1981, a woman was living with my husband and me. She had just separated and wanted to rent a room in a family home. She was renting one of our bedrooms for her son and herself - it was just a mother and young son duo that were living with us. She had met our daughter, who had told her that we had a room available in our home. When she asked us if she might live with us, we thought it could work well... and it did. She was not the only one to benefit from getting a cheap room in a family home. But there was something in it for us as well. For one thing, she was a dependable presence in our home. That way, our (by now fourteen years old) daughter could be in the city whenever she wanted, instead of feeling stuck at our Galiano Island home, which was often too isolated for her liking. Better, she didn't have to wander around the city any longer, trying to find a place to sleep in the home of one of our friends or relatives. Another plus was that this woman's son became a new friend for our three-year-old son, Colin.

Our new roommate had recently met a man who had just completed the EST Training and was encouraging her also to take the course. She asked me if I would consider going with her to an Introduction to the course – to which I agreed... although at that time I had no idea what I was saying 'Yes' to. After taking the introductory class that evening, she and I decided to take the next course together - and the rest was history. After we started this course, neither of our lives were the same ever again. We developed a close bond with each other as well, out of having shared the course together. While she lived with us, it was very nice to have a friend live with me who had shared the experience of the EST Training. However, she soon moved out and married her boyfriend, but while she was there, we both became really good friends. Throughout our lives, as we develop - emotionally, psychologically, spiritually - some of our experiences have more impact on our maturation than others. We can't eliminate this process - but we can slow it down or speed it up by our degree of consciousness. For myself, once I started taking courses that were classified as "personal development courses," I feel like I sped up my maturation process exponentially.

During these courses, two major things happened. First, I got insights into my life development - I could see where I had grown. As I looked back, I could evaluate where I had stayed stuck as witnessed in my seemingly mature or immature responses. I learned about the places that were holding me back because I was immaturely still holding on to those old feelings in my life. Second, the thing that excited me most was that during those courses, I had a chance to have another go at these places where I felt stuck in life and to heal them and let them go.

"My attitude to myself needed a make-over..."

The ways where I was positively affected by my "work" in these courses were huge and far-reaching. My prevailing attitude had been very negative about my capabilities. I honestly did not know if the skills I possessed were good enough...or not. On the other hand, people who knew me were strong and sure in their praises of my abilities, work, projects, talents, impact on others. Their list of praises about me went on and on, but I "knew" they were just being nice and kind and didn't really know me. During these courses, even though it was really difficult to acknowledge so many great things about myself, I gradually came to see that people were right. When growing up, I had had a strong dose of indoctrination of not tooting one's own horn and being humble. For sure, there is a place for this thinking, but I discovered that I had gone overboard!

"The EST Training was the first of many such courses..."

Over the years, I have taken a great number of courses, and I have used them all to become emotionally lighter and more fully expressed. I used them to dig into myself to discover what is still there that is obsolete (thoughts, feelings, judgments, beliefs, decisions). I have used the support of these kinds of courses to let go of the old and to create and allow a new, current reality to show up. I had no idea that I could "complete" those old relationships - let alone "how." In addition to that, I learned how to create a whole different and honest relationship with them in the way I wanted. However, even more importantly, I was no longer negatively affected by the "stuff" that had happened in the time between my birth and the present. This was exciting to me - and still is, to this day, because no matter how much I complete and even think (or hope) that I am done for all time, there is still more. I must admit, though, there is much less, now, than at the beginning of my work on myself in the EST Training.

During the EST Training, I began to discover and complete my reactive, incomplete stuff that I was harboring, particularly about my Mom and my Dad. This "stuff" had been growing from the day I was born...and I had built a strong set of negative beliefs about myself and the people in my life by the time I was forty-three at the beginning of these courses. By the end of the EST Training, I began to be in touch with the strong feelings of love that I had for my parents; whereas, over the years, my love had become covered over and buried deep down in my heart, which resulted in me being more aware of their "faults" and my reactions rather than of my love for them.

"I knew I loved my mom and dad..."

If you had asked if I knew that they loved me - well, of course, I would answer, "Yes." However, I wasn't aware of the depth of what I felt for them. These buried feelings began to rise as I got more complete about "my stuff" in my past. By the end of that first course, all I was aware of was my love for them. I still remember how I felt on the day after I finished my course. As I was driving down the freeway for a half hour to see them, I got more and more excited until I felt nearly ready to explode by the time I arrived.

That was all a revelation to me - how deadened I had become to the many things lying under my emotional surface and all the ways these hidden emotions were impacting my life. One small example of this is that for some time, I had stopped kissing my mother. It was something that we always used to do when I would go see her or when we would see each other off at the end of each visit. But that habit had gotten lost over time. I became always searching for my authenticity, my truth. Looking back, it seems ludicrous, but somehow, I got it in my head that I didn't want her lipstick - and her meat bacteria - on my lips (I was a vegetarian at that time). She was great - never questioning or pushing herself on me. It was as if she knew I'd come around on my own. Sure enough, I did - but when I think about it, I marvel at what my mother was able to put up with from me - and not take personally - or worse, take out on me.

I was amused, delighted, sometimes taken aback by the difference it was making in me. People who know me now find it hard to comprehend the difference as I describe myself in my old reality. I was horrified at some of my initial discoveries. My worst one was what I call being a "martyred bitch." I'll describe a common scenario. I was discontented and frustrated by so much in my life, but when my family would offer to help me – or offer to look after their young brother and give me some time off, I turned most of their offers down. Then, what was even worse, I made them pay for it in a whole host of subtle and covert ways.

Apparently, it was a common mask or emotional reaction, but common or not, I was very upset with this discovery.

Another part of me was a "people pleaser." I learned that I didn't like people thinking badly of me. It would bother me very much if somebody was unhappy with me. So, I was often afraid to stand up for myself or to tell the truth for fear that I would be thought of as stupid or not nice – or even worse, as a bad person.

"Deeper and deeper – and lighter and lighter…"

As I began to take these various courses, I discovered that even though I thought of myself as a positive person, deeper down, my thoughts - and even my words - were often negative and self-limiting. I often uttered - and believed to be true - words such as can't, not able, not capable, and other equally self-defacing words. These new discoveries that I was the opposite had an incredibly liberating effect on my life and emotions.

This, in turn, brought about increased happiness, productivity, and all manner of other great outcomes. Feeling negative about myself has been an on-going struggle in my life, and these courses didn't totally eliminate that struggle. However, they did give me some insight into the workings of my psyche, which helped me, more and more, to defy my internal negative verdict. I have had to be ever vigilant - we don't get to have a free ride just because we have become more aware. The point being that in every person's life, there must be, for their own betterment, the realization that they have, within them, a plethora of negative emotions - self-doubt and self-criticism being the most prominent among them. So…to deal with this, first, a person needs to be aware of that and only after that can they identify when it is happening and possibly bring about a different outcome.

Usually, when it happens, it is hard to notice because it is a part of one's mannerisms and history of what we know ourselves to be…we assume these negative thoughts about ourselves to be true, and our limitations thus become real. These courses gave me the ability to discover these negative beliefs and then gradually to strip myself of them. This resulted in me feeling lighter, happy, freed up from these untruths. Sometimes they would come back to haunt me and try to get control again. What helped me return quickly to my new self and new awareness was a growing arsenal of new practices plus new friends who would remind me of who I had become.

"The ten-evening seminars were the best…"

The EST organization encouraged us to take a seminar (ten evenings over three months) as soon as possible after the initial course because that was when we were very vulnerable and needed a safe place to share our discoveries (upside and downside) as well as to explore new directions and receive feedback. Part of our vulnerability was that we were "new" and yet we were still surrounded by friends and family who didn't always understand, like, believe in, or support our new ways and views. In my case, my two children at the age of fourteen and sixteen, and my husband all took the course immediately following my "graduation." Therefore, with my whole household taking these courses, I had more support and understanding than most did.

Three years later, our youngest at six years of age took the Young Person's Training. Their course is quite a bit shorter because apparently it doesn't take them as long as their parents to "get it." One example of that showed up for us when he was about five. During the three years while he was waiting, he was like a little sponge, soaking it all up from us. There were many fun times when he would throw things back in our face, reminding us of some lesson or other. Some of these things had been so difficult for us to learn, but not for him. He picked stuff up like a breeze.

One that we all struggled with was the principle of "getting off it" when we were stuck and dug in about something. One day, he was exasperated with one of us and said to his sibling, "get off it." They glared at him and said it was easy for him to say. He returned, "it IS easy...see...like this" - and he leaned down and drew an imaginary line on the floor and jumped over it. "See...like that." We were floored that he had, without a course or seminar, already understood the lesson completely. We were also a little peeved about the ease with which he "got it" while we were still struggling!

For two solid years, I spent a lot of time with the EST organization, taking courses, and taking deaf persons through the EST Training as well as through seminars (as their interpreter). This struck me funny at the time, because my husband's first language was sign language, as he had deaf parents. Whereas, to deaf people, I am only a "second language" signer. Therefore, I thought that my husband should be doing the interpreting that I was doing. However, when I was first asked to interpret, he hadn't taken the course yet, so he wasn't eligible to interpret for it. Then later, after he had taken it, he wasn't free to do so. Therefore, I kept on interpreting - although my husband did interpret for one deaf girl for a Communication course because she begged him to do that for her – but that was the only interpreting he ever did for the EST organization.

"Our divided life began..."

While I was spending two weekends with these people, interpreting, plus three evenings as well as ten evenings of the seminar following their course, I was in my glory. When I was doing that, it felt like I was making some difference in the world and not just for my family (this was what I had been longing for).

Whereas, while I was busy, my husband needed time in nature - to offset his work-life that took place almost totally indoors in meetings, mentoring, researching, and writing. He would take our two sons (our daughter usually wanted to stay in town), and they would head for our island home…where he would later also take his new partner.

"Our family life - was changing…"

By 1981, when our youngest son was four, we all began to live between Galiano and Vancouver - according to our individual needs. Initially, we had set up a house in town because our daughter needed more time in Vancouver. When I think about it, so did I - and our eldest was doing a part-time course that took place in Vancouver. Our daughter was starting to want to stay in town where there were fewer responsibilities and more action. By that time, she was a young adult with interests, friends, and desires that differed from her Dad's, two brothers' and mine.

My husband needed town for work, but Galiano was his love and relaxation. Our older son needed a bit of Vancouver time for schooling, but mostly he sided with his father's love of the land - and they would travel back and forth together to Galiano. That was when we had decided to share our Vancouver house with a single mother and son - and when she had left us to be married (to the man who had introduced her to the EST Training), we replaced her with a couple who were mutual friends. The house-sharing was a perfect arrangement because there was always company for our children when they were without us in town, and therefore we were all free to come and go as we wished.

I (and also my family members) continued to take personal development courses. To get a large dose of being present to life was intoxicating, and I wanted more and more of it. It was very relieving to have something in life that was giving me comfort. It all began for me a long time ago with EST (1981) and has been a fairly continuous process since that fateful, fortuitous day when my friend asked me to attend the introductory meeting. Only in my late sixties/early seventies did I begin to let a few years go by, in between, without taking any courses or volunteering with the Landmark organization to assist in the putting on of their courses (it's the only personal development organization I ever volunteered to assist in various ways).

In the early days, following the courses, sometimes I would join a group of us that met regularly, and we would work on our "stuff" – as a group. Later on, in my life, I was drawn to some different one-on-one personal growth work such as bodywork or sessions with a psychologist. It was only a few times that I used a "mind-altering" substance, and on those occasions, that substance was recommended by a friend and was done so with a professional's guidance. However, four times was enough to satisfy my desire to know, through experience, what these substances felt like. I was glad I had experienced them, but the mind-altering quality didn't appeal to me. However, I will say that they had their place because they showed me that more than anything, I wanted to be fully conscious during my experiences as I put my past in its place and "grew up."

The way I seemed to respond the best was in a group course or program, such as EST ('81), The Sterling Women's Course ('87) - and a host of other courses in between and since. The most recent institutes from which I have taken many courses are Landmark Education ('98), Peaks Potentials ('04), the Enlightened Wealth Institute (EWI) with Robert Allan ('05). I feel blessed by my experiences with all these personal development programs. I took a few shorter but also highly impactful courses. I took them all to achieve one goal: to experience transformative processes and to receive the resulting growth.

"I reflect…"

I am extremely grateful for having been introduced to these kinds of courses and for having the courage to participate in them. My experiences have allowed me to create a very different life than I otherwise would have. All around me, I hear people uttering things that sound like the "old" me. Each time I hear them, I am newly grateful for the chances I took to put my old "hurts" behind me. Early on in my process, I decided that I wanted a "current" life, which meant getting complete with these old hurts. As a result, my life became startlingly different and delightfully new. As I said before, I am not the same person.

Chapter 14
A Community Emerging…
And Changing Times

Out of my experiences resulting from the EST "Training," I had become clear that living an isolated life was not part of my life purpose! Upon leaving this first course, I declared that I wouldn't go back to live on Galiano until I went with a community of people. Before the EST Training, I had already begun thinking about the possibility of creating a community. However, people often think about doing great things, changing their lives, the way they live…but only idly, in a musing fashion – not with any commitment to change their lifestyle and make it happen. True, they are thinking about being the person they aspire to be. But it's more of a daydream or a bucket-list goal and not something for which they give dates and create action plans. They see these as dreams - and sometimes not even as possible.

A common fear, along with the self-limiting beliefs people have, frequently doesn't allow them to get their dreams off the ground…and that is the fact that people hate change. That is because they don't know what lies on the other end of that change, and they let their fear of the unknown stop them. The change could be everything that they dreamed of, or it could be a complete disaster, and the chance of it being a complete disaster is what stops them and hinders their growth. However, it is worth considering that everything we do in life has a chance of failing…that is just a part of life; failing is what makes us grow and gives us a chance to turn into a better person. As is said famously;

"Success is not final, failure is not fatal: it is the courage to continue that counts."

-Winston Churchill

Around about this time, Robert and our friend, GP (former owner of our property and with much experience in community building), began to draft for us some guiding principles of our future community. There were many drafts and many conversations - heated and otherwise - over many months in the next couple of years.

About that time, the couple who lived with us in Vancouver expressed interest in our Galiano home as a possible "community" for themselves, so they became part of the discussions - both on Galiano with GP, as well as in

Vancouver, where we all talked long hours about how a community can work. We used Robert's and GP's ideas as our guide…and gathered new ones during discussions with our Vancouver friends.

These ideas all got written down and worked over between the four of us – as well as with other friends who were interested in the ideas of perhaps living that way, and of course, GP. We tried it out for a year with this couple, when unexpectedly, their spiritual community, which, up until then, was based in Vancouver and California – with almost no notice - decided to form a physical community on Salt Spring Island (another Gulf island near our Galiano Island home). So, instead, our friends moved to Salt Spring Island - another of our possible new members gone.

We advertised for potential members – and some interested people visited our island home. After mutually interviewing each other, and over a few months of meeting prospective community members, we did not find anyone with whom we had consensus. This was an uncomfortable time for us – being in the position of judges of other people's ideas and lifestyle choices – and then voting them not suitable. However, we knew that it was better to wait for people to show up who were aligned with us, than to say 'yes' too soon and end up having to live with people with whom we had nothing in common. We knew that that would lead us to regret the entire plan - and that was something we did not want to do because we wanted this to work out for our future. Therefore, we soon realized that we must not compromise on the sort of people that were to live with us.

By that time, we had already experienced a horror story and hopefully, once was enough. The experience was very discouraging for us - and just about ruined our faith in community…and, therefore, our dream. It had happened that we liked what we read on paper about this one family and invited them to join with us. They had two young children which seemed like they could be great company for our youngest - and that at least was true…but that was the only thing that worked out well.

By the time we realized that there were too many of the deep things in which we diverged, which made them unsuitable to be a part of our community…it was no longer possible to part easily or amicably. They were totally enjoying the experience of being with us and didn't agree with how we saw things…in fact, our parting was not only sticky but got quite ugly before we succeeded in removing them from our property. After that experience, we didn't feel quite so optimistic…and we went back to the drawing board for a while before feeling brave enough to begin the process again.

"Therah Village Developments Ltd was born (1982) - for better or worse…"

Within a couple of years, though, we had much more clarity as to what we were looking for - and not…and had had many more conversations with our friend, GP, as well as with other friends with whom we were engaged in conversation about "community." As we attended EST seminars, we began to meet people in our EST community who expressed interest in such an idea as an "intentional" community.

During that year, we set up several information evenings in Vancouver and then arranged for people who were seriously interested to visit the island, be toured around, getting their questions answered. Enrolment/membership began. The first couple of members were personal friends of ours (one had previously taken the EST Training - and her mother had not). The next few members who joined after them were amongst our friends whom we met in the EST Training and seminars.

All were intrigued by the idea of living in an intentional community, as well as sharing an interest in living a healthy and alternative lifestyle. For the early members, there was the bonus of a communication style in common (as an aside, any who joined later during that first year or two, who had not already taken the EST Training, did so fairly soon after joining - probably out of self-defense)! We found that this one thing in common gave us powerful communication tools. This didn't mean that we always agreed with each other or believed the same things – or that we never hit bumps. But we had something between us that made our community work (meaning that we could work out anything – better than we had even imagined…it was exciting to experience our "inner" work in action.

"A name was chosen…"

It wasn't long before we had chosen the name, Thera Village Developments Limited (TVDL for short), set up a Board of Directors, and we were holding regular, monthly meetings (mostly in Vancouver). Even the choice of a name was after long deliberations. We called ourselves Thera, which went back to the Therapeutae of Greek times. After some months, the numerology enthusiasts of our community (there were about four or five) finally won out, and we added an "H" to our name making it, Therah! The first members all lived in Vancouver, which was fine because we didn't have a meeting place on Galiano Island yet, so our earlier meetings took place in Vancouver. There were two structures on the property – the dome where our family lived, and a kitchen/ dining/living space with a bathroom on the backside. It had been the old shed where our van used to be parked in the early days before undergoing quite a bit of renovation. Eventually, members donated couches and chairs so that we could meet there.

"Our first Thanksgiving…"

A very memorable occasion was our first community Thanksgiving. We held it on Galiano Island in our community home. The day was mellow; love, joy, and thankfulness were palpable. We cooked the turkey in the old wood stove in the community kitchen. There wasn't room for anything else in the oven, so we cooked other things on the stovetop. In those days, none of the members had built their homes yet, so all the hot things had to be made right there or prepared at home before they traveled and just heated up – or served as is. It was our first community meal on the island, and for this occasion, there were many additional people – relatives, friends of friends. We weren't prepared yet for such a large gathering, so we did lots of makeshift seating. Many of us sat around on blankets; some brought patio chairs; a select few (mostly elders - my mother and father, included) sat at the one bona fide picnic table – although a couple more, rather shaky tables were constructed with sawhorses and a couple of old doors.

I remember it was a perfect weather day - a sunny and perfect, mellow October day. We ate mid-afternoon to accommodate people who had just come for that day and needed to leave early to catch the evening ferry. Added advantages of eating early were that it was still warm and prior to the damp fall evening air descending. Also, those who were staying overnight had a nice long evening to enjoy one another – visiting, nibbling on treats, singing around the piano, which was my specialty, and jamming on instruments. I remember there being a couple of flutes, a sax, a guitar, and a few made-up percussion instruments...a wonderful memory of our first community gathering.

"Alternative schooling for our third child..."

In 1983, it was time for our youngest to go to school. We were, by then, dealing with the demanding circumstances of Robert's illness. Therefore, we had concluded that because our focus was almost entirely on Robert's health by then...we were no longer in a position to home-school and would need something different for our youngest. We explored various situations and settled on a school that an acquaintance's son was attending, Windsor House, an alternative school in the North Vancouver district...a half hour drive from our home.

It was certainly a drawback being so far from school - I drove back and forth for at least half of that year because he was only going half days, and there weren't any other youngsters his age that lived in Vancouver. By midpoint, though, the school allowed our son to switch from half days to full-time and so our friend's son, who lived nearby, was able to take him to and from school to finish out his Kindergarten year.

In hindsight, we would have been better off if I had continued driving him because my husband and I suffered every day until he arrived safely home…and we didn't find out what really was happening until it was too late to do anything different. Our son had been enjoying his taste of freedom and had talked the older boy into wandering the downtown streets of Vancouver and window shopping before coming home. The boy couldn't control our son and was afraid of the responsibility of looking after him – but rather than share what was going on, he just kept taking him to and from school. Somehow, we all managed until the end of June.

"Wondertree was born…"

September rolled around, and we had to face this unsatisfactory situation once again. The other little boy (only nine years old) wasn't happy having to try to control our little fellow (just six years old), who was sprouting his "freedom wings." Just at the point that my husband and I had concluded we could no longer tolerate the situation a second year, Wondertree came into being and into our lives. One day, someone asked Brent if he had met Robert Boese; and at the same time, someone asked Robert if he had met Brent. The two fathers met, and the Wondertree alternative school for lifelong learning was officially born with two pupils, Brent and Maria's daughter, Irena, and Robert and Maren's son, Colin.

Whew! Just in the nick of time. By the end of Wondertree's school year, the numbers had grown to three and a half (one child went half days) – and by the end of the following year, to seven and within another year or two, it was capped at eleven students. What a wonderful experience this turned out to be for the entire family of each student who was enrolled. Colin went to Wondertree for eight years, at which point, all (parents, students, and their teacher) were in agreement that it was time to graduate the eleven students - it seemed that each of them was ready to explore what was next in their education and their life…as was Brent.

"Transition to Post Marriage"

This all took place at a time that I was transitioning out of my marriage. A large part of my transition was about men, particularly when I was meeting so many men in the EST personal development community. From July '81 (when I took the EST Training), until Jan. '82, I had stars in my eyes instead of sense. It was an exciting time for me, and I didn't want to be tied down with Robert and his needs any longer. I was excited by life, and I wanted out of the marriage to discover myself – who I was, what I was up to, without Robert. By late fall of 1981, it became apparent to us both that I was no longer in the marriage. I was willing to stay and help Robert with his recovery, but at the same time, I was the cause of undue stress for him. Robert, being sick, couldn't afford that, and therefore, he requested that I leave. I understood – and agreed - and we soon separated after that.

At many points in our lives, we reflect on the things we have done. This is usually following some event that has transpired or just from the sheer realization that we have been in a rut for such a long time. This was one of those times for me. Even though I deeply loved Robert, I knew that I was no longer committed to our marriage and that it was no longer working for either of us. Instead of dragging it out, it seemed best just to pull the plug, as he was requesting.

Even though I was finding it extremely difficult to admit this, I had begun to see that it would be easier for both of us. Once done, it would allow both of us to carry on more easily.

People seem to think that inevitably, there will be regret once such a momentous step is taken. However, if it is not taken, then there will be even more regret. At that point, the "what ifs" inevitably came into effect - and my fear of change loomed large. However, I could see his point, and as Robert requested, I pulled the plug, without allowing more regrets or what-ifs to get in the way.

It wasn't ideal...but it was the end of a chapter.

Chapter 15
"1983... In Came Val Contini..."

I experimented and explored who I was for a couple of years - many different men, courses, jobs. One of my jobs was the Therah community coordinator – and with that job, I set up tours to and from mainland Vancouver and Galiano Island – usually, day trips on Sundays. Because I lived in Vancouver at this time, I led the tours. On one of these tours for prospective members (June 1983), I met Val (Osvaldo) Contini. He was considering becoming an Associate member of the community...and we were immediately drawn to each other.

After a half-hour drive from the ferry to the north end of the island, we arrived on the community property. According to plan, a few community members were already there to help me present information about the community. After the prospective members asked questions so that they could get clear if it was a fit for them, we then toured them around the community land - showing them what the land-in-common looked like and what people had built on their private pieces of land - as well as the single lot that had been set aside for the Associate membership category to time-share. Then there was free time until I gathered the group late that afternoon, and we returned to the ferry.

"Like bees to honey…"

During our free time, Val and I laid out a blanket off to the side of the main gathering area - and began to talk. I had been reading relationship books, taken two Relationship courses, and had made a list of qualities of a future partner, pin-pointing any deal-breakers. I went everywhere with this list and was constantly mulling it over, adding and subtracting. By this time, I had noticed that the list was feeling quite complete - so I was both excited and nervous to go over it with a tangible prospect in mind. I checked with Val to see if he'd be interested in looking it over with me and to see what he thought.

With every person, there are things that are non-negotiable. Most people are not aware of these until they are already too emotionally invested in the relationship, so much so that they try everything in their power to make sure that it works out. However, if your partner refuses to compromise on that particular item or requirement, then it becomes a huge problem. You can't very easily be with a person who does things that you don't believe in…or doesn't believe in things you do…and if you try to ignore it, there will inevitably come a time when you will have had enough. When that happens, you will feel compelled to leave, because by then, you can sense that it is going to get worse if you choose to stay. Therefore, it is best to deal with non-negotiables in the beginning if you can see them. That's a great thought; however, they are often hidden initially and only show up later.

"My list…"

I remember that there were a couple of things on my list that he wasn't strong on - but I also remember that my list was long…and that the two missing things were of minimal consequence - neither were what I call deal-breakers. Going through this list was a very intimate thing to do on a first meeting. However, this was no usual, first meeting. Nor did we feel casual about each other - right away. Val agreed with me that we were a high match for each other according to my list. He also said that although he had never made a list like mine, my list seemed very close to one that he would write about a future partner he would like to attract. I remember our reluctance to leave, but it was time for our little group to gather and make our way own to the ferry. I don't remember what the vehicle was like, but it must have been a cargo van because some people sat on a bench along one side, and the rest sat on the floor. Val sat on the side, and he pulled me onto the floor close to him. That was our introduction - we were soon lovers.

"Unbelievable...but true…"

By the time I met Val, my husband was already in a new relationship, and we were in the process of going our different directions. Our youngest son and I were sharing a two-bedroom apartment with my husband and his new partner, and they were soon expecting their first baby (his fourth child). My husband's partner, Maharra, was my best woman friend, so we weren't strangers, and as unbelievable as this might be, all of us got along really well. My husband had been seriously ill for some time - and the part of all this that worked for me was that his new partner relieved me of the pressure of being the only one who could help Robert.

For so long, I had felt pressured to spend more time at home and also to help Robert more than I wanted. I loved him, so I just did it. However, when Maharra came along, she relieved me of so much that she was my "saving grace." There were difficulties in separating, but the separating had a lot of up-sides…and for me, the main one was that I felt relieved to know that Robert had many more of his needs met by this new partnership than I was able or willing to fulfill.

Their baby was born in June and after that, we soon fell into a routine that suited us all. I would come home from work and walk their baby - and often dance him to sleep. All this helped Maharra and Robert a lot because she loved to cook and make meals for all of us - and the baby was usually fussy right at this time and, of course, interrupted her. For me, going for a walk after work suited me perfectly - and it felt so good for me to be able to dance him to sleep. A further upside for Maharra and Robert was they got to spend a mealtime together in peace.

"It couldn't have been more perfectly designed for us if we had tried…"

The place we were living in was a ground-level two-bedroom apartment. The master ensuite bedroom/bathroom/walk-in closet were on one end of the apartment with its own entrance. We put a lock on the inner door…which I never did use…and moved my old piano in, along with a new futon bed. Then our son could go back and forth from my "bachelor" suite to his dad's "one-bedroom" apartment. We couldn't have created a much better arrangement than this if we had set out to do so!

"What's up with Val and me…"

My new friend, Val, and I just dated for quite a while. Then, we began to want our own place. First, I started staying over at his place on the odd overnight - and then we decided that we'd try living together. It lasted about three days before I became homesick. In a few weeks, we tried it once more (with the same result). Most men would have said "goodbye" at that point…but Val was not "most men" and was very patient with me. So, we continued to just be lovers for a while longer.

Chapter 15
Robert's last days

This was late summer by now (1984) and Robert's health was going downhill. It was about the time when their baby was just over three months old, when the three of them flew to a health spa in Germany. Robert looked fabulous when he returned. However, in hindsight, for his regained health to last, he probably would have had to stay at the spa much longer - but he ran out of money, and also, he felt that our community needed him (I think he also missed his seven year old son).

Sadly, by Christmas time he was sinking again; and Robert and Maharra (and babe) bought a trailer, pulled it onto Therah's community land on Galiano Island and made that into their home for his final days, for about another three months. I, on the other hand, decided to stay in Vancouver with our seven-year-old son…his teacher's family invited us to move in with them until the summer holidays.

"Robert died March tenth of that year (1985) … It was a big loss for us all…"

Robert was our community's visionary and the inspiration for community life as well as for vision and dreams. It took a few years of us limping along before we sorted things out and began to move forward again as a community - although it was never the same. Robert hadn't been around for long enough for the community to develop, build and stabilize - which would have meant, in our case, that other leaders had come forward. We had quite a few people among our members who were powerful people and leaders within their own world…but not leaders in Therah. As I said, losing him was a huge loss for all of us. However, as it turned out, unexpectedly, it was especially devastating for me.

Having spent the greater part of my adult life with him, and having had children with him, and going through the ups and downs of my own health with him…all of those suddenly became just memories. Instead of an actual person, alive, that I could see breathing, walking and talking in front of me - he was gone. Death is an inescapable reality for all of us, no matter if a person promises to spend their life with you (or not). They will leave you - or you will leave them -

at some point. One part of me fully understood this…but I had trouble dealing with it just the same. Even though Robert and I had already separated a few years prior, his death brought about remorse in me…all over again…for the course of actions I took - much more than when he had been alive. I had chosen those actions carefully after much deep consideration - and in the end, it had seemed to work out for both of us. I got to grow as an individual and Robert got what he wanted with his new partner.

He had wanted something from me that I did not have the will to give any longer. Believing that it was much better to pull the plug than to just drag on - as I had been doing - I felt strongly that he had been much better off without me than he would have been, with me. Even so, I was devastated by his passing, and for some time after, wondered if I had been responsible for his early demise.

Now, much later, I am able to be more objective and philosophical about Robert's passing. For one thing, about thirty years later, I am more mature about "dying." Now, I can better understand and accept death as a part of life…perhaps the only thing in life that we work towards, our entire lifetime. Now, I see it as something to accept, gracefully, when our time comes, and accept that landmark on other's (our loved ones') behalf, as well. Now I can see - and understand that...whereas I couldn't at the time.

Another thing I had to deal with was...standing by one's decisions - particularly during deeply troubled times. It's something that most people find very difficult to do. It is sometimes, only after years of life experience, that people really come to terms with the course of actions their lives took. Somehow, like it or not at the time, everything that happens is for the best. Even if one cannot see it then, even if it tears you apart at the time, it is very important to know that what happened, happened for the best.

The decisions you made in the past are unchangeable. Therefore, there is good reason not to dwell on them or to look for convoluted ways to atone for them. However, that is not to say that those past decisions should feel great...but it is very important to let life teach you. One important thing that Robert's passing taught me was to accept and to stand by my decisions (even if my mind, or others', disagreed) and to be at peace with them.

The community, to this day, is still going strong...but is a very different community than what Robert and I - and the other originals - had envisaged. No one since has had the mix of visionary and leadership that Robert did. Together, he and I were powerful in bringing visions about - but alone, I wasn't there for it, nor has anyone else been since that time. The community was our life and soul. It was the product of both our vastly different personalities and different ideas. I couldn't have done it without him, nor could he have done it without me. His passing left a hole in the leadership, which could not be fulfilled by anyone.

I think that our son, Gordon has come the closest, but I'm guessing that his age was against him and not enough of the members gave him their complete support. Some openly resented him (and worse) during his tenure as Chairperson of the Board. His sister, Shelagh, also spent a term as Chairperson - and her experience of non-support (even abuse) was the same. Other members have stepped forward, for a time, and in various capacities…but none, to this day, have become a replacement for Robert.

Post Marriage
"Val and I felt ready to live together…"

After Robert's passing, I felt that it was time to move on with my life. In July 1985, Val and I found an old house to rent, just off of Oak and King Edward in Vancouver; and moved in, together with my youngest son plus Val's fourteen-year old son. The reason I moved in with Val so soon after Robert's passing was, that right from the beginning, I felt that I had found the man I could be with, who wanted the same things as I did and who was compatible with me. Initially, those reasons were not enough to make it work because I had not totally closed my chapter with Robert. However, now that he was gone, there was no reason to postpone moving in together.

We made it for a whole year this time! I didn't have any other work going on, so I began working with Val – organizing his office, typing letters for him, and doing other typical office work. Then on weekends, we spent a lot of time on Galiano Island on the Therah Community property. My husband's partner did not need (or want) their trailer any longer, and I bought it so that Val and I had a place to stay when we were on Galiano.

"Massage came forth - for us as a couple as well as for clients…"

Val didn't need me for full-time work in his office, so I had time to do other things. During Therah's community meetings, I had found myself drawn into massaging community members. A few of them began to see me as "clients." A friend gave me a massage table, my mother sewed special, shaped sheets with face holes, and I began to work from home doing massage and giving bodywork sessions. I seemed a natural at massage and eventually added a treatment called Reiki to that. For those of you who are not familiar with Reiki, it is a hands-on method of healing – no motion – with a few different positions on the body. Most of my clients liked a mixture of these two methods as it felt good to be receiving the massage - something tangible. I would then add in the Reiki when I felt it was the right moment - and the combination turned out to be a particularly powerful treatment.

"All was not rosy…"

We had a very interesting and satisfying year, but also turbulent. We had much in common. We had both done the EST Training and therefore shared a skill set and "language" in common for communication as a couple. We both loved spending time at Therah community (Val became a member). Two of our favorite activities were listening to classical music and giving each other a massage. And we were excellent communicators. This was a lot in common - and if commonality were the only criteria for a winning relationship, we would have succeeded.

One item that was on my relationship list when we met was my need for an open, non-exclusive relationship. We talked about it then and thought it was perfect that we both wanted this. That was fine until one of us, Val, moved over to the mutually exclusive philosophy, without raising it into the open. It took a fight before I woke up to the fact that things had changed. When we calmed down and talked about it, Val admitted he no longer wanted to date anyone else – just me.

And to make things worse for me, he was soon going away on a family trip to Italy for about a month and wanted me to be faithful to him during that time. I agonized over that for a while…but then I agreed to try it on for size – and be committed to Val for that month while he was gone - as long as he was willing to talk about it all when he returned, giving us a chance to recommit (or not) at that time. Val agreed.

The point that I was grappling with was that Val had changed the manner of our commitment with each other, without even thinking of taking into account my perspective about it...and discussing the change with me. To be fair to him, he told me that he was unaware of this change in himself until the issue became relevant. I had gone into the relationship thinking that both of us wanted the same thing, which was true in the beginning...but it just did not stay that way. What happens, inevitably, in a relationship is that people change. However, I was not willing to change on this point, as it had already taken me so long to become happy with the sort of person I was.

I was always a free spirit, and one person was just not enough for me. I thought the same thing was true for Val... that one woman would not be enough for him. He, however, changed his mind. While I did like to date around - on the other hand, I was still very much attracted to Val and did not want to lose him as a partner, So I had to give his request a try...I hoped that my strong feelings for him...plus my newly professed commitment to him alone would enable me to readjust myself back into the constraints of a monogamous relationship…

"Infidelity became a deal-breaker…"

It was an interesting month - many opportunities came up to "play around" with different men. Once, I remember getting myself in a pickle - and then out of it…just in the nick of time. I also remember I had many discussions with various male friends that month, as I turned them down, one by one. That's when I realized that I had to take a stand - either commit to my relationship with Val…or not. I also needed to take the consequences of whatever choice I made. I chose Val - and never cheated on him again, after I committed to be faithful to him.

Funnily enough, in the end, he was the one who "fell off the wagon" - but only once. Without me knowing it, he wasn't feeling very connected to me at one point in our relationship. I was too busy and not spending enough time communicating with him or taking care of his relationship needs. That's when I discovered what commitment is really about…and that's "trust" - because it was some time before I found I could trust him again. I couldn't emotionally relax with him for some time, either. Also, a big one for me was the fear of STD's - and so I asked him to wear a condom and have a test. He never blamed me for my reaction and did what I asked. That was a good lesson that I learned - and it has been with me ever since. I have been in many relationships since that time...and infidelity was always a deal breaker for me after that.

Much later in my life, there was a man I was dating for over a year, and I found out, after we had parted, that he had gone back to his wife behind my back while still dating me - and all the while saying he was done with their marriage. I felt so deeply betrayed - and it wasn't anything about him going back to his wife which later he did openly. I could accept that he wanted to go back to her - and even agreed that it was best for them. It was the lying about it - that's what felt like a huge betrayal. I realized, then, that I couldn't trust the truth of anything he had said in the bit over a year that we dated. Distrust has very deep, deadly consequences in a relationship. Trust makes or breaks a relationship; only commitment supports trust.

You'd be surprised what your partner might be open to once you start to be open and honest about what you are doing and thinking and wanting. That is not to say that your partner would necessarily be open to a polygamous relationship, as most people still hold very dearly to the ideology that they have to commit to one person and that is called true love. However, your partner could be open to much more than you think. Most people tend to make very simple, yet deep mistakes that become the reason that the relationship breaks into a mound of heartbreak, regret, and shame. It could be over anything…however, a simple lie means that your partner can no longer trust you - and everything you say is brought into question. That is when you will especially learn that everything you say (and do) in a relationship deeply matters - and even the slightest slip can cause deep troubles.

For Val's and my relationship…on the domestic side, all was not rosy. A big issue was that Val's son, about fourteen years old, was bullying and scaring my son who was seven years old at the time. It was worse on days when both Val and I would come home late in the afternoon, which left the two boys alone after school on those days. We seemed unable to rectify things between them, so my son's teacher allowed him to stay at their house after school, until I picked him up after work each day.

In addition to this, there were things going on between Val and myself that we needed to sort out; in the end, some of our issues couldn't seem to be resolved. The outcome was that we exploded apart at about the one-year mark. I didn't want to see Val after that. I was angry and disappointed - and I didn't feel ready (or willing) to work things through.

"Val moved out, and Mary moved in..."

It was 1986 when Val moved out. Very soon after that, I bumped into an old friend who was looking for a place to live, and I invited her and her daughter to live with me and my son. They took over the top floor, and Colin and I had the main floor. At that time, I had only one piano, so there was room in the large living room for my musician friend to move her piano in. She had been a piano teacher on Salt Spring Island but was taking a hiatus as bad back problems from a former injury had reappeared. She offered to give my son piano lessons, and because my son had become at odds with his teacher, he was very happy to quit and take lessons, instead, with my friend.

"A musical house…"

Eventually, she was sorry she had offered - because his way of learning a piece of music drove her crazy. I called it the 'shotgun approach,' which meant that he would hear his teacher play the piece, and having a good enough ear to remember it, he would proceed to try this, that, and anything until he heard the right sound. Then he'd try it again – with more 'shotgun' trials until he finally got it right every time that he played it. My friend said to me, "he'll never learn to read that way." He didn't…and admits that to this day, he never did… and regrets that he didn't. Moreover, his young son (my grandson) is dealing with the same thing…and I am doing my best to help him learn (even my daughter-in-law tells my grandson that it's a useful skill to learn - and she wishes she had!

We obviously couldn't force my son. Sooner than later, my friend admitted she had to stop teaching him because when he wasn't following her requests and suggestions, that was disturbing for her. I could see the point in her argument, and of course, I couldn't force her. But – I could see that my son was learning and using her teaching sessions as structures to keep himself going…but my friend couldn't see it…and he never did learn to read music!

We then resumed lessons with his former teacher for some of the remaining year until my son again refused to continue with her - and quit about three months before the final recital. Upon inquiring about his reason to quit, he told me that he found her too strict and rigid. Finally, I assisted him at home with his pieces until he had them all perfected – since he had promised his teacher that he would still play in her recital if he had them up to par. I think it irked her that he arrived at the recital, played his pieces perfectly, without lessons, and moreover, had quit - given the amount of talent that he demonstrated.

At about the one-year mark, my friend was ready to move back to her island home and "pick up her pieces" where she had left off. This meant that I was back to just one piano again – and I missed the second piano more than I would have thought. As I am writing this, I am struck by this fact and began reminiscing about the place of pianos in my life. Let me digress for a moment and explore that thought.

Chapter 16
The Significance of Pianos in My Life
Val - Second Round...

At age seven, I began a life of piano lessons, recitals, and informal family performances until I completed my Grade Ten piano exam at the end of my Grade Ten year at school. I continued the following year but with a fairly high level of disinterest. Near the end of my Grade Eleven year, my mother asked me if I would be interested in learning the organ because our church had installed a new pipe organ and hired an organist from England who wanted to give lessons.

I jumped at the chance and dropped my piano studies in favor of learning how to play the organ. That was my Grade Twelve year of school when I completed my Grade Ten Organ exam at the end of that year. That was followed by four years of being an Organist and Choir Director for the Unitarian Church in Vancouver - which kept me in pocket money throughout my university years (I was living at home for free - bless my parents - and fees were minimal in those days). Once I had earned my B.Ed., I continued to play the organ, this time in North Vancouver where I had moved for my first teaching job. However, that winter, I became very ill for a few months and had to give up on my teaching job as well as being an organist. But it wasn't all bad, because this meant I had a lot of free time (and when you learn what I got up to, I'm sure you'll agree with me that I didn't have time to work!).

My husband and I had become involved with a group of deaf young people (we called ourselves, the Pacific Deaf Fellowship - or PDF). In addition, I had a research job with my husband. Soon, I began a sign-singing group with my deaf PDF members that turned into a deaf choir and our group began to put on regular Sunday services for our deaf PDF young people. I sometimes sang - meaning, "signed" the solo – which meant that someone else sang while I "signed" it in rhythm.

We often joined other congregations - usually the churches of the parents of our own young people. In addition, we would be joined by "hearing" relatives and friends of our group and ourselves. Consequently, the congregation was predominantly "hearing." I have become more of a singer now, than I was then, whereas, at the time, I was happy to sign-sing my interpretation of the solo at each service. Sometimes, I had a particular song I wished to sign sing (with my hands) and I would approach the hearing choir to find someone who would sing the solo along with me, which was the reverse of me interpreting their solos.

Musically, this was a happy time for me - I felt very at home with sign language and felt totally at ease and inspired when interpreting the songs into "signs." Even though my mother came to love my sign interpretations of the music, at first, she was taken aback and even horrified that I wasn't playing the piano any longer. I told her not to worry - that it was just a phase and I was sure the piano would come back into my life.

I knew that I would be back at the piano, however, I am a personality that is always drawn into trying new things, and also, jumping into them totally. I have never been satisfied with just standing in one place, or slowly testing the waters…There is always something more to learn and to experience…some other way to grow and another way to be better. That yearning to learn and to grow was vastly important for me to get to where I am today - which is being happy…and I think that's what we're all after. Happiness is the one thing that is in short supply these days…and we'll never know, but possibly has been in short supply since the beginning of time. For me, and probably for you, too, whatever you are going through…learning…growing…just being better than you were the day before…I'm convinced that that'll give you happiness.

"My old family piano came back home…"

Soon, I also became a mother, and in our baby's first year of his life, I sang a lot to him. He seemed to always respond to my singing…would begin bouncing in rhythm. My mom and dad had decided long ago that they no longer needed their piano and put it down in their basement until, one day they asked me if I would like to have it. My response, of course, was an excited "yes." That piano was a part of my childhood memories and I had been longing for a piano for some time - I never thought of asking Mum and Dad about that piano.

I had thought about it for a long time and I realized that deep down, I really wanted a piano in my home. When I was seven, my mom and dad had deliberated over a piano. They came to the conclusion that because they didn't know how my sister and I would take to learning to play the piano, it was best to buy an inexpensive "practice" piano. Now as a twenty-six years old adult and a mother, I was now about to make that same inadvertent error of judgment because of money. However, when they asked me - and I said 'yes' - I did it with my eyes wide open. And I happily accepted my old piano.

"My Soul Mate…"

Since then, pianos have come and gone for me - including my first old piano…and, I might add, from then on, they were never chosen on the basis of their monetary value, but rather, a balance between cost, tone and touch - and sometimes the size. One story, however, stands out.

It was 1986-87 when my friend, Mary, who had been living with me and my son, Colin, moved out. With her, went her baby grand piano. I had become used to her piano being there and enjoyed playing on hers way more than I did on my old upright piano at the time. I had begun to play duets and two piano works with a couple of people, so that when Mary's piano was gone, a piece of my life was also missing.

One day, I commiserated with my friend, Aran as he tuned my upright piano. After he heard my story, he invited me to visit his collection of pianos on display and see if I might find a piano that suited me. I was familiar with Aran's display room, because I had played there a few times - but always on the same piano and always for the same particular reason - to accompany my friend's singing. I had never looked around at the other pianos, nor had I ever played any of the rest of them.

"My friend's used piano showroom…"

A couple of weeks later, I woke up thinking of Aran's suggestion. I phoned him and found out that that day worked for him, so I got ready and went over. His room had about twenty pianos in it. The first thing I did was I to go around to each one and play a few chords from top to bottom to hear the tone and feel the touch. I narrowed it quickly down to about six. Then I took out a piece of music I had brought with me. I played the same page or two on all six pianos. Then I knocked out two more pianos. Next I played a new piece of music on the four remaining pianos until I narrowed it down to two of them.

"It was time to make the choice – or so I thought…"

At that point, I called upstairs to my friend to see if he was free to come downstairs and listen. His opinion was worth a lot, given that he was blind so that listening was one of his strong points. After he sat down, I played a page or two of the same music on both pianos. Then I chose another piece and repeated my ritual. At this point, I turned to my friend for feedback. I was interested in how I sounded, comparatively, because the ease of my playing, accuracy of notes and expression, coupled with the tone of the piano was different on each. I had my own feelings and opinions, but I kept these to myself and instead I looked at my friend and waited for him to comment.

He didn't. Instead he asked me a question, "Why not the grand?" The grand he was referring to, was the piano I always played on when accompanying his singing. "Well, for starters, it's your personal piano. But it is too much money for me, it's too big, and the keys are too stiff."

He looked amused, "To respond to each of your points, I have thought of it as my piano, in that I don't let it out to rent along with all the others in the room. However, I would let it go to you. Next, it isn't much more money than the one that I think you are favoring - only a couple of hundred more.

As for size, it is only a "baby" grand - and that's identical to the piano your friend used to have in your living room - so I don't think that its size is a problem. And finally, I can weight the keys lighter than they are, so they will no longer feel stiff."

"A big surprise…"

I just sat there for a minute, thinking about what he had said. Finally, I asked him to go back upstairs and said I would call when I was ready for him. I took up my music again and moved onto the grand piano's bench. I began to play...and tears ran down my face. I felt stunned. Of course, Aran was right. To think what a near miss it almost was. The "narrowing" exercise that I had gone through with the rest of the pianos was really a bit of a pointless exercise - because from my first notes on the grand, it was so acutely obvious that this one was my soul mate.

It was a little superfluous to call Aran down, but it seemed the proper thing to do, in order to be complete. I played for him on the one I had previously chosen. After that, I played on the grand and when I had finished and everything went silent, Aran was also quiet. I looked over at him and he had this little smirk on his face. I laughed and asked, "Is it that obvious?" "Yes!" he said...and then we talked business...the only thing needed to tidy up the deal.

My "soul mate" was with me for twenty-three years - longer than my husband was; and longer by far than all the other men in my life!

All along, music - and the playing of a piano, in particular - is the thing that has given me peace of mind...it restores my soul to order, you might say. Dancing, now, also does that for me. The thing is, everyone needs to have that one thing they can grab to restore themselves. Where playing the piano has been "it" for me, make sure that you always know... and have ready access to that special thing for yourself...the point being that even though your life goes on in this direction or that...no matter what, you need to have something in it that helps you focus and returns you to yourself. It is imperative to know that when life throws some challenge at you, you have something you can rely on to get you through that...as my piano has done for me.

"It was time to move on..."

Ironically, I gave it up when I met, loved, and moved into my final partner's home. It was a one-bedroom suite in a 4-plex and is a cute little place with no space for a piano, certainly not either of the pianos I had at that time. Therefore, I gave up both my small upright piano as well as my baby grand piano. At first it was lonely being without a piano, but I got along without one for two years. Finally, I bought another piano…a digital piano this time…and therefore, really different from any piano I have ever owned before. I've been a pianist for almost seventy years, but even I am impressed with my own determination!

Although I never thought I would have a digital piano; a couple of years into the relationship, not having had a piano to play in my home for almost two years, I was hungry for one. Buying a digital piano or keyboard had been one of my goals for a while. However, after a year or so, I had given up on the idea due to it not being practical so long as we lived in our "cottage" and I scratched it off my list. One day, however a magical event happened. My partner and I were walking in a nearby mall. We wandered into one of his usual haunts, and as I rounded a corner inside the store, there, a few feet in front of me, was a piano, all set up in the aisle -

in front of a counter. It was the smallest, slimmest one I had ever seen - and I immediately wondered if it might fit somewhere in our suite. I asked the clerk if I could play it and found myself enjoying it. I called my partner over to join me in my exploration and admiration of the piano. He asked the clerk for a measuring tape and with those measurements we walked home to see if it might fit. After looking our place over, we decided on the place we would put it and measured the space. The only space we could possibly fit it was going to have the new piano slightly in our way when walking from our front door into the kitchen, so we put some stools in the way, marking where the piano would be.

Having decided that we could probably live with the inconvenience as a trade-off for the value added, we went back to the store. I thought that there was very little deliberation left for us to do but just when I thought we had come to a "yes," my partner admitted that he really didn't feel comfortable with the whole thing. I was a bit stunned, and on an impulse said that was that then. I said that I wouldn't raise it again and asked to be taken home. My partner muttered something about having to do a bit more measuring - which I ignored, because I didn't see that any more measuring would change anything.

Back home again, I withdrew into our bedroom. When I regained myself, I went back out into the living room - and found him measuring. I still said nothing. Then he looked at me and said, "Well, I think maybe we can try it and see if it works."

Back we went again, and this time around he agreed to buy it (not that he was the one putting out the money - but there was more than money involved in this purchase). It turned out to be the last one they had, and therefore they could give us the floor model - all set up. It fit into our car, so two men from the store carried it, as is, with a plastic over it (a slight drizzle of rain was falling). When we arrived home, Dave and I easily carried it into the house, and because it had been set-up by the store, we had nothing more to do!

"The proud owners of a new digital piano…"

It was dinnertime, so I contained my excitement until after we had eaten. Then, we had pie and ice cream to celebrate our acquisition, followed by our first little sing-along in our living room. Then I played a Chopin waltz, and our new piano was properly christened!

It didn't play like an acoustic piano, but I seem to be in a different phase of my life and more into playing as an accompaniment as I sing. I sing all kinds of songs, such as Gershwin, a few modern songs, old folk tunes - all of it. Sometimes I like to play a Chopin waltz or Beethoven's Moonlight Sonata, but those occasions are too rare to be longing for a real piano for those few moments. I am in a new stage of life and I'm enjoying it immensely.

Anyway, I feel complete with my piano detour and hope you can read between the lines and learn something about yourself through my experience. In any case, I feel ready to resume my Val story.

"In came Val once more (now 1987)..."

Initially, after we had parted so angrily, we didn't contact each other for quite a while. I guess neither of us had anything new to say nor could we face each other after all that had happened. But I remember that at one point, I became sick with a very bad cold, and after some hesitation, I phoned Val and asked if he would consider coming over and giving me a massage. My condition was pretty bad... and I don't know if it was the fact that I just wasn't thinking straight or that I really wanted to see him...regardless, he said he would like to do that. I remember that his massage felt mind-blowingly wonderful and I asked him if he would consider massaging me each day for a couple more days. I think it may have been the only time that he, or anyone else for that matter, ever did this experiment on me. I must have intuitively known what it would be like because it certainly wasn't out of any previous experience. Each time built on the previous one and by the third massage, I was in a state of pure bliss.

This contact reconnected us and we began spending time together again. It wasn't long before we began to talk of getting back together. That would be, of course, without his son...I think there was a cousin's family for him to stay with. I said that I was only interested if we were going to commit and get engaged this time. It felt very important for me to have a commitment from his side. He agreed. Val bought me a gorgeous ring (a beautiful, modern design) - and although we had a couple of outstanding years, it became clear that it wasn't a 'go.' It was so obvious… and therefore I had to be practical about it… and just accept it this time.

The main crux was on Val's side…his non-negotiable criteria (which rather typically had not shown up clearly enough) had become impossible for him to live without. This was that he longed to have a partner who followed the same spiritual master as he did. When we got together, he knew I was a spiritual person and he had hoped that I would come to follow his particular path. I really enjoyed listening to his guru speak - his ideas and I loved his sense of humor. However, over time, I knew that the community and spiritual practices weren't for me. For myself, I didn't need or want a particular person or path to follow.

This time we parted amicably. Since that time, I have only bumped into him a couple of times and contacted him by phone twice. Whether that makes us 'friends' or 'friendly,' is questionable. However, that is the dynamic of the relationship and the way we preferred to leave it. Nevertheless, it was a wonderful two additional years; much gained and no regrets. During that time, we worked together again, which had stopped during the year we were apart…and we continued to spend many weekends on

Galiano Island. We took courses - relationship as well as other personal development ones. We were deep communicators and loved to share with each other our deepest thoughts and inner struggles. And he was my best lover ever – regretfully given up. However, all these wonderfully workable aspects could not balance out the one deal breaker for Val: his partner in life had to be part of his spiritual community.

"The end came unexpectedly and easily…"

By the end, I was holding on for dear life, struggling to admit that we weren't a good match any longer. And just as it seemed that it would never happen, the end came upon me suddenly. Val left for a week at a retreat center with his spiritual leader, in the hills of Southern California. He wasn't gone more than a few hours when a thought came to me…that if I worked really steadily, I could be gone by the time he returned. With the thought came a rush of energy as I realized that this would be a really easy way to let go of him - I couldn't seem to do it when he was there.

"When I was complete, there was nothing left but ease and love…"

I phoned my parents and told them what I was planning to do and wondered if they might find any way to help me. My parents, in their usual style, when something had to be done, arrived by 9:00 the next morning. I masterminded and they did most of the "doing." They came daily and the three of us kept at it most of the week. At that time, my daughter, just over twenty, took her eleven-year old brother to her place, indefinitely, until I could relocate.

We also cleaned the house as we sorted, emptied and packed. I knew I could leave my two pianos in the living room until I properly re-located, which wouldn't be for about another four or five months. When the boxes were all packed and stored in the basement, except for the few things I was taking with me to a friend's, the house was neat and clean. There just remained the yard. I cut the grass, weeded the flower beds and rockery, wrote a note of completion - and left for my friend's house.

I felt really good about the way I had left - I knew that Val would get that I had left in friendship, not anger. I left just because it was the right thing to do...we both knew that, but neither of us could actually do it. Being the one to always come up with plans and take action, I knew it was on me to do this. Though I was mainly the one who had been resisting the truth, just one moment of clarity was all that was needed to get me going. My son could not stay with me during this phase…but his schoolteacher's family offered to be my daughter's back-up whenever it didn't work for her to have him. Everyone was very good to both of us at this time. However, I wasn't able to stay at my first friend's home for long, so then I moved in with another friend.

"The beginning of more than twenty years of running shared houses…"

Eventually, a third friend and I decided we would like to live in a large Shaughnessy home. When we began looking, we quickly realized that we would have to involve a couple of other people. The homes were financially out of our range - but we liked the idea of living in that kind of house. By September of 1989, we moved into "our house" - and it was more than time for my son and me to be re-united, and his sister to be freed up again.

Chapter 17
1989 - In Came Jhake Stokink

"Shared housing - a rich and interesting experience..."

Years earlier, I had been introduced to Jhake by Val at some personal development event we were all attending. He kept me in his sights for a few years until I was single again. At first, we just kept it light and only dated. By the fall of that year, my friend and I were ready to rent a large old house. We asked Jhake if he also would like to move in with us. It had three bedrooms, plus a small dormer room that my son claimed. I had one room, my friend had one, and that left one room for Jhake. He wondered if we would wait for his answer until he returned from his planned trip. We decided we could wait that long.

When he arrived, I remember giving him a tour of the place, and showing him all the rooms, ending off with my room. Then I asked him which one he wanted, and he said, "this one." I said, "I was afraid of that." It was simple really...I asked which he wanted...and he answered. I was fine with that. There were no overtly complicated or romantic moves involved, just a simple question and an answer. With that we were in a relationship. In all my years, that was the most backhanded way I have ever gotten into a relationship!

"The house was a-buzzing…"

What a wonderful year that was. The house was amazing. We could never have imagined owning it outright so that only by renting could any of us ever experience the magnificence of such a home. Now that Jhake didn't need a room, we quickly found someone to rent the third bedroom. It was time to move my two pianos out of Val's home…and I put them in the living room, which was like a ballroom. We had the best informal sing-alongs there, usually initiated by me. We also hosted all kinds of meetings and events for speakers, a singing workshop, all types of healing events and friends' birthday parties.

"We were enamored with having a pool - until it turned green…!"

With these large houses came many interesting features such as…enormous decks for sun-bathing or dining; lovely dens, family rooms, enormous living-rooms, extraordinary kitchens, alcoves, stained-glass windows, gorgeous grounds. Not all these features came in any one house – but all of our houses had many of them.

For example, our first house came with a pool. We loved the idea of having a pool, however, it didn't take us long to find out that the idea that a pool is wonderful, was pure fantasy. We worked very hard at keeping the pool clean but every time we turned around, it would become green again! That was a great disappointment for us all. After a while, we just let it go - it cost too much and took too much time to keep it healthy - and we had learned our lesson about pools, the hard way!

Another thing about these large houses was that they took a lot of time to maintain. I have an idea that original owners probably had money to pay for a housekeeper and a grounds-man. But we didn't have that kind of money...plus roommates were not usually into helping with the space in common - some of them barely maintained their personal rooms...so we were lucky if any of them helped with cleaning bathrooms and kitchens or mowing the lawn. Except for the odd offer, the bulk of the upkeep of the house and grounds fell on Jhake and me.

The thing about these shared houses was that they were large and had interesting little spaces that smaller, two- or three-bedroom family homes usually do not have. It seemed that we could always find a nook or cranny for special purposes. On the top floor of this first house, there was a room that extended off the side of the house, like a solarium. Even though we didn't do it professionally, both Jhake and I often gave massages and we both used this room for our massage and bodywork sessions - most of our clients would come to our house for these. If it was cold, because the room had no insulation and was very cold in the winter, it seemed adequate to use an electric blanket on the table and under a sheet. Usually we entertained clients on an individual basis, but ever so rarely we gave a joint session (a two-on-one massage), which apparently was to die for.

"Canadian Centre for Attitudinal Healing"

Jhake ran the Canadian Centre for Attitudinal Healing from our home. For years he had held regular weekly meetings at another location but when he moved into our house, we all agreed that it would make sense for him to move the Centre and its meetings into our main living room.

The Centre was holding an event called Hug for Peace on Valentine's Day and so we also held all the planning meetings for that. We were intending there to be one thousand people in a downtown parking lot, joined in a giant hug for peace. Thus, to achieve that, we advertised like crazy, flyers everywhere and we felt ready. We woke up on the morning of the big day to hear snow warnings, and by late morning it was already snowing hard. By late afternoon, things were a mess.

By evening rush hour, things were impossible. We somehow got our car out of the driveway and started driving downtown. Our direction (north) was moving, slowly, but we passed the rush hour cars going south, trying to get home...and they were mostly gridlocked, at a standstill caused by cars ahead of them that had spun out of control. All the advertising and planning we had done went right down the drain in front of our eyes.

When we arrived at the designated space, there were just a couple of people there - and that was only because they lived nearby and had walked to the event. When we saw only a couple of people in the lot, at first, we thought we had arrived late to our event and that everyone had gone home.

Then we realized that people just weren't able to get there. We were stunned. A few more dribbled in over the next hour, and they had also walked or ditched their cars when the going got too tough…and walked the rest of the way. Altogether, there were about twenty-five of us, out of our hoped-for one thousand. What a disappointment that was for all of us. However, for those of us who were able to get there, it was a touching event. When we initially created this event, our hearts were definitely in the right place!

"My monthly sing-alongs were born…"

One of the events that had the most lasting impact, from that more "public" part of my life, was the monthly sing-along evening. Small sing-alongs had been spontaneously happening right from the beginning. My friend, who shared the house with us, had a songbook of about forty songs she had inherited from her father. Sometimes, she'd ask me to play and we'd both sing together. Also, there were often parties in the house, mostly put on because an acquaintance of one of our household members would request that they be allowed to put on a birthday party in our home. During the evening, my friend would get a bit bored and suggest that we sing for a while and before we knew it, a group would be gathered around the piano to sing along with us.

Jhake was always very supportive of me having the life that I wanted, sometimes even outspokenly expressing that I wasn't aiming high enough. He shared with me an on-going dream he had of me being on stage as a speaker and performer. Already he had experienced me creating sing-alongs in our large and ideal house whenever we hosted birthday parties. At first, these party sing-alongs sprang into being, spontaneously. Then the word got out and friends (or even friends of friends) would phone us and ask if they could have their birthday party at our house...and if we would include a sing-along.

One day in the spring of 1990, Jhake asked me if I had considered putting on regular sing-alongs. This idea had also been brewing inside of me, so when he brought it up, I decided to go for it. He urged me to name a date, and then he put it out to his Attitudinal Healing group and encouraged them to attend. I thought I was prepared to put it on once a month. However, on my first one, when no one showed up, I was ready to give up at such a little thing. Not Jhake...he insisted that I had to set up a pattern and give it a while to catch on. I chose Sunday evenings, once a month, about four or five weeks apart. He was right…for the next sing-along, a couple of people attended. I also started putting out invitations to a few of my friends - and everyone in our house followed suit. Gradually, my friends and their friends got the idea that I was committed to put on sing-alongs once a month. After that, every house I moved into, the sing-along moved there, too…until exactly thirty years later, they are still happening!

After a few years, I even put on some public ones. A sing-along friend of mine got me an interview with CBC's Afternoon Show. That evening, of the one hundred people who showed up, ten came because of hearing my interview that afternoon on the radio. They said it sounded like it would be a safe environment for them to sing. I was thrilled that that aspect of the sing-alongs came across so strongly to them, because it was something I felt very strongly about.

Then for a while, I moved my sing-alongs out of my home and into public spaces like a church fellowship room and later to another hall. However, however, once I quit hosting the public sing-alongs, which seemed to "feed" our regular singalong events, the numbers began dwindling. I wondered if I should move them back into my home again because eventually, we were barely covering the room costs. The first time I had one in my home, about forty people showed up and I had my answer as to where people wanted it to take place. A few years ago, I moved outside of Vancouver, and it took me a while to find a new home where the sing-alongs could take place again. Therefore, for a year, I wasn't very regular - but that's the only time I was irregular during my past thirty years!

"Suddenly, my life was inundated by changes…!"

About this time, Winter of 1990, I was hired by the Naturopathic Association of BC. It seemed a great match for my abilities and interests… for about a year and a half. That was when they decided I wasn't such a great match after all. Around about this time - that summer - I changed my name, a granddaughter was born, I went on a Vision Quest, and I began my final profession. Let me tell you all about these, one at a time, beginning with my tenure with the Naturopathic Association.

"I had sixty-plus bosses - and we didn't always see eye to eye..."

Early in 1990, I began working for the Naturopathic Doctors of BC. I answered to a Board of Directors, which comprised of about eight of the doctors and served about sixty-five doctors all told. I was their only staff person, although they had had a part-time person before me who did her best with the amount of work...but didn't do much organizationally. So that was a large part of my job, and that being my forte...I enjoyed organizing the office and the work into systems. Over the course of a year and a half, it became evident that there was more work than I could handle in reasonable hours. Not being one to quit, I worked long hours in order to handle it all, which of course, made my family and social life suffer.

The doctors and I had different priorities in two areas in particular. First, the Board expected me to produce their meeting minutes within a couple of days following the Board meeting. Rarely did I find myself willing to prioritize that activity over other activities that were competing for my time. They were adamant, and it was a constant complaint of the Board.

The other on-going complaint of theirs was about referrals. When a person phoned into the office to receive a doctor referral, the doctors wanted me to give them the closest doctor's office to the caller, period. However, over time, I came to know more and more of the doctors' specializations...and after asking a few questions and listening to the caller's needs, I often thought that the nearest doctor wasn't the most suitable for the caller's needs. Then I would offer them a couple of alternates and explain why I was suggesting the match. I believed that if I increased the caller's understanding and got them engaged in their own process, complaints against the doctors might decrease... instead of continuing to increase.

Also, when anyone phoned in with a doctor complaint, I did the same thing, which was to take some time getting to the bottom of things, trying to understand the root of their complaint. Then I'd help them see some possible approaches as a solution. They'd get off the phone, calm, with more perception and a better attitude. Given my way of working, public complaints did decrease. I thought that was worth a lot; however, the Board didn't appreciate the correlation, and something had to give.

"My home life was about to transform…"

Apart from the fact that my social and home life were suffering, there was additional stress in my home. Out of the blue, our landlords delivered us an eviction notice to be effective September of 1990. There was nothing wrong on our part, just that they wanted the house back for family use, which happens to be one of the few allowable eviction reasons governed by tenant-landlord rights, even now. That put us all in a bit of an upheaval. I did a quick assessment with everyone to see where they were at and what they were thinking of doing next. I had to know who wanted to find another house to continue the shared living experiment, and who had other ideas.

Much to my surprise, I found that no one wanted to continue, including Jhake. A male friend of my girlfriend had expressed some interest in joining us in our next shared house, but Jhake didn't really want him in on it. This was because he felt nervous about the dynamics. In addition, we were at the power struggle stage of our relationship and weren't doing very well. So Jhake not wanting to continue wasn't a complete surprise, but it was a painful moment of truth.

"I was caught off-guard - but good for her..."

As for the rest, my girlfriend was the biggest surprise. She wanted to change her lifestyle completely...sell all her things. Then...Maybe go sailing? Move east? Work for herself? "Maybe" was the keyword. She wasn't really clear on what she wanted - except she did know that she didn't want to be a part of the group in our next shared house. The other friend decided he would rather live on his own again as he felt ready for it and had the income for it now. All that news meant that my son and I were on our own again.

I don't remember where, how, or when Jhake moved out, but I do remember it was a rather painful process for us both. I wasn't that happy about the separation, but I do remember thinking that he was completely emotional and unreasonable. I thought that we were being hasty in giving up on our relationship - but Jhake wouldn't talk about it anymore and began looking for a place for himself. I think he moved in with a friend - or some very temporary arrangement. As soon as Jhake made his decision to leave, I got in touch with my girlfriend's friend, Matthew, to see if he was still interested in looking for a house. He said, "yes," so we came up with an action plan and began to look.

"A new look...but the same life..."

Matthew found the house first. It was brand new and modern, very unlike the heritage quality of the previous house - in fact, it was different in almost every aspect from my previous house. It had a moderately-sized living room - unlike the ballroom-like living room of the other. It had a sunken atrium off of it, which we all liked a lot. We couldn't see ourselves using the formal dining room, so we turned that into the piano area for me, which wasn't really a room, rather a hub or an intersection of hallways leading from five areas from the front door: one, from my piano area; two, from the sunken living-room and atrium; three, from the isolated master bedroom that my friend Matthew chose; four, from the five bedrooms above; and five, from the kitchen/family room that consisted of a long, wide, pass-through counter dividing the large open area into one/third kitchen and two-thirds dining and family area.

For a few months, I didn't get any privacy when playing the piano. However, for my sing-alongs, the openness was an asset because people could spread out into the foyer beyond the piano, and even sit on the stairs. Later on, we erected a ceiling track and attached a drapery to wall off the piano area to give some privacy whenever I wanted.

Before we even moved into the house, we had begun broadcasting our interest in finding housemates. Our efforts came up with results, and people were beginning to ask us about it. We were also bumping into prospects, personally. Most came by word of mouth through friends of friends. I think we found only one of our final choices by a more distant process like the UBC Housing Rental. By the time we moved in, our rent was totally covered by the four adults (they agreed that the adults would cover Colin's share.

For my son and me, it felt lonely without Jhake, but we were survivors and got on with our lives without him. For the first month or two, we didn't even hear from him. However, as it turned out, by mid-fall, Jhake was having serious second thoughts about living without us. He began to phone me almost daily at my work, and eventually, we met for lunch.

"Jhake and I decided to have another go at it…"

I had been really reluctant to change the status quo, so we had left things on a talking-only basis, along with the odd meet-up. However, after a couple of months, Jhake asked if he could come and see the new house where we lived. My son and I had missed him, so I finally agreed to him coming over for a visit. That, however, turned out to be the beginning of the end of me being in control. I had always said that if he came, he would have to have a bedroom of his own, and there wasn't one. However, when he saw the house, he saw that there was one very small room that was empty. He inquired about it, and I said that because there was no closet and it was super small, we had decided to leave it empty so that all of us could use it for massage and meditation.

He expressed interest in moving into this room, and I agreed, on the condition that it was agreeable with the rest of the house. I knew my goose was cooked, so to speak…and sure enough, the others agreed. He soon moved his things into the little room. I don't remember what he used as a bed, but I think it was his massage table with the legs folded to flatten the table on the floor. What I do remember is that it wasn't long before he was back in my bed – what a pushover I was where Jhake was concerned!

After being there with my son and me again, for almost a year, Jhake raised with me the possibility of the three of us finding a house on our own and running it as a shared house ourselves. He envisaged filling the bedrooms mostly with foreign students needing a caring home to live in while away from their home. I agreed in principle, and in the fall of '91, we set out on our own, this time about two miles east but still well within Vancouver's West-side. Once again, we were in the Shaughnessy area of Vancouver, quite close to our original house. The new house was, like the house before last, in an area of the city I felt very comfortable in. This house had more bedrooms than that house and also a finished basement plus two bedrooms, which meant there was a lot more rentable space.

My son had one of the rooms in the basement, along with another roommate, and there was a family room down there that we set up as a TV room. Because I wanted a room on my own and because no one except my son used the family room, Jhake soon began to use the "hideaway" bed down there as his bed…and set up his desk in the L-shaped part of the living-room. We were all set!

"Jhake made a good father figure…"

It suited Jhake to be the "master" of the house. In the previous house, we had all been white middle class and either had grown up in Vancouver - or had lived there for years. We were all practitioners or leaders in the personal growth movement, and therefore, peers. Jhake suited better being in the role of leader, where he was an authority figure. While running shared houses, we rarely had roommates over 40 years old - and mostly they were young people, coming to Vancouver for English instruction as well as to experience the Canadian way of life. Once we had a Native young man - only sixteen - he was just emerging from a life of foster homes, and he had trouble integrating into our household (he didn't stay long). Another was a young French man, here from eastern Canada to improve his English, having grown up in a French speaking household and having gone only to French speaking schools.

Mixed in were a few working people - but I noticed that they didn't fit in as well as the foreign students who were here to learn English…and usually didn't last long, either. They didn't want or appreciate what we had to offer - they mostly would arrive home, make a meal in our shared kitchen (or bring it home from a deli), just heat it up - and disappear into their room. They didn't add anything to our living experience - just to the rent!

The students and young people all welcomed the homey environment that we offered, along with the freedom of eating what they wanted and having no curfew. We offered the feel of the family away from home. It wasn't really a typical home; two adult "friends" sharing responsibilities for the son of one of them. However, we were empathetic and took time to help them with their English and also often made meals for them and even took them shopping and on tourist outings. We made sure they had a good time while they were with us. They usually made friends with my son, which enriched his life and theirs but was hard on him when they left.

"A major change in the relationship was called for…"
Jhake and I had a lot of things in common; however, the first time around, I got clear that I didn't want a romantic

relationship with him any longer. He didn't like talking about our relationship; rather, just wanted it to happen. I, on the other hand, was done with that kind of relationship with Jhake. He was 18 years older than I was, and it felt like I had completed my "father" relationship in being with him and was now done with my "teenager" relationship with him. We were an excellent team in our running of a shared house, and between the two of us, we just naturally covered all the bases. But having a romantic relationship seemed to get things really muddy.

Things suddenly changed when about a month or two into our second year in this house, we were given a three months' notice to vacate...there are enough loopholes for owners to easily and legally evict tenants. It seemed to happen quite often with the kind of large houses that we rented - often from an offshore owner who was more of an investor than an owner. The most common reasons that owners used were to move the family in, to renovate, or to sell. We eventually experienced them all. We soon found a new place about a mile away, so we could relax again - at least for a while. Just like our first shared house experience, the move shook people up so that we had to start all over with a new slate.

One woman moved with us, and she found a friend to move in - and for the rest, we put out an ad and filled our rooms...as usual, it was easy. My son...and I... still stay in touch with two of those roommates - a young woman from Mexico and a young man from Australia. Once in a while, I see the woman who had moved with us from the previous house - the last time I saw her was in a Lindy Hop dance class!

Life has a way of putting things into perspective. I've learned that you must never stop moving in life. You always have to grow and take on challenges. That being said, living in these shared houses was a really good experience for our son. He learned early on, seeing his mom tackling different challenges and running large shared houses with their constant problems: that I deal with things as they arise...and keep moving on with my life. Children do as they see... and it is always great if a parent can give them something worthwhile to see!

Chapter 18
I Am Tough
And Strong Of Character

I don't know how I kept my job, managing the Naturopathic Association office through all the turmoil going on at home in my first shared house. However, I somehow managed to keep it going through the moving and separating process from Jhake. I am strong and resilient - which I might not have known at the time, but looking back, it is clear to me now. By this time, I had taken a few personal development courses in addition to the original one, the EST Training - and I was learning not only to believe in my own abilities but also to build my life forward on my new-found courage and knowledge of myself.

I have become a strong believer in the fact that you are what you believe yourself to be. I hadn't always been so clear about my strengths, but by now, I had learned to think of myself as all of those things…and obviously, people who embody those qualities never give up. They go on even when there are a seemingly insurmountable number of difficulties piling up…and even when there seems to be nothing in their favor. Anyway, in 1991, a year into the job, there were struggles and rumblings going on there. After much frustration on each side, the Naturopathic doctors finally asked me to leave at the end of July/91. When they informed me, they said I could leave on the spot and didn't have to show up again to train the new person - who was the wife of one of the doctors. I was horrified. I didn't want her to have to go through the same hardships that I went through, initially and said, of course, I would train her.

Additionally, after all the care I had put into organizing and developing the office and the public service for the doctors, I thought it would be a terrible waste not to introduce my replacement to the set-ups and systems I had put in place. Moreover, it would be a shame not to make her life easier so that she didn't have to figure out so much – or worse, force her to reinvent the wheel by starting from scratch each time she couldn't figure out something important.

"I was stunned, shocked, dismayed…"

As soon as the doctor, who dismissed me, left my office, I burst into tears. It was lunchtime...and about then, a friend phoned. I was still sniffling, and when I told him the story, his reaction was, "Hallelujah! Let's go out and celebrate!" I was shocked and asked what he meant. He said, "It's about time you got out of there – you have been telling me for a long time that you are overworked and underpaid…and by now, you are burnt out."

At first, I was stunned, but as I let that sink in, I realized that he was right, and for some reason, I had been willing to cast a blind eye to all that. However, if my friend was so clear about my situation, even though I was ignoring my plight – like an ostrich with its head in the sand – I must have been talking, and probably complaining, to all those around me. Not good! We went out for dinner to celebrate.

"Auspicious moment…out with the old, in with the new!"

The following week, I showed up all week so that I could train the doctor's wife. She was amazed at the amount of organization and procedures there were to go over. After our first week of training, there was a holiday, BC Day, which was a provincial holiday weekend. On the third and final day of the August holiday weekend, I changed my name to

Maren Dancer, which was one of the best things I ever did. It took me on a new journey, there's a story to this, but first, let me finish with the naturopathic doctors. After three weeks, altogether, the job was done, and I felt that I had shared enough with the woman who was taking over my job so that she was prepared for it. She was thrilled that I had taken that time because, at the end of the three weeks, she realized that she would have limped along for some time if I hadn't given her the thorough orientation that I gave her. During the three-week-long process, one or the other of us documented each aspect of the job. By the end of those three weeks, between us, we had produced and completed a job manual.

"Appreciation from an unexpected source..."

We were more like gifts to each other – I made her job entry extremely smooth and easy. Likewise, she made my exodus very easy - she provided me with the missing appreciation and acknowledgment that the doctors never gave me – they were too caught up in what was missing, or the glass half empty. Because of this, I had lost sight of my accomplishment in the year and a half and had doubted the job I had done. She set me straight on that one – because she had temporarily held down the fort in the early days (before I came along) and therefore knew better than anyone, what I had turned the office into, and the service that I had been giving the public.

I think we could have been good friends, but I didn't keep in touch with her – I thought it was best for me to just move on and create what was next for me. As an aside, I do know that sometime after I was gone, the Naturopathic Association realized that their legal and governmental accreditation matters were becoming too important to mix in with their daily, general office business. The outcome was that they created two separate offices to handle all their Association's business needs, separately from their legal needs. Knowing that, seemed to complete things for me - it confirmed for me that it was no wonder that I had felt so overworked and in need of assistance in order to handle the workload and demands!

Chapter 19
Grandma' Or 'Nanny'
It All Depends On The Child!

Fired, Change of Name, Vision Quest...WOW

By this time, the arrival of grandchildren had begun. My elder son moved in with a woman who had two daughters from a previous relationship. Then together, they had a daughter.

June was born near the end of my tenure with the naturopathic doctors. Her birth heralded a new era in my life. I hadn't been able to build a stellar relationship with my bonus granddaughters, who were two and four years old at the time when my elder son joined with their mother. But with June's arrival, everything sort of fell into place...From that moment onwards, the other two started to call me Grandma.

I know I didn't visit them often. It's quite a long trip made even more difficult because I had to take a ferry to get there, and at that time, I had a job in Vancouver. Plus, it meant going in the opposite direction, north, rather than the path that the rest of my life took me. For example, I went south to see my mom and dad, south-west to see my sister and brother-in-law. Visiting my part-time home on Galiano Island took me even further southwest, which was also a ferry trip. Sometimes, I even went south across the US/Canadian border on trips to jazz festivals…but almost never north, where my elder son resided.

Also, I had a big life with the running of a shared house, looking after my youngest son, who still had "parental" needs, and doing some bodywork after hours. However, if I am honest with myself, it was probably just a big justification for some other emotional reason. Over the years, I have felt a lot of guilt over the way I chose to do "Grandma" in those days…although I have come to terms with all that now.

"Christening of the great-grandchild…"

Sometime in early September or late August, right after I had completed my naturopathic staff training, my granddaughter, June, was christened. It was a significant event and an especially important one for my Mom and Dad, as she was their first great-grandchild. At this point, I hadn't told many people about changing my name, and I wanted to keep it that way for the time being. I was adamant about the event not being about my name change but rather, be only about June's christening and her family. I remember my youngest whining about what he was going to call me. I don't really know why because he always called me mom - and that is what I, unsympathetically, said to him, "Call me 'Mom' like you always do!"

"A numerologist got my attention…"

A third of the way through my completion process in passing the baton at my job, I had changed my name. It was a life-changing and transformative event. I had hoped it would be that way...and I certainly wasn't disappointed. It had all started about three months earlier when I was playing the piano at a birthday sing-along of a friend. A friend of his sat down beside me where I was sitting after the singing, eating some birthday cake. He began to doodle on a napkin.

At first, I paid only mild interest to him until he started to ask me questions about my name: How did I spell it, Did I have a different maiden name; What month, day, and year was I born. As I answered each question, he would make notes about my answers. Then there were some silent moments as he seemed to study my answers, and he began saying things that he was thinking and noticing. I asked him what he was doing. He introduced himself as Clayne Conings and said that he was a Numerologist and was doing an analysis of my name, based on the numbers of my name and my birthdate. He had my attention; the things he said were very interesting to me.

He told me some things about myself…stuff that I was familiar with, but he couldn't possibly have known. I realized that he had figured it all out by the answers I had given him. It didn't make sense that he could know so much about me when it was only the first time we'd ever met. More interestingly though, he told me some things about myself that I hadn't "known" until that moment…but what he said made a lot of sense.

I recognized myself in what he was telling me, as I sat there, listening to him and connecting the dots and reflecting on how I reacted in the different situations that he was describing. Everything he said made sense. I was shocked at his solid grasp of myself and my life, just by applying the principles of Numerology. He made me realize, for the first time, that my name had an undeniable power over my life…and I couldn't help but recognize the truth in what he was sharing with me.

"I knew I had to change my name…"

A thought suddenly entered my mind that night…I had to change my name. I recognized that the main issues I had had all my life sprang from what this man called "the vibration" of my name. In addition, as I reflected on this information that he was giving me, I knew he spoke the truth…I was always working on these issues in personal development workshops or getting some expensive therapy to deal with them as well. My question of myself was, "How much more time and money do I want to spend to deal with these negative, "unbalanced vibrations" - that had only partially been resolved in these ways?"

My answer was quick and straightforward, "None!"

And I decided, there and then, to change my name.

"No time to wait…"

I took this stranger's name and number and got in touch with him the next day. His suggestion to me was to take his beginner's Numerology course. An even faster approach was to buy his tapes…and being the pro-active kind of person that I am, I did both. Once I started to get the hang of it, I was insatiable. I doodled every person's name in my close circle. I couldn't gain enough knowledge fast enough. I was in this doodling/analyzing frenzy for weeks. My teacher/friend had developed sheets of suggested names, with each sheet having names with a "recommended vibration," as he called it. He gave me two of these sheets with possibilities for first name choices, from his numerological point of view and one sheet for last name choices.

He had also shown me how I could take currently unbalanced names and add certain letters to balance them. Some names didn't lend themselves to that, but lots did. When people choose to go that route, often the spelling seems strange or unusual. Some examples are Allice for Alice; Carrelyn for Carolyn, Barrey for Barry. With these changes, the names could become numerologically balanced. This seemed bogus to me, but my teacher assured me that the name becomes balanced according to the Science of Numerology with these changes. I could have applied a couple of changes to my old name to balance it, but I chose not to do that. Even with the additions and changes, they still sounded the same, and somehow, when I thought about it, sounding the same wouldn't achieve what I wanted. I felt that I needed to be called an entirely different name so that every time I heard my new name, I would be aware that I had put something old behind me and was welcoming in the new.

Some people tend to make resolutions and leave the change to tomorrow. I, however, knew that for me to be what I truly wanted to be, resolutions and promises weren't going to cut it. I needed to act. I wanted my new name to reflect the kind of person I had become. Moreover, I wanted to be sure that every time I got called out with this new name, it would serve as a reminder to me that I had left my old self behind. I had no intention of getting her back…sometimes when people are curious about what my old name was - I tell them, "She died!"

"Stressed out and time for a holiday…"

By the August holiday weekend, I had been mulling this over for more than three months. I was beginning to feel stressed out. Added to that, the excessive pressure of dealing with the loss of a job and beginning the intense training of the person taking over from me in the naturopathic office, I needed a holiday…so I decided to go to my trailer in the woods on Galiano Island for the three days of the holiday weekend. I easily found a ride over from one of my community friends. The weather was lovely, it was peaceful, and I walked, swam, and slept a lot over the weekend. On Monday, the final day of the holiday, I had a dream in which my teacher called me by a new name.

It was an unusual name that I hadn't heard before. I woke up with a start and bolted upright. In the woods, at night, it is pitch black, unlike in the city. I couldn't see the clock, so I got out my flashlight...and saw that it was four in the morning. My dream felt so real that I thought I would see my teacher standing there, but no…there was no one - it was just a dream.

"There it was on the shortlist…"

By now, I was wide awake and wanted to see my name sheets, particularly the pieces of paper where I had some names short-listed. In those days, I took my numerology file everywhere. With the help of my flashlight, I found the file with the "first names" sheet. There I found the name "Maren," which I remembered him calling me in my dream. I was so excited by now that I was just scrambling around in the dark. Next, I found the short-list. Sure enough, there was "Maren" handwritten on that list, too. How could I have it on both lists and never have "noticed" it before?! Much later, I figured that because my old name began with "Mar" just like this one, when I first went through Clayne's list and short-listed any possibilities, I saw all the "Mar" names, of which there were about four or five of them. I just posted them all on my short-list sheet without really looking at any of them or even thinking about them consciously.

Back to the task at hand, I took out my "last names" sheet and examined it in detail, thinking about each name and saying them all out loud. A few struck me as possible. Now came the big moment. I went back a second time and said "Maren" with each name on the list. There must have been fifty or so names on there. By now, I was both excited as well as impatient for the process to be done. However, I knew that this shouldn't be rushed, so I started at the top, short-listing the ones I was interested in. By the end, I had about fifteen possibilities, which I reviewed from the top, trying each on for size. "Maren Dancer" jumped out at me, but I made myself continue to the bottom. Then, the moment of truth...I paused...and smiled and said once more, "Maren Dancer" – and just like that, I had a new name.

As an aside, Later, I asked my teacher if he ever chose or suggested names for people. He said, "No," most emphatically. He explained that that wasn't his interest. Instead, he just showed people the way, and then they had to take the step of choosing, by themselves. He felt it would be less potent for them if he got involved in the selection part. I conjectured that he also might have feared he might be the focus of blame if they had doubts or any hard times with the name change.

"I witnessed the power of the mind first-hand..."

So that my dream was just that, "my" dream...because my mind had seen the name before – even though the name hadn't consciously registered. I am guessing that it was my mind's way of coming to peace with the process and declaring its readiness to get on with it. Up until that time, from the moment that I had looked at the names on the sheet my teacher had given me, I had been "kicking and screaming," so to speak, about choosing a new name. I was behind the idea, but at first glance, I didn't like any of the names on the sheet. However, because my new name turned out to have been on the sheet (as well as on the shortlist), perhaps I hadn't been entirely ready for the change – and my inaction proved that to me.

When the day finally dawned, it was a lovely, mellow, and hot August day. I passed through it in a daze. I walked a few small ridges over to see my sister and brother-in-law on their nearby lot where they were doing some preliminary development, but I didn't visit them. I just left them a note that said that I was leaving that night. I walked back to my trailer, gathered a few things like some snacks, a bathing suit, and a towel, preparing for my favorite walk to the beach called Coon Bay on Porlier Pass.

After spending a relaxing and introspective afternoon, in and out of the water, daydreaming on the rocks, in the sun, I finally walked back "home" again to my trailer in the woods. I ate, packed up, and was ready, early, for my ride.

"Two perfect acknowledgments…"

Finally, there was her van. I hopped in and hugged my friend. She said, "Hi" and of course, called me by my old name.

I looked at her and said, "I changed my name today." "Oh," she said, "Did you? What is your new name?"

I told her, "Maren Dancer." There was a moment of silence as she took it in.

"That's a beautiful name," she said...and so I was christened with my new name.

She took me home and dropped me off at my door. Jhake was there and helped bring my stuff inside. After being back for about an hour, with Jhake telling me all about his weekend – what he and my son, Colin, had been doing while I was gone...I couldn't stand the suspense any longer. Finally, I blurted out, "Jhake, I changed my name today." He stuck his hands in his pockets in a typical Jhake stance and stood there, looking at me with a little smile on his face, "I know," he said. And thus, I was twice christened!

"My Vision Quest…"

Speaking of "christenings," Jhake, my son Colin and I had driven all the way to the ferry and then driven about twenty minutes more on the other side for the beautiful christening of June - very touching and moving for our family (as an aside, she is in her late twenties now!) After the ceremony, we all hung out, visiting and celebrating, and then the three of us set off back home where Jhake and I had left our bags all packed…we were excited and hopeful to get on the road without delays.

It was Fall, and school had just started up again after the summer holidays. Otherwise, Colin would have gone on a holiday of his own and stayed with an aunt and uncle in eastern Canada (which would have been his preference)! Once home, we settled Colin in with his caretakers, who lived in our "shared" house. That made things smooth and easy. We grabbed our packed bags…and off we set on my Vision Quest! I had decided that I was so burnt-out from my last few months that I owed myself this holiday before even thinking about what I was going to do next.

Right from the beginning, I thought of it as a Vision Quest, and, initially, had wanted to go alone. Jhake, however, insisted that he go with me as my protector. I asked him if, for any reason, it didn't work for me, would he be willing to let me deliver him to a bus depot and pay his way home. He very good-naturedly agreed, although I always thought that if I had actually done it - dropped him off at a bus depot - he would have been shocked…and not too pleased. Anyway, that didn't happen. As it turned out, he helped me a lot, doing most of the driving, all the shopping, and most of the food preparation and dishes and clean-up afterward. He was an extremely good sport about just serving me and then staying out of my hair. When he needed company, he would head into town and do his own thing, because I was deep in writing and thinking.

"A lingering fear – and getting used to my newness…"

This was a wonderful way to break into my new name. People didn't know me, so I got lots of practice saying my name as I introduced myself. However, I felt a little shy about saying it sometimes. Perhaps that came from my initial phone calls home. I always did them "collect" so I had to tell the operator my name when calling. The first two times, the operator didn't understand what I said when I told her my name. Funny, it never happened again - after that, the operator always understood right off the bat!

Because I had not told my Mom and Dad before we left, that I had changed my name, I hesitated to place a long-distance call to them because I would either have to announce my old name - and I didn't want to go back to that, even if it was just for a minute. Or I would have to declare my new name and confuse them, which I didn't want to do, either. Therefore, I wrote them a very long letter, explaining why I had changed my name. Intuitively I knew that my mother would be upset to some degree.

However, I let them know that I liked the name they chose for me, but at the same time, I wanted to put some things behind me and welcome a new life…and a change of name seemed a great way to do this - from many points of view! Thirteen pages later, I completed my epistle and mailed it off - promising to stop in to see them on the return trip. They lived just across the border, so it was on our way home to Vancouver. I did phone them before returning, but I let it go long enough that I was pretty sure they would have received my letter...because I really didn't want to upset them at all –

or at least not on a phone call…I thought it would be better to be from a letter.

"One of my adventures…"

I had the time of my life on that trip. Jhake and I were most often on a similar wavelength, intuitively, and spontaneously. We would be driving along...and then suddenly we'd be off on a back-roads side trip. They were the best ones because we never knew when they were going to happen and what we'd find on the side-trip. Sometimes it was the name of the highway, or the look of the countryside beside us, or just an inner impulse that made us do the things we did.

One of those places was the Apple Valley campground or something like that in Idaho. Nothing in its name or the surrounding countryside was an obvious turn-on. But we dove off the highway and just kept driving through the grounds, slowly, high above a creek. Suddenly I saw it…a little road that led off to the side and down a little hill to the creek bed at the bottom. There we set up our tent, I got out my writing stuff, and we were set for a few happy days there.

"Oh my…"

On the second day, Jhake set off for the town - to explore, have a bit of social time, and to get some supplies. It was a hot day, even in the filtered sunlight under the canopy of birch trees that hung over the creek. I sat naked on a rock in the creek, dipping my toes in the cold water to keep myself cool. After a while, I heard a truck drive along a road above me, on the opposite side of the creek that we came in. It was high above my head and at the top of a steep embankment, so I hadn't even known it was there until that moment. The truck came to a stop…and in a bit, I could see a State Patrol clambering down the sloping cliff beside the far side of "my" creek.

He was a real gentleman and apologized for intruding and wondered if he might talk with me for a minute or two. I said, "Sure," and asked if he wanted me to cover myself, and he said it didn't matter to him…so I didn't. I stood up on a couple of the rocks while he walked, balancing carefully on each rock until he was standing "in" the creek near me. We carried on a short conversation, standing there in the creek. He was a California State Patrol and said he was just doing a routine check of his territory.

I expressed wonderment that this was California. He said that we must have driven beyond the campground, which is officially in Oregon, and he had wondered if I realized that. "No, I didn't - but we were planning on driving into California next." At that, he excused himself, climbed back up the cliff to his truck, and came back down with a map in his hand. There we were, me naked, pouring over a map with the patrol officer, while he showed me a short cut to get to California and back on our highway, without having to retrace our steps. When Jhake returned, he soon realized that he had missed way more excitement than he had encountered on his journey to town!

"Washington and Oregon were for me…California for Jhake…"

We stayed there for a couple more days. When we finally packed up and, following the Patrol's directions, we found our way along this very bumpy, rarely traveled country road back onto the highway. After being so secluded for so long, it was a gentle way to start our day. It was equally pastoral, full of deciduous trees, their leaves shimmering in the early fall breeze. The Washington/Oregon part of the trip was what I really needed, whereas the California part was more for Jhake, having lived there for a while.

Jhake had lived just outside of San Francisco and had fond memories of many of the places we visited. One place that we both loved was a Spa that was built around a natural hot spring. We spent a couple of days there, enjoying the hot spring - and lovely, organic, healthy meals - which I appreciated for the change from our very simple meals (these were gourmet)! On the third day we reluctantly left the hot springs (we couldn't really afford to stay longer - it was fairly pricey).

I don't remember going as far south as the Los Angeles area - I think, after our stay at the Spa, we started working our way west to some of Jhake's San Francisco's "haunts" - like the Centre for Attitudinal Healing that Dr. Jerry Jampolsky had created and had trained Jhake. We stopped in to see the former director of Jhake's Vancouver center, Phoebe, who had been Jhake's boss that he had "worked" for in Vancouver before the center closed. After leaving Phoebe, we worked our way north from there.

"To my Mom, a name change did make a difference - and it didn't…"

On our way home, on the last day, just after we crossed the border, we stopped in at Mom and Dad's as I had promised in my letter. There are a couple of stories that I still remember from that visit. A question that my mother asked me was, "Why did you change your last name to Dancer?" I think, out of my nervousness, I jumped to the wrong conclusion - and that was that she didn't like my choice. Even though there was an element of truth in that (she didn't like that I had changed it, period, no matter what the name), but that didn't turn out to be the direction she was going, this time.

"That's what I'm going to be…"

Rather, she told me a story that happened when I was a young girl, about five years old. My mother had taken me to an afternoon concert in the Art Gallery. When it was over, I hippity hopped down the hall and was standing, transfixed, in a doorway. When she caught up with me, I asked her what they were doing. "They are dancing," said my mother, "they are practicing so they can become dancers someday."

Then, apparently, I uttered the classic statement, "That's what I'm going to be when I grow up." I was blown away by Mom's story...because I didn't consciously choose my last name for the meaning of the name…although maybe I had, unconsciously. In the moment of choosing, to my knowledge, I had gone only by the sound of it with the first name I had chosen, "Maren."

The second story was about her contention that a name change didn't make any difference. Even though I had gone over everything in my thirteen-page letter that had preceded me, I still had to explain to her once more why I chose to change my name, and how this change could impact my life.

However, even though she stuck firmly to her opinion, she related to Jhake and me a personal story about the effect of name changes. She shared that in her lifetime, she had experienced three different names, Emily, Rose, and Rose Emily. Her family first called her Emily. Then when she met my dad, he called her by her middle name, Rose. Then her family called her Rose Emily. She confessed that she felt entirely different, depending on which name she was called. I had a lot of compassion for her, realizing that she couldn't see the lack of logic as she tried to come to terms with my decision. We all have blind spots - I just wasn't used to seeing them in one of my parents!

"Post Vision Quest - inspired to begin my final career, piano teacher..."

That trip was all that I intuitively knew it would be. After deliberating over everything - and nothing, I returned refreshed, my sparkle back, as well as being full of ideas, focus, and motivation. Going on a Vision Quest had cleared out the old energy, rested my body and spirit, and brought me clarity and vision.

Chapter 20
Post Vision Quest - a New Career

"A New Career…A New Man…And India…"

When we returned that late September, I knew what I wanted to do.

The first task on my list was to start giving piano lessons. I didn't feel very competent as I wasn't trained to teach the piano…I only played it. However, I was a qualified schoolteacher with my Bachelor of Education degree, and was motivated, passionate, and inspired about teaching the piano. I drew up an action plan and set to it. It took me about six months - until early the following spring - for me to start teaching, but the important thing is that I immediately began the actions that soon led me to teach.

Now that I was ready to give classes, one of the first things was to design a flyer. That turned out to be the easiest thing of all. I was talking with my sister after I returned from my trip. She had been wondering what I was going to do next and asked me if I had thought of piano teaching. I said, "As a matter of fact, I have been thinking about it." To me, this was yet another sign that I was on the right path. She continued, "Well I have designed a flyer for you, and I will drop it off soon." I was ecstatic - and felt extremely supported by her. I could hardly wait to see the flyer. She dropped it by in a few days - and as it turned out, it was the only flyer that I ever used in my twenty-some years of teaching. Over the years, the most changes that I made were a few words...just trivial things.

The next thing was to see if I could discover any teachers who would allow me to sit in on their lessons. I looked up my friend, Mary, the one who had lived with my son and me years earlier and taught him for a few months. She was very open to showing me what she knew, and the adventure was that I had to take a ferry to visit her. I just sat in the background of her lessons for a few days. Looking back at that time, it was the most productive and inspiring "training" I received. Back in town, I sat in on an afternoon of my sister's niece's classes and got some useful ideas from her. My third mentor was a woman I discovered who taught at a nearby community center - and she was also very helpful. And that was it - I was ready.

"A marketing plan is always the big one for success..."

Marketing was going to be the most critical element of my teaching venture. Word of mouth being the most powerful, my first students were the children of my best friend (including my late husband's fourth child). In addition, my son and I delivered flyers around our neighborhood, and from that, another student turned up from a block away.

When I visited my friend on Salt Spring Island, she helped me work out my first lesson. After I had delivered that first lesson, I phoned her up in a panic to see what was next. She laughed and said it won't take you long before you instinctively (with your background) just know what to do. She was right. Once I had those first two lessons under my belt, I calmed down quite a bit when I realized that I had enough specific knowledge about the piano, general life experience, and intuition to be able to work my way through the rest of the lessons.

The little neighboring boy didn't return in the fall. However, that wasn't through any lack of effort on my part. It's just that he wasn't committed to practicing - and the father considered it a waste of money to keep sending him. I continued teaching my friend's children for a couple of years until they, too, lost interest. Over the years, I learned that teaching piano works like this, and I must not take it personally. However, I had two stellar students. They stayed with me for ten and twelve years, respectively. Usually, students stuck with me for three to five years.

To break into a different "market" and get beyond my immediate neighborhood and friend's children, I used the Yellow Pages (yes – we still had them in those days prior to Google) and decided a radius beyond my house that people would probably drive their children for lessons. Then I flipped to the section on Elementary schools and wrote down addresses that were close enough. Once this was done, I figured out my driving route.

In schools, the rule is a visitor must first say hello at the school's office and state their reason for being there. I did that…I would present myself, show the secretary my flyer and ask if I might put my fit on their school's Parent Board. In all cases, I was met with enthusiasm and was told to just go and make room for my flyer on their board. I was thrilled that it was that easy.

I loved teaching the piano so much that I found it hard to believe that I had so actively avoided it over the years. Part of the reason, Clayne, my numerologist friend, pointed out to me was that, according to the Science of Numerology, I hadn't been in the best birth path cycle previously. Now, however, I was just coming into the perfect cycle for me to begin teaching, and also for other creative pursuits, music being only one of them. Any time I would talk with Clayne, he would want updates, and I could hear his smugness over the phone when I would tell him the great things that were happening in my life. "Of course!" was his usual response.

"In 1994, (one house later)
In Came Maurice to My (or Our) Life…"

My five-week trip to India soon followed. I know that I learned much…although I'm not entirely sure what, but I do know that I observed a lot. When I tell the story from a relationship point of view, it is a mixture of sordid, pathetic, and hilarious events. If told only from that point of view, it would be quite a short story, because the relationship was brief…and, more than anything else, a fiasco. My trip began about two months before when I met a man who was all set to go to India. He had his ticket and was about to leave for India within the month. We were soon getting along like wildfire, and he urged me to join him on my Christmas holiday. I usually took time off for four or five weeks anyway…and the more I thought about it, the more extraordinary the idea sounded to me. I had never done such a thing, all of it was so new and scary; going to the Orient, on such short notice, and with a man I barely knew.

It was outrageous – regardless, I set the plan in motion, and everything began to happen, all at the same time. We hadn't even heard of each other two weeks before he unexpectedly sold his place. It had been on the market for a long time without any leads, so he had somewhat given up. But then a buyer suddenly showed up, out of the blue…and they wanted immediate possession. Therefore, Maurice, my new friend, had to get out of it, and he was looking for alternative accommodations.

I approached Jhake - who had become only my business partner, no longer my partner in life - to see what he thought about my new friend staying with me in "our|" house. This arrangement would be for just two weeks until Maurice left for India. Jhake, bless him, agreed. Those two weeks were full of drama. Both men were Dutch, Jhake from Amsterdam, and Maurice from a small area in the north of Holland (Friesland) where they considered themselves the elite of Holland. What a set-up that was!

The first morning that my new friend was with us, the two men sat in the kitchen and had breakfast. I'm not much of a breakfast person, but I joined them anyway. It was fun, moving back and forth from stove to table, helping make breakfast, and listening to the two of them. At one point, my new friend asked my business partner, and former boyfriend, how it felt to be number two.

I wasn't going to stand for that and flew over to the table and confronted him - I was so mad and taken aback that I spoke very heatedly! "Neither of you is number one, or number two. You are both my friends - and I care for you both, and there won't be any more talk about favorites!" I should have known then that I was in for trouble with Maurice. But the thing is, love is blind, and I still had rose-colored glasses on. We had a very connected relationship, with lots of karma, lots of emotion, and heat of all kinds!

That had been kind of the thing with Maurice...he was erratic, emotional and impulsive (to name a few of his qualities). In hindsight, I realized that he didn't know how to deal with emotionally charged situations and would let his emotions get the best of him. He was possessive about me, as was apparent by his comment about being 'number one,' which is never a good quality in a man. It also showed me that he was confrontational and didn't think things through. Over the years, I have met others like him…they think that all of their emotions are justified and that they are allowed to say anything that comes into their head (we had a few like that in our Therah community)!

For some, possessiveness might be an attractive quality in a man; however, that sort of intensity soon burns out. Love that matures over time doesn't burn out, and even when it does, it often turns into something sweet. That ensures that even if things do go wrong, there will be equal efforts from both sides to keep their dealings kind and respectful. However, with the type of passion that Maurice exhibited… that kind of love goes as quickly as it comes. I knew that…but I was yet to truly understand by personally experiencing it!

Have you ever been to India? I have rarely traveled in my lifetime, and when I have, they were mostly short, somewhat "local" trips. Some of them were to the States such as southern California and one trip each to New York and Chicago…plus a couple of trips to eastern Canada. Therefore, this was a real adventure…India sounded right out of this world. Even though it had never been on my radar as a holiday destination, I was intrigued. However, if I am being sincere, I was, in large part, attracted to India because of my new friend.

"I was very touched by my meetings with Mother Teresa…"

This man was going for his fifth time; he went every year – and always helped Mother Teresa. He would go to her hospice and work with the other volunteers - most of whom were there, having given up their holidays to help, as well as the sisters who were there to be of service, as directed by Mother Teresa. A few of the patients were there to be healed. Mostly, though, they were afflicted by TB (so that meant that I would have to have a check-up when I returned home). Some were found on the street - or brought in by relatives who were unable to care for them any longer.

In either case, this was their final - and short - residence. The most significant number of them were quite clearly there to die. They mostly arrived in such a dirty state that the first thing to do was to clean them up and help them be warm and comfortable. My friend worked mainly in the men's section, shaving them and giving haircuts, though he would do whatever he was asked to do. The entire set-up was very touching and inspiring to me.

"INDIA: I cannot save the world...
but I can do my part."

My friend, Maurice, set off a month before me - I would need the month to do what was needed to get me there. I particularly needed to get my ticket, find out if I needed shots, and sort out my finances and affairs. The biggest thing was that I was leaving behind a teenage son, and I wanted him to be comfortable with all the arrangements.

In what seemed no time at all, the day had arrived for me to set out on my journey. It was a long plane ride that stopped down in Singapore, so I had to stay overnight there, in a hotel, before setting off again for the last part of the journey. It all seemed very glamorous (little did I know)! Maurice met me at the airport; a couple of Mother Teresa's nuns were arriving on the same plane, and because Maurice "worked" at their hospice, he learned of the arrival and got a ride with them to the airport. On their return trip, they were able to fit us all in and dropped Maurice and me off at the hotel where he had been staying, which was relatively close to the hospice. It had been a long and tiring journey so far, and I was just so thankful for that "taxi" ride.

Within a week, we had had our first falling out. It was because he thought that I was not grateful - it was a little vague to me exactly what I was not "grateful" for. My friend was fit to be tied. He didn't want me around, and moreover, he didn't want me to stay. He started saying things like, "Get out of here...leave...go home." My counter-reaction was that I wasn't going anywhere. I had just arrived…no, I was not just about to leave.

The rose-colored glasses, through which I had viewed him, started to clear up. Here I was, in an entirely different country, on the other side of the world, mostly in order to enjoy his company…and his reaction was immediately to tell me to go away. After spending all that time and money to get there, I was staying. Moreover, I was there for more than to be with him, and I could always get another place on my own - even if it would be a financial burden.

My friend became upset and began acting erratically. When I questioned him, trying to get clear about his issue - that only increased his agitation. He wasn't making any sense to me, so I couldn't understand his upset, which was over some way he perceived me acting the day before.

He steamed off - not very happy about my response. I was feeling quite upset - running into this big a challenge in our relationship so early in the game. After all, he was my only anchor in this country, and there was a long while to go before returning home. He wasn't my only reason for going...but he certainly was the biggest part of it.

"To be so upset nearly cost me my life..."

Realizing I was very thirsty, I looked around for water. When flying, I wasn't allowed to have my own water bottle and hadn't been shopping for any since landing in India. I spotted a water bottle on the floor that was quite full. Still agitated, I quickly put the bottle to my mouth. As the first mouthful of it began to go down my throat, I realized it wasn't water, and in a reflex action, I threw it up immediately; it just exploded out of my mouth. In a panic, I dashed out of our accommodation onto the rooftop where people were sitting around tables, and making food on hibachis, eating, chatting, and so on.

I was in tremendous distress and went running over to one table where two men were talking. I shared with them my plight and my panic, and they said they thought I should eat something - like potatoes and bread. This would coat my stomach and membranes and should help suppress the aftereffects of whatever that foul liquid was. Maurice and I hadn't become very domestic yet, so we didn't have anything to eat. During our trip, we mostly ate out of nearby cafes. But those kind men shared what they had with me, even rounding up some food from people around. Gradually, with all this help and attention, I managed to calm down a bit.

Later, I kept a close eye on my condition, concluding that at most, probably only a minuscule amount had gone down. I was doing a lot of thinking, and I realized rather belatedly that India wasn't the easiest place for me. I began to wonder if I should give in to Maurice's wishes…and return.

However, I was upset and confused and hadn't made up my mind just yet.

"A partial change of heart…"

About this time, Maurice came back, and when he heard that I had had an accident and that I had almost swallowed kerosene, he was in even more of a fury. He couldn't believe that I would do such a thing, and he blamed me for being stupid and a drama queen. He said I was just trying to make trouble, and he stormed off once again.

Of course, it wasn't a good idea to drink kerosene, but in the face of Maurice's upset with me, I wasn't acting normally or coherently. This happens often, when something goes wrong in life, you just do something stupid or dangerous in reaction…like drugs or get a tattoo… or just something that in the heat of the moment seems like a good idea that they come to regret later. It's kind of like going through a bad breakup and going out to a bar to get drunk. At the time, I was too quick - and not at all careful - and certainly not in my right mind. Now I was full of regrets over how it was all going for Michael and for me.

The first time, my friend had been gone for an hour or two. This time he was gone for another couple of hours. When he returned, he told me - in a sullen, unhappy, and upset voice - that I could stay. He said that he would make the best of it and that I didn't have to leave. I wasn't sure that I wanted to stay under those terms as he didn't sound like a very good company. However, my options weren't great, so I thought I would start out by staying and see how things went.

The next day, we went shopping - walking, buses, streetcars…we had a couple of things we were looking for in particular. One was a harmonium, which is a bit like an accordion, with ivory keys and bellows. Only it is a wooden box that sits on the ground or on a low table. Also, we wanted to find a cloth like a bedspread or a tablecloth. That way we could walk to a nearby park and lay the harmonium, first on the cloth on the ground…and then we could sit on the cloth while we played and sang.

"Nearly calamity number two…"

Maurice held my hand as we walked along, and when we came to the curb, he began to cross the street, pulling me with him. I panicked and pulled my hand out of his because I didn't feel ready to cross. I hadn't yet become used to the different direction that traffic would come at me on the roads. He let go of my hand and stormed across by himself. To me, it felt like they were driving on the wrong side of the street, and to them, I was dangerous. I was having difficulty in figuring out this street, but I finally decided to brave it and go across. It was extremely wide, which made it hard for me to get a sense of where I was looking for the traffic. Not only was it wide, but it had an access road running beside it on the far side. This made it seem like two streets in one that I had to negotiate...which made the traffic all the more confusing. Additionally, I had to contend with Maurice, steaming, and fuming - not being easy or pleasant to get along with.

So here I was, beginning to gingerly pick my way across this road. Suddenly, without warning, I unconsciously and intuitively sucked in my stomach, jumped back, and turned my head in time to see a large truck go lumbering by. As it turned out, I hadn't been watching for traffic in the correct direction. It didn't slow down a speck. In India, people look out for themselves, and drivers are used to that - and moreover, expect that. Everything was new here, and none of it made sense. Back home, I understood the system to follow, and everything seemed orderly…if you had common sense, you could just about find your way to navigate any situation. But here, people seemed to be going more by instincts and survival skills… both of which I lacked. Moreover, with Maurice being by my side, and being a pain in the behind, I was not at all happy.

When the traffic cleared, I mustered up the courage to finish picking my way to the other side of the street where Maurice was. However, as soon as I reached him, he lit into me and yelled and screamed… and then screamed some more. He had been so sure that when the truck passed, I would be lying dead on the road, and he was pretty close to being right…and this was how his panic expressed itself. He couldn't fathom how I couldn't figure out the traffic directions better than that - it was beyond him - and he was having all kinds of reactions.

I found out later that he felt responsible for my being there - much more than I wanted, needed, or expected him to be. Moreover, he felt like he wasn't doing very well in showing me a good time and a safe trip and was feeling guilty. Nice as that would have been, I didn't need or expect that from him either. His reaction was somewhat understandable but not at all appreciated. I did not want to feel like a kid being scolded by their parent because they made a stupid mistake. Everything was new there, and it would also take some getting used to him yelling and raging at me. Even if it was out of concern, his reaction was not making things any better.

"All of that...and only week number one..."

That was how we began...all of that took place before even one week was up. I was a complete mess, just standing there, flabbergasted, listening to him yell instead of consoling me. I was speechless, couldn't talk, nor could I even think. My friend hated that I needed him in any way, and he didn't want to look after me. I was pretty ignorant when it came to travel. However, I was very determined to learn to do things by myself, which took me the better part of that first week. After that, I did okay on my own, which was helpful to us both.

As an aside, I've had a couple of other travel experiences more recently that were somewhat similar...where I was traveling with people who were much more travel-experienced, and I was not nearly as well versed as they were. I would feel somewhat scared when I wasn't in control of my situation...and then I tended not to do very well, interactively, with my friends.

That was at least the underlying flavor for a good part of the trip - although, for the next six weeks, my friend and I did manage to have a good time (on the surface). After we got over those first few incidents, we didn't have any more like that. Even when we had incidents…the odd one here and there…he didn't react quite so strongly ever again. Also, by now, I knew what pushed his buttons, so I tried hard to recognize a potential trouble spot before things escalated from bad to worse.

Chapter 21
Other Riches That India
Brought To Me...

I'll shift gears now and talk about some of my experiences for which Maurice was a catalyst. While in India, even though most of our relatedness was an abysmal failure, some of the things we explored together were the height of joy and connection. For example, we discovered that we loved to sing together. When we sang, it was just pure bliss; both us were transported.

I guess that was one of the things that got us so into each other and what made it even partially bearable to get together at all while we were there in India. Early in my trip, I had successfully found a harmonium...and a satiny bed-throw. My friend knew where to find one - and it was a bargain. We were very pleased with this purchase - I never expected to find a harmonium so easily – let alone at such a good price.

Singing and playing my harmonium allowed Maurice and me, naturally and easily, to break through barriers caused by language and culture. We would head for a nearby park, spread out our cloth, and settle down on it. I would lay out the sing-along book that I had brought with me on the trip. Maurice would handle the bellows at the back of the harmonium, leaving my hands free to play both parts of the music as I was used to, as a pianist. Whereas, usually with a harmonium, the player manages the whole thing themselves - operates the bellows with the left hand and then plays both the tune and chords with the right hand, only - a bit like an accordion.

After a while, a crowd would gather - most of them stood around in a semicircle to listen while a few sat down on the grass - if you could call it that. It was yellow from lack of rain and all trodden down from constant foot traffic. We had a lot of fun playing for our listeners. We would mostly ignore the crowd and simply play and sing to our heart's content, just because we loved it. Maybe that was why we would always get listeners because they realized that we were singing from our hearts...we weren't just some street performers who were there to gather the biggest crowd...as well as make a living.

I think that in our lives, too often, when we set out to do something, it is to gain recognition and not solely because we want to do it. Of course, the recognition is always good but running after it just makes it that much harder to get. Also, while you are looking to gain that recognition, you forget how much you loved doing the thing in the first place. If you get the recognition, that's a plus, but if you don't, and you've been pressuring yourself, your tendency will be to feel dissatisfied and negative about the whole thing and perhaps put you under more pressure. When under pressure, you have no room for creativity, and the vicious circle begins again. Therefore, it seems best to just focus on your thing, do your best - and that includes enjoying yourself…and let it play out how it will. That was one of those times for me.

We'll never know, of course, if any of them understood our English songs, I personally doubt it. Nevertheless, they seemed to be curious or interested in our singing. A lot of busking goes on in North America, but at least in the part of India where we were, Calcutta, I noticed there seemed to be more "soap boxes" and orators rather than music on the streets, so maybe we were a novelty. As for ourselves…we loved to sing duets as it gave us a chance to find a way to harmonize our spirits!

Another thing we loved to do was to wander through the streets, find a place to lay the harmonium down on the curb, and start playing and singing. Again, people would gather round because many people lived on the street and families would live under makeshift cardboard "houses." As soon as we laid down the harmonium, these families would be the first to gather around us. The children always wanted to touch and play the harmonium while the parents were forever trying to stop them. I always put them at ease and had the children take turns playing notes on the instrument...I just loved seeing the excitement on their adorable little faces.

Another highlight with my harmonium was at Mother Teresa's. After my first week, once I had got over my jet lag, on many days, I went with Maurice to the hospice. Most of the patients there were dying of tuberculosis. My job was just to "be" with dying people - hold them to keep them warm and comforted. After all, they had no visitors, no one to love them, and so Mother Teresa's hospice had taken on being that source of love and comfort.

Sometimes, instead of holding them, I would bring music to them. Starting at one end of the room, one by one, I would lay my harmonium on the bottom of each cot, in turn. Because it was Christmastime, and because they were religious, I played and sang Christmas carols to them. It didn't matter that they didn't know the words - they knew the tunes, and the music lit up the room, and peace came over the room like a blanket - for the nuns and the volunteers, as well. After playing in the hospice for a few days, the nuns asked me to play for their Christmas service. I felt honored.

"The British legacy (not all bad) was strongly in evidence..."

We were there at Christmas time - the month of December - and in Calcutta, there were a lot of concerts. With their British background, there was a strong connection between India and London. Many nights of each week, British soloists were booked for concerts in the various Embassies. We went to them all. Also, there were Festival of Lights shows and concerts in other palatial settings...and the local symphony played.

We noticed that they had a lot of young people, and we asked to get the story behind that. There was, apparently, a local orphanage that, for years, had taken homeless boys off the street. Long ago, the school struck up a bargain with them - if the children would be committed to the musical program, they would be schooled and given room and board. This program was so successful that these boys became the future source of replacements for the Calcutta orchestra. There were concerts all over the city, which was marvelous for both my friend and me - he liked the concerts as much as I did. That was a highlight! The first three weeks of December were packed with events to attend - but festivities, concerts, events all slowed down after that (we missed them a lot when they ended - after Christmas Day)!

Sometimes, as we were wandering through hotel lobbies, usually on our way to or from a concert, we would pass by a grand piano in a foyer. Maurice was very encouraging of me to play, but I didn't feel comfortable playing publicly…I didn't have my music with me, and I was nowhere near the caliber of pianist that all the concert pianists were. But eventually, I gave in - it was a new experience for me, and I didn't want to miss out. I knew that stepping out of one's comfort zone and having new experiences is very important. So eventually, I played a piece or two on some of these "public" pianos.

Mother Teresa's hospice were central to my many life-changing moments. However, almost everything I experienced in India turned out to be life-changing - and not just the obvious big things. Maurice's and my habit of wandering the streets at night for something to do with our time turned out to be one of those. He would sometimes let me wander by myself because we had different things we were interested in browsing. What I didn't know till a bit later was that he was keeping an eye out for my safety - and, consequently, noticed a lot of things going on that I was oblivious to.

"Sleeping baby story was an eye-opener…"

This particular night, a woman in her twenties tapped me on the shoulder and said, "Misses, misses, please, milk for my baby?" She had a "sleeping" youngster draped over her shoulder. I decided to buy some milk for her baby and signaled her to follow me to a booth. There I purchased a can of milk from a vendor and gave it to her. Apparently, what really happened is that after I was out of sight, the woman went back to the milk vendor and handed her the can in exchange for the money that I had given for the purchase. Then she walked over to another booth and handed in the money, and off she went to find another "victim." I had only lengthened her process by buying the can rather than giving her the money. If I thought I could beat the system already in place, think again!

"Buying a young man a meal was another eye- opener…"

Next, I was approached by a young man to see if I would give him money to buy some food. Again, I took him to a vendor of his choice and ordered a meal. I paid for the meal and stayed long enough to make sure he got the food, thinking that that was the end of the matter. Again, my friend hung around in the background to see what transpired next. When I had left, the man handed the meal back, and they returned the money that I had paid for it. He went to another booth, turned in "my' money…and then skedaddled over to the same place where I had found him - to suck in his next victim. When I heard the whole story from my friend, I felt devastated. I had really hoped that I could beat the game. However, I learned that night that the system was way bigger than I was. Clang went my heart.

After that I shrugged off the touch of the beggars and I shunned the babies and their "mothers." The worst part, for me, of this "charade" was that there was no guarantee that these women holding the babies were actually their mothers. There was, instead, a high probability that they just used the babies as a sure way to get money off of people. I found this out through a Dutch businessman who frequently came to Calcutta: he said that for sure, the "mothers" were not their baby's mother. Vendors were the same - they gave money to the mafia...it was like insurance money for their protection. The babies were just loaned around by the mafia to different women and kept drugged so they would stay asleep and not make any fuss. When they were too heavy for any of the women to carry, they were gotten rid of - moved into another system of begging - they were now in the system for the remainder of their lives. The thought broke my heart!

Once, I saw the torso of a man - no arms or legs. I learned that every morning, someone would deliver him to his spot, set him on a cloth, and set his money hat in front of him. It was all worked out how he would get fed, and then at night, someone picked him up, collected his money, and deposited him somewhere to sleep. The next day, the same scenario would be repeated. I felt numb. I would give nothing after that. I knew I could not really help them - and I felt duped by them all. I was in shock - this coldness I had put over my heart was not natural or comfortable for me.

"The Dutch businessman could be wrong, but…"

I didn't entirely understand it all, yet, but I had met a Dutch businessman who filled me in on a lot more reality. He had been coming to India for many years, and in doing business there, he learned many things that tourists like me are not privy to. We are there for such a short time and are living at such a superficial level, and therefore, most of the realities are invisible. This Dutchman described to me a little more of the depths of the system of which I had had only a bare glimpse. He said it was what he called the mafia who were controlling the streets. If the beggars would give the mafia their earnings, they would be fed, clothed, and offered a place to sleep. The most important thing is…they would be protected. The alternative was to be hurt or worse.

I found out how these beggars were not to be blamed for this; they didn't really have a choice, because their situation would most definitely be made worse if they refused to hand over their earnings - they could even lose their lives.

"My heart broke…"

The mafia and the street cons were not all that I saw and heard. Every day, as I walked around, I would see little groups of children, of ages ranging from about four to ten years old. They would be huddled on the curbside and shooting up drugs. I found it hard to believe that no one would save them. Then there were the lanes where garbage was strewn all around and rats were running from pile to pile of garbage… it makes me shiver just to think about it all, now. If I learned only one thing from all this, I learned just how good we had it back in our country.

I could see that these kids were living in situations no one would get them out of. I know that there is never really a good reason for doing drugs, but I could understand it in the case of these children. They had nothing going for them…it didn't take rocket science to figure that out - one glance was enough. On a daily basis…being controlled by the mafia, they would be given just the meager necessitates to be kept alive…and they were given drugs, so their minds would be enslaved so as not to understand anything except what they were being told. I just felt very bad for the kids who had to grow up with this way of life. It was all so pitiful; however, there was nothing I could do about it, so I decided to let it go as best I could.

From then on, I became sick with the usual tourist "trots," and gradually, my sickness became worse. I think it was a culmination of feeling helpless to do anything about all the shocking things I was learning about…that, coupled with the unhappiness going on under the surface between my friend and me. The combination was intensely stressful - so it didn't surprise me that I became sick. At first, the trots weren't enough to stop me from having fun. However, finding out about the pathetic conditions that those kids and women were living in began to take a huge toll on me.

I realized that our first world problems are nothing compared to theirs…and that changed me. Maybe that was the part of me that matured… learning to be happy with what I've got. I was basically a happy person, but I was always chasing after something or other. Admittedly, it was so that I'd be better at life, but after my experiences in India, I learned to be thankful for all that I had, as well.

"Oh yes - the water..."

I drank bottled water, but there were stories circulating about not being able to trust even the bottled water. It apparently turned out that there were a couple of Indian water companies that used water straight out of the tap rather than purifying it first. We were supposed to eat very spicy food to combat this…I think the idea is that no self-respecting bugs could survive the heat. That being said, neither could I. I would choke and feel like I was about to have a heart attack from the spice. So that wasn't an option.

The other thing we were supposed to do was to eat only at "western" restaurants. This was too costly for our budget. Also, the food wasn't as interesting as the Indian food. But some Indian cafes served American-style food like traditional breakfast food and hamburgers - if that's what you wanted (which I didn't). The café, where we ate most of our meals, was largely full of Caucasian people - European, British, Canadian, and American. The food was a mixture, with many Indian dishes. I naively trusted their food practices, until one day, as I arrived at the restaurant. I passed by the lane and a cook was outside washing his sieve of cooked rice under the water tap. After that, I knew I could no longer trust the cleanliness of their food anymore, either.

"Homeopathy 'saved' me..."

There was a German tourist who also had a room off of the rooftop as we did. He realized one day that I had become very sick though I don't remember what gave it away. At that time, Maurice was away at the hospice. The fellow knocked on my open door. He found me lying on the bed - and by this time, I was nearly comatose.

This man had come from Germany to study homeopathy with an Indian homeopathy master - and was going to be studying with him for a few months. He asked me a few questions that would help him (and his master) determine what remedies would be best for me and left me, saying that he would be back shortly. When he returned, he brought me some remedies that he said should work on the fever and diarrhea within twenty-four hours.

He was right, and it wasn't long before I began to feel more like myself. I got instructions from this German fellow on how to find his teacher's medical office. He gave me directions and advice on the best times to go to the office, in that the doctor saw people on a first-come-first-served basis. Apparently, I chose a good time because there were only a couple of people ahead of me. The homeopathic doctor was pleased by my progress under his student's care. He also gave me remedies to further strengthen me. I went to see him a couple more times during my visit to India and never got sick like that again. But funny enough, I had one more bout of diarrhea on the airplane, and then that was the end of it. It will always be a mystery...why once more...but it seems like it was more emotionally induced than physically.

There were a few happier moments. As our relationship quieted down, I began to relax. When I wasn't so stressed, I started to feel better about exploring on my own. I loved going to the nearby market - not to buy things so much as to just be part of the life of the people. I was in a whole other world and wanted to see how these people lived on a day to day basis. The hustle and bustle of daily life excited me at another level because there was nothing like that back home. Most vendors would negotiate on the prices - nothing was set. People were excellent negotiators, and I would sometimes notice them going to a couple of stalls before getting the best price and buying what they wanted. I didn't go to the hospice for as many hours or nearly every day like my friend did. That meant that I often had a day, or at least a few hours, on my own.

"My windmills..."

One day, early on, I spotted a vendor with a pole full of little windmills - a plastic wind-vane at the top of a stick. I bought two of them and from then on, I carried one in each hand, holding them high in the air as I walked (fast) to the market, each of them whirling around over my head.

One lane that I walked through had a stone wall down one side of it, and men (middle-aged and older), using it as a bench, sat talking. I didn't realize the impression I was making on at least some of them until one day when I went to the market without my little "windmills." When I came to this "bench," one man put both of his arms in the air (as if he was carrying a windmill in each) and then raised his eyebrows. I guess I had become "the windmill lady" for the people around that area!

"Charitable organizations in India..."

A phenomenon in Calcutta was there are many charitable organizations such as Mother Teresa's hospices. They all had some sort of organized tour or office where you could get your questions answered and where they could request single or on-going donations. Mostly they were run with volunteer help because the recipients gave nothing, and therefore these organizations depended on donations - both money and time. Many were attached to a particular church, but some weren't attached or supported by any organization and ran solely on donations from visitors.

Over my six weeks in India, I met many of the volunteers from different charities. Quite a large percentage of the volunteers came annually - some of them for their annual holiday, and others took time off from their jobs or quit. It was a beautiful gathering in all the charities. You could tell that everyone who surrounded you was there just to make lives better for other human beings.

It was a rare experience, being among so many people who just wanted to do good in the world. I know that people volunteer for a lot of reasons…they could be there because they want to feel good about themselves…or feel like they are contributing something to the world. However, that didn't negate what they were doing, even if it was just to feel good about themselves. The thing is, most people don't even think about it, whereas these people were there, taking time out of their presumably busy lives to serve those who were a lot less fortunate than themselves.

I met one couple at the hotel where I was staying with my friend. On the rooftop of the hotel, right outside of my hotel room door, there were tables and chairs set around, and any of the residents could visit or cook meals up there. The husband was often there, reading, and we got talking. He told me that they had decided to retire, sell their home, and pull up stakes from their home in Holland. It was mostly his wife's dream that he was supporting… she had been a nurse, and she had always wanted to "work" as a volunteer in Dr. Michael's street clinic.

As an aside, this was not a rare experience, there, in Calcutta. Most of the people we met at our little pension had come to volunteer at one of the charities, but most of them were young, in their twenties…and most had learned of it through their church, which was a supporting donor. Some others had learned of it through a friend (like I had), or run across it online or through literature. There was a predominance of Europeans and North Americans amongst the volunteers. I found all of this volunteering interesting -

not a phenomenon that I had run across in Canada. It may be that some of the charities in my city also have volunteers from other countries, but I think that was unique to India, or at least, to Calcutta. Particularly the large numbers of youth in their twenties.

After talking at length with the Dutchman, Maurice and I decided we wanted to go to see the clinic where his wife volunteered (called Dr. Michaels) and see how it was set up. As it turned out, it was literally a "street" clinic. For the line-up, they had snaking lines in order to get the maximum people into the small area beside the street. People waited, on their feet, all day, or many days if there were a lot of people ahead of them in the line-up.

At closing time, if they hadn't been seen, they had to stay until the next day or lose their place in line. In addition to the line-up and the examination areas, there was also a dispensing area to fill their prescriptions. These were also free - having been donated or bought with donations. I was amazed that on this little piece of dirt, so much goodwill and so much real-life was present.

We also visited an orphanage that was another charity where many of our hotel friends worked - and we felt the same sense of generosity and love amongst the volunteers. It was mind-boggling to me, to say the least. Seeing all of that, being a part of it… just learning through all that I saw…those experiences really matured me. I hadn't considered before that I lived a cushy life. However, being a part of all this opened my eyes, and I returned home with a greater sense of appreciation of life - and my life in particular. In addition, I developed a greater love and appreciation for those who aren't as fortunate to have the things and experiences that I take so for granted.

"The leprosy sanatorium - a touching experience..."

One of my most touching experiences that took place in Calcutta was my visit to the leprosy sanatorium. My friend and I had to take an underground train, then a streetcar, and then another train to get there. It was outside of the city of Calcutta, whereas we were staying in the heart of it. Mother Teresa, I was told, was the person responsible for getting the lepers out of shunned colonies and into this sanatorium. At first, she and the nuns of her order ran the sanatorium themselves. Later, once it was established and running smoothly, Mother Teresa persuaded the Priests' Order to take it over.

When we first arrived, we were given a little talk by a priest, both to orientate and educate us. The most surprising thing that I learned was that leprosy was highly curable. However, to cure them was one thing, but of course, it was not possible to reverse deformities. Therefore, they would be free of the disease but were ultimately left to live out their lives with their deformities.

It was heart-breaking for me to know that - although it was also very inspiring to see those who had been afflicted with it and didn't let that stop their lives. Of course, they had to go through an adjustment period, getting used to their new way of life. Plus, they had been left with a huge challenge, and that was to be accepted back into their families and village communities. Their families and friends had to take the priests' word that they were healed…because their healing was invisible, whereas their deformities were still visible.

Mother Teresa's solution was to give the healed leper the choice of returning home or staying in the sanatorium. The priests informed us that, understandably, a high percentage opted to stay. They knew that they wouldn't be accepted back, at least they wouldn't be accepted back as "normal," so they opted to stay with those who had the same affliction as they did…where there was acceptance and a sense of belonging.

They became the caretakers of the sanatorium, with an enormous variety of tasks to choose from. The newly cured ones were trained for the tasks they could do. These tasks ranged from housekeeping, to medical, to helping in the clinic, to weaving the cloth for making habits for the nuns of Mother Teresa's order all over the world. In addition, they worked with leather for supplying all the leather needs of the people inside the sanatorium, shoes, belts, pouches, etc.

There was also a multitude of outdoor tasks needed to run the gardens and small farm that surrounded the sanatorium. Then there was the school dormitory where the children of lepers were taught and looked after, which meant there were needs for teacher's aides as well as housekeeping and child-care in that section.

The atmosphere was very light-hearted and happy everywhere we were taken inside the sanatorium. The ones who were not cured yet were sitting on their bed in large dormitories. We paraded past the bottoms of their beds and smiled at them, and they smiled back. They were happy to see people not afraid to look at them and who smiled at them. Their whole life had been one of being ostracized, being banished, and being cast away and isolated. Their gratitude and joy were touching. Everyone they had known - as well as strangers – had been afraid of them, and no one had wanted them. How touching it all was.

Then, outside of the hospital part of the sanatorium were all the cured ones. They always kept themselves busy, working at this or that (as well as their assigned jobs) both inside and out on the farm surrounding the sanatorium. They were so grateful for their regained health and for the loving attitude that surrounded them.

From then on, after I had seen all this, I vowed that I would never complain again. Of course, being human, this was not possible, but it reflected what I had experienced. However, I noticed, after that trip, every time I got the desire to complain, I did think about them…and I would like to think that I at least managed to curb my tongue and not complain as much after that because I had become grateful for my health and all my opportunities.

It was time to say goodbye to India…and to Michael. We had managed to have no more flare-ups or major drama, like in the beginning of my trip…for which I was grateful. The trip had turned out to be extremely interesting after we got over the initial hurdles.

"However, that was just the tip of the iceberg..."

Things had gotten much better after that...or so I had thought…but five weeks later, on the taxi ride to the airport, Maurice opened up both barrels and let loose, right between my eyeballs. He told me exactly what he thought of me, which wasn't exactly high praise. He kept up his tirade all the way to the airport, and after we parted, I was an emotional mess - so much so that it took most of the trip home to regain some composure.

One of the nuns who worked at Mother Teresa's was also on the plane and she befriended me. The plane wasn't full, so we found two seats together. Plus, we also spent about six hours of a stopover in the middle of the night, together. Being with her was very helpful - I began to calm down. I think she had sized things up, and very kindly, picked up my pieces. She got me talking and laughing again. I was sorry to say goodbye to her when she got off at the next stop. But she had been with me long enough to make a huge difference for me - so that I was able to make the rest of the journey by myself and not fall apart anymore.

Even though I wasn't that emotionally attached to him, hearing someone say all these things about me had taken a toll on me. It made me realize my mistakes and my shortcomings, even ones that weren't there...and I began to think that everything was my fault. In that moment, my new friend's kindness and perception were extremely helpful in picking up my broken pieces and putting me back together again.

It's funny about this man and me. We tried to get into a relationship once more, or maybe even twice, after our India trip. It was never as ugly as it had been initially, but it was still steamy. I didn't know why I even gave it another shot after the way he had treated me in India...but I did, and it ended exactly the way I had thought it might. We just couldn't seem to get on an even keel, and it always turned out to be difficult...it seemed like we were inextricably bound by fate or karma.

Now, however, many years later, it is completely different between us, and if we ever see each other, we light up. Somewhere along the way, we both have let things be bygones. Well, I guess we always did that...light up. But for some unknown reason, other stuff in the past was not easy. There was just something about it, I can't exactly pinpoint it...but some part of us did connect - and what did connect was much greater than what didn't.

As I said, now it's easy - we meet up, have a wonderful few minutes or a few hours, and we part company, happily. There is usually a year or more goes by before we see each other again, but there's no more negative stuff between us any longer. We have both worked that stuff through and out. But, earlier, we certainly had a hard time getting along on a day-to-day basis.

"I will never be the same person again..."

My trip to India was certainly not a light-hearted holiday. Rather, it has given me much to think about, and the experiences have given me enough food for thought to last an entire lifetime. That trip created much personal development. It took me the better part of a year to get myself back to normal. I had worn myself down - had a lowered immune system and increased allergies, a topsy-turvy sleep pattern, as well as feeling emotionally depressed, unmotivated, and unbalanced. Not to mention that I had come back with scabies. I was a bit of a mess.

I worked on the obvious first - scabies and my upside-down sleeping, which were the easiest. One day, a friend heard me talking about how messed up I was in my sleeping rhythms. She suggested using an alarm clock, mostly, to force me awake at the "right" time. This didn't always work - but I blessed her for giving me the idea because it did help, sooner, to bring me back to Pacific Standard Time inside my body.

"The seven-year itch..."

As for scabies, a roommate in the shared house I lived in was willing to take on the anti-scabies project. Sweet woman that she was, she'd come into my room and we'd go into action. She got really good at spotting the little bugs trying to hide out in my hair, which after my seven weeks away, had grown very long. She was patient and very kind and never suggested that I cut it to make her job easier. There were lots of related activities to this project, like boiling the comb and brush after we were done (we melted more than one of them); extra laundry with the towels we spread over both of us and the bed.

In addition, there were visits to the GP and the skin specialist. The latter had interesting things to say - one that I still remember is that he called it the "seven-year itch." I asked the doctor why he called it that, and he told me that after seven years, the itch still remains (comes and goes with stress, mostly) - long after the scabies are gone. This is now about twenty years later - and it still comes back once in a while.

"Even though it was an invaluable experience..."

With what I know now about India and myself, I don't think I will ever return. However, there's so much diversity to the parts of India that I didn't see - which is most of it - so sometimes (but rarely), I think about going again. However, my memory alone of that difficult year after I returned is probably enough of a deterrent. I wonder, though, if most of the difficulties during the six weeks that I was in India, stemmed from the turbulence in Maurice's and my relationship - and very little from my feelings about the sad state of affairs I saw between the street people and the "force" that controlled them.

I'm speculating that our emotional stuff probably at least weakened me and made me more susceptible to the unfamiliar organisms that I had succumbed to. If I were to go again, I would think that all the street stuff would not affect me as much on a second trip, now that my veil of innocence has been pierced. Only time will tell which wins - my curiosity about the rest of India, or my fear of a repeat performance of a fight for my health.

Chapter 22
The Purpose, For Me,
Of Being In A Relationship

When I returned from India, I had no interest in spending any more time with Maurice. However, a fear that I often faced over the years was of being on my own - and this fear usually led me to dating right away. My habit was to jump as fast as I could from one relationship into the next one. Now I jokingly, refer to those as "serial relationships." However, it is no joke, rather a very serious matter. I was just so miserable when I wasn't in one and thought I needed to be in a relationship to feel happy. I was just immediately jumping into the next.

Gradually, I realized that the time period when I was first out of it was the best time to complete the previous one and to learn what I could before I was busy with the next romance. Otherwise, there were too many of the "same" patterns showing up in the next one. The hard part seemed to be to give myself enough time between relationships to heal and complete everything and balance this with my need to be in another relationship.

A secondary - yet compelling - reason for my too quickly entering another relationship was that I deeply believed that I must be in a relationship for my best spiritual and psychological growth. Any time over the years that I was on my own, and there were many of these, it seemed largely a selfish time in that I only had to consider myself at any given moment. I only needed to think about my own likes or dislikes, my own feelings, wants, or needs. Obviously, upsets didn't occur between me and myself – and I noticed that being with myself gave me little to rub the rough edges off my diamond, so to speak. It didn't seem like it was the path I was here for.

It seemed too slow a spiritual journey for me. It wasn't that I knew that I had a lot of "rough edges" - or more than other people had. However, it was up to them how these people wanted to deal with the immature aspects of themselves and travel their spiritual journey. But I had come to believe that my spiritual path lies within relationship…and attempted to honor that. What I wasn't giving time for, in all this…when jumping so quickly into the next…was healing and completion time. Somehow, I needed to consider including this time in my "relationship" beliefs.

"Two unworkable patterns…"

Therefore, one of my newest lessons that I realized I needed to come to terms with was that I don't 'need' to be in a relationship, rather, I 'choose' to be in one. Being in a relationship feels good, and most people have this need hardwired in them - to have companionship. However, the thing is, this need tends to pop up hardest in the worst possible time…which is when you've just gotten out of a relationship, and the wounds of the last breakup are still fresh. I was only just beginning to see this…I hadn't realized this before.

I also saw that unless you stay very conscious, you will subconsciously start to project those wounds on your new partner. In the beginning, your partner is probably understanding… however, they will grow tired of your emotional baggage. So, it was time for me to include this "healing" time in my beliefs and give myself time to heal in between. Then when I can see and feel that I am back in a healthy frame of mind, then, and only then, I am ready to get into another relationship.

However, even with this new realization, it took many years before I began to get a bit of grip on myself so that I would let the much-needed time pass. This seemed to be a big one for me. My head knew what to do (or not), but emotionally, I would just keep going for it, too soon. The result was always predictable. However, I just had to play it out until my emotions, and my head became aligned.

Meanwhile, I continued to manage shared houses with Jhake - probably for about three more years - and continued to date other men, but not seriously enough to develop any deep and lasting relationships. However, I was learning to put my new understanding into action with more success than after previous breakups - I was learning to examine my actions and reactions - and to grow up, bit by bit. I was satisfied with my progress.

"Time to go on my own..."

After I returned from India - and for many years after this - Jhake and I continued to run shared houses, until my relationship with him had run its course. When that time came, I moved out of the house, leaving my 17-year-old son with Jhake as well as my furniture and pianos. All the dining and living room furniture was mine - Jhake only had a desk. I didn't want to take any of that, and Jhake had agreeably accepted to keep it and my pianos till such time that he also wanted to move elsewhere. I continued to have the Sing-alongs as well as do my piano teaching from there. I was grateful to have the parting all work so easily. The only downside about all this was that my short-term living spaces felt unsatisfactory and made me long for my own shared house again - just not with family any longer…and I wanted to run it myself.

I liked the shared arrangement: we were strangers, and yet we shared space together. I was not responsible for their lives…but there was company at hand and at the same time, distance from them. It suited me just fine. Immediately following living with Jhake, I had moved into a bedroom in a shared house. This felt weird - someone else being the one who laid out the rules and dictated how things were to be handled. This didn't last more than a few months when I decided to find a house where I could live as I wanted.

I found a small house about six blocks from Jhake's - with two bedrooms. Jhake had been feeling like moving on and finding a small place where he could live by himself - he wasn't enjoying running the household by himself without me to partner in it. My son had graduated and was working as a sous-chef, and he and two of the fellows in the house also wanted to go out on their own. So Jhake and I agreed the timing was good for us to disband the house and pack it all up. My first step was to get hold of my favorite piano moving company, and they packed both pianos out of there and moved them the six blocks east to my new place. I also had a new man in my life, and he was as strong as an ox - he moved my furniture out of Jhake's house like it was doll furniture!

My relationship with Daegles didn't last long - less than a year. He had bouts of an on-going struggle with mental instability brought on by a brutal ambush and beating he had suffered long before we met. How it played out with us was that for days at a time, he would become like another person. Reluctantly, I soon parted from him. He had been more of a helpmate than a lover. He saved me a lot of energy - and time, particularly in my role as business manager of my community when I had to go back and forth to Galiano Island as part of my role. Daegles took on all the packing up, driving me over on the ferry, unloading, etc. and then a repeat performance on the return trip home again.

I didn't miss the tormented side of him, but I missed his physical helpmate side. At his best, he was a loving, caring man; at his worst, he was jealous and insecure. That came out when we went dancing. In those days, I was into what was called "Contra Dancing." He didn't like to share me with other partners. Shortly, I quit the dancing - I didn't like the jealous scenes, and even though I didn't like being controlled on this matter, that's what I chose at that moment. Even after Daegles was gone, I didn't go back to dancing for a few years - until after I had begun taking programs with Landmark Education. Then, it magically appeared again - and this time in a different context…and I am still dancing, about twenty years later.

After Daegles was gone and I was again on my own, I began longing for a shared house. I had no need for all that space, plus I had great memories of the time I lived with Jhake in shared houses. In those days, most of our tenants had been young and from different places in the world, and I loved how much I learned from them. Also, during the years that I was a single mom raising my third child, it gave my son greater options than I could offer him by myself. Particularly when he got old enough not to need a babysitter, there were always people and activities going on, so he didn't feel lonely.

Shared housing enriched our lives in so many ways. However, running shared houses now - and on my own was a totally different thing. I had really different needs now. For one thing, my son had grown up. Now he wanted to sprout his own wings and had moved from the house that Jhake had been running into a place that he shared with two of his fellow housemates. I had full-time work and had no time to take care of anyone else - different from before when I worked from my home and Jhake was there to help me give the foreign students a great experience.

Moreover, shared houses, from now on, had a very different context for me...this lifestyle was the only way I saw of being able to live in a house so that I could continue to teach piano from home. I still had the two pianos - as I previously explained, one piano was for teaching...and the other was my soul mate, entirely for my own enjoyment and for sing-alongs.

My solution was to find a room-mate - which I did, quickly and easily (a friend of a friend). I had a bedroom to myself - plus the exclusive use of the living room, which happened simply because my pianos filled up the room, and it didn't feel inviting to anyone else. Also, it seemed over the years that renters, when home, seemed to just be there to do their "quiet" thing and not to socialize with me or each other. That was particularly true of older roommates - and now, that was what I leaned towards…older, self-sufficient persons who all lived our lives somewhat anonymously, having little to do with each other, by choice.

I soon initiated another change because I quickly realized that it would take three of us sharing to make this house viable financially. Energetically, a threesome also increased the anonymity - which suited me fine. I wanted to increase my focus on my own stuff. I cleared "my" bedroom and totally moved into the living-room – which essentially turned it into a bachelor suite.

It was quickly and easily done because nearly everything I needed was already there - my pianos, my desk, and my little bit of office furniture. I left the bed for the new roommate and slept on a foam that I rolled up and down daily. As for my clothes…I had an enormous dresser which handled everything that could be folded up – including tops. But I no longer picture where I hung things that needed more care than to be stuffed in a drawer! Somehow, (because in a shared house, everyone gets into the action – like it or not, it comes with the territory) I/we found a solution.

During the seven years, I was in this house, my life took a big turn. The first year was about settling into my new life, running the house, holding my sing-alongs, holding down jobs such as receptionist, or managing different businesses for their owners. Then something major happened…I took Landmark Education's initial course…and my life didn't look the same anymore! That had happened about twenty years earlier when I took the EST Training…but twenty years is a long time and I had forgotten this aspect of transformational courses.

The biggest change was adding Swing dancing to my life. That brought a long line of new boyfriends - all whom I had met on the dance floor!

I ran two houses like these, and the first one was great until, in the seventh year, it developed mold (it was probably always there, just waiting for an excuse to get going). One of my two tenants was a young man who was not very well mentally, and he closed himself up in his room for many days at a time. With the lack of ventilation, the mold got running rampant in his room - and gradually spread in vulnerable places throughout the house.

The insulation in the walls was poor, and we didn't know that we shouldn't put anything up against it. In places, furniture had been placed too close, and in a few cases, even leaning against the wall. When I discovered what the mold was doing in his room, I had to ask the fellow to leave…and attempted to clean up the mess. Then I went around the whole house, examining walls and windowsills for mold.

I reported my findings to my landlord - and at the same time, served him my own notice to leave in a month. I had decided that for my own health, I needed to get out of there. In the end, I decided to stay a bit longer to help my landlord to replace me. My other tenant (who had been with me the whole time) decided it would be best to leave at the same time. My landlord went into prompt action - cleaned the walls anywhere that the mold was in evidence…and painted (in the bedroom only). After this was all done and I had found a new tenant for him (who was happy to take over the whole house), my tenant and I moved on, each in different directions.

I moved things that I cared about into either a friend's house or my son's - one piano into each - and became a bit of a gypsy for some months until my son offered me to take over the house he had lived in for a couple of years with an Australian friend. The friend was returning to his home in Australia, and my son had a new girlfriend who wanted to find a more suitable place just for themselves. She had been generous in letting me stay there quite often, but my other options for a place to sleep were dwindling, and therefore, I was spending too much time at my son's and girlfriend's house. I had realized that she wasn't thrilled when I would show up, increasingly more often. So...I wasn't surprised, but rather, was delighted with their offer.

Because their landlords had met me several times in the previous months, they felt comfortable with me assuming my son's lease. I soon found a roommate to share the expenses of the house...my son's girlfriend left me a bed and a couple of other things...and my friend moved all the rest of my things out of his storage space over to my new home...and eventually my grand piano. I had missed it; it was my soulmate. The other piano didn't give me much pleasure (but it was perfect for my teaching). I was soon set up again to run another shared house. This time, I decided to keep the numbers down to two persons - which was more difficult, financially, but somehow, I managed to make it work.

This house - as did the previous one - served me well for about five or six more years (bringing the total to twelve years) of running shared houses by myself. During these years, many life-changing things happened.

While I was still in the "moldy" house, I began another round of courses on Self Development. I felt I was overdue for some refresher experiences. For one thing, I noticed that I was beginning to become "crabby" - complaining about things, with a "victim" mentality beginning to set in (and I didn't want to add another "bitchy" old woman to the planet)! I had dealt with my "complain-y" attitude in the EST Training and thought I had put it behind me forever.

Landmark Education was the first of these "personal development" kind of courses that I took this time round and over a few years. This was followed by Peaks Potentials (a financial "overhaul" including learning about my money "blueprint"). Then a whole host of others, mostly business-oriented, like Robert Allan's and Robert Kiyosaki's enlightenment courses. I loved them - the discovering of and grappling with business and wealth (or lack of) in our life…exciting stuff! It all helped to some degree - but I felt that no matter what helpful things I discovered about myself in these areas, that I was past my business and money-amassing years.

I was in my early seventies by this time. At that time, I had other priorities that I was unwilling to give up in order to turn this part of my life upside down. I had to accept my inner voice on these matters - even if emotionally I wanted things to be different. But bottom line, I wasn't willing to do what it would take to change this area of money and business in my life. I'm glad I took the courses and gave myself the chance. Beside expanding my vision and adding to my knowledge, I learned some invaluable lessons, met some inspiring people, and I made many changes that are still helping me…that alone was worth it!

It was out of the Landmark Education's first course that I began dancing which introduced a whole new level of fun and passion - and notably a set of four men that radically impacted my life (TB, DP, JS, FM). I have no regrets about any of them - each one was a unique gift to my life and spirit! I met three of them in a local swing dance club and one at a jazz festival. All my other short relationships began on a dance floor at a jazz festival…both Canadian and American.

For a few years I danced swing - east coast, west coast, and jive. But it was Lindy Hop that "put me over the moon." I've tried all the major dance forms - including all Ballroom, Salsa, Tango, West Coast Swing…but none of them give me the rush or on-going pleasure that Lindy Hop swing dancing does. With dance, every person has to find their dance…the mix of music and steps…that feeds their soul!

One new and interesting development that happened was that I had almost no romantic relationships after joined the Lindy Hop dance community. I began to exclusively dance Lindy Hop. Previously, most of my relationships had developed on the Jazz Festival dance floors, but Lindy Hoppers are predominantly young (twenties and thirties) and therefore are not an eligible age for a relationship with me. Instead, my final relationship was with a man I met online. But that is a story that deserves to have its own chapter.

Chapter 23
Boy Friend: The Final Stage?

This relationship that I embarked on is what I so much wanted to think of as my last one. It was different from all the others...which difference I didn't always like...but saw it as what I needed, not always wanted. I sensed that it was time to stabilize, come to a halt, and express my life from this stable place. However, it took a lot to get used to the lack of change, the little excitement, and to begin creating variety from stability. Moreover, I found it challenging for me to keep the relationship together, strong and viable, as it became more and more apparent how little we had in common that we liked to do together.

Back in early October of 2010, I met Dave (online). We started corresponding, and I intuitively "knew" that he was right for me. On Sunday, October 17th, I met him in person. I knew, even as I watched him come down the small hillock beside his house and as he looked in my car window, that he was the one. We spent from noon till about 6:30, having lunch and talking, then walking the beach and talking, and dancing for three hours and again talking. The belief that he was the one got stronger with every passing second…until I just knew that he was the next man in my life…and hopefully the last one.

"The clincher was that Dave had known my mother and father"

I'll begin at the beginning and allow myself to wander on side paths as I go along. It didn't take us very long to discover that Dave and his ex-wife and children knew my Mom and Dad. The thing they all had in common was the church they attended. Religious beliefs and spirituality are one of the earliest topics that I bring up on a first date with a potential long-term romantic partner. I feel as if that is one topic that is very important to discuss and be on the same wavelength because it is a very sensitive topic.

Some men might not be okay with the things I strongly believe, or I might not be okay with theirs…that is a relationship which is very apt to fail. If it is someone who I am not going to spend much time with, then it is not so high on the list - but it's very high on my checklist for a future best friend. In exploring, I found out that in Dave's case, as in mine, he wasn't currently a churchgoer, nor did he want to be. This was one of the many things we talked about early on during our first day together. He had lived in the little community called Crescent Beach, and we happened to drive right past his former church, both coming and going on our beach walk that first day. Also, the Legion, where we later went dancing to a traditional jazz band (one of my passions), was situated right behind this little church.

"A match made in heaven…"

When Dave mentioned that this had been his church, I said, "That was the church where my mother and father went."

He gave me a funny look and then asked, "And what were their names?"

When I told him, "Rose and Frank Rudd," he looked at me in disbelief. Not only had they known each other, but Mom, for some reason, had once invited Dave's eldest daughter to their home for tea one afternoon. It was something about an idea the church had that involved elders building relationships with the church's youth.

The first time that Dave's children all came over to our place, I showed them a picture I had of Mom and Dad. It was one of those pictures that their church took of their members every year, if they wished. His children all remembered them, even though it was many years prior that they had last seen them. They were amazed that their Dad and I had met up, completing that circle so many years later. That one thing alone was a big factor in Dave and me jumping in so quickly. I think it handled the trust factor that many people don't get past - and particularly older people, as both of us obviously were. It was as if my parents had given us their blessing. I often wondered if they were smiling.

"Thinking we ought to be sensible – but not really wanting to…"

I think we had to miss a week seeing each other; then I visited him again - still a go. I stayed overnight the next week, and the following week…I stayed for three weeks. At the end of that time, I looked at Dave in amazement and said, I have a place where I live, somewhere - but I can barely remember it, and I don't much care. We both laughed.

When we first met, I was in the process of leaving that house I had lived in for about five years. Things had changed and I no longer felt like it was my home, for a number of reasons. However, by this time, we were nearing the end of November and I had declared to myself, that I would be out of my place by the first of January. That gave me about five days to get my notice in to my landlord.

"My birthday marked the spot..."

In the five days that followed, we had many conversations about what would be best. By the 29th of November (I remember, because that was my birthday), Dave and I had the final, clinching conversation. In my mind was the fact that I had already "lived" with Dave for almost the entire month of November. I thought it could be strongly possible that I could move into another place and never darken its door (which would make it a very expensive storage locker that I would then move out of without ever having needed to use it).

My final argument was that I would rather move only once. So…if I moved in with Dave as a first step, we could see what worked and what didn't - if there was anything at all. Things had been going so smoothly for us that that thought seemed ridiculous at this moment - but I conceded…it was always possible - just not probable. I had many years of experience under my belt, in terms of relationships, and knew how to handle the little stuff before it turned into big stuff. With the added fact that both of us were very happy with each other, and there was just that click that made us so sure that it would work out. However, we both agreed that it would be best to have a contingency plan if all didn't go well.

If we were able to work everything out as we went along, then great. If we found that we needed more space, we could move to a new, larger place together. Or if I was missing Vancouver and wanted to be somewhere that was easier and quicker to get there, I could move back to Vancouver or somewhere on the transit path that would make it easier to get to both Vancouver and Dave's.

"We took the step – and I moved in…"

The opposing advice is something that most people are familiar with...it's wise to take it slowly and cautiously. However, at our age, the opposite could also be true -

because we don't know how long we have - so we just got on with it. We chose to move in together, formally, by January first, 2011, although the date we think of, as our anniversary, is the Sunday closest to October 17th, 2010. By the time I officially moved in, we had already done quite a lot of living together. The experiences we had had by the time we made our decision to live together had already revealed the things that we were each still dealing with, our 'dragons,' one might say. I had already experienced my own upsets, knew the nature of them. Most importantly, I had experienced how we worked through these, individually and together.

Of all the men I have lived with, Dave has been the slowest to react out loud. He believes, and puts into practice, that it is wise to keep blame and name-calling out of it, and rather, sit and ponder and look quietly inside for insights. This is really helpful for me because I can quietly do the same, rather than getting all tangled up in surviving the onslaught, as was the case in most previous relationships.

"Three upsets largely completed what I had yet to handle..."

Three upsets come to mind: the earliest one was over sexual differences and expectations; the second one was about a perceived criticism; the third was when I didn't take his asked for advice...oops. By now, we had experienced a range of upsets, and I liked what I both saw and felt about the way we worked our way through them.

Generally speaking, in emotional matters, Dave is, to use a cliché, the strong silent type. I sometimes have an opposite style - become very vocal, in a negative way - but I'd say that I predominantly shut down and say nothing. In the past, it has never been good if I shut down because I am doing it in reaction and will possibly explode later. With Dave's style, though, it has usually been quite easy to just go off and work it out by myself (which is the most appropriate way to work it through, anyway).

Dave's upset, over sexual expectation, happened on my first overnight. Dave encountered a situation between us that I will call an unfulfilled expectation, and he wanted to end everything before we went any further. How it went was this. He couldn't sleep because of being upset, and got dressed and went into the living room. I'm a deep sleeper and knew nothing of this. Later, he popped his head into the bedroom about 7:30 or 8:00, and I said "hi". From his response, I knew right away that something was bothering him. I asked him what was going on for him, and he said he'd been thinking and he thought it would be best if I went home. I was stunned as this came out of the left field for me. I asked him if he would be willing to talk about it...and he said he would.

Even though it was kind of offensive being asked to leave just like that, I knew that our kind of relationship was hard to come by. I was nowhere near ready to let it go that easily, and somewhere deep down, I knew that he wasn't, as well. In the past, I would probably have just gotten up and left; however, this time was different, and I knew we needed to see if we could talk it out.

Something I have learned being with Dave (and others) is that in a relationship, almost all problems or upsets can be handled just by talking about them. There is no grand gesture needed, just commitment from both sides to quietly hash things out - honestly and sincerely.

"Communication and willingness were of prime importance…"

I sat up in bed - and Dave sat on a chair beside the bed and I asked him if he would begin and share the essence of his upset, which he did. He said he had thought that I was open to being sexual, and I said I was, but with reservations. I elaborated, and we tossed the ball back and forth as we explored where we were both at. The outcome was that Dave said that he thought it would be okay if I stayed and that we could give ourselves some time on this…and continue talking, sharing, and exploring what was possible and what felt good.

Eventually, there was another upset about all this, and again, I encouraged him to share about his upset, and again we worked it through - this time, with more knowledge about each other… just going deeper and clearer each time it came up. After a few months, we had worked things out so well that there weren't any more upsets over our sexual life.

After that, if something came up for one of us, we had developed enough trust and experience with each other to know we could just raise it and explore it. Caring communication, and willingness to make things work were the answer, every time. In every relationship, the basic desire is to be carnal…and being both close to, as well as passionate with your partner is essential and works as a catalyst for a great many things. It was necessary to get things in order before we could move forward. I had to make some compromises, as did he…and out of this, we were able to find our sweet spot.

Another early upset went like this. I was shopping for a car and Dave was my sounding board. I had narrowed it down to a particular car. Only it was my worst color, black. They phoned around and reported that it seemed to be the only car left of its kind amongst their dealers. I sat down with their business manager so she could "crunch numbers" for me. It was past their quitting time, and I asked if I could have until the morning to think about it, and she replied that I'd need to put $500 dollars down on it for them to hold that car.

I talked with Dave to see what he thought, and he was dead against that. I went back to the manager, and she stuck with her story. Her rationale was that because there was only one of those cars left in the area, it wasn't a wise business move on their part to let me go without pinning things down.

I thought about it for a minute and then said I'd give her the money to hold it. Dave walked off in a fury to the far side of the showroom. I was flabbergasted at his reaction. When I was done with the business manager, I joined Dave. On the way home, we stopped to pick up some food first and then went home. He had stopped talking to me, except for the bare essentials. I had a counter-upset going on. We had both flared up, which resulted in both of us shutting down emotionally.

We had been reading a relationship book together, off and on, for about three or four weeks. It had some quite unusual premises and was different from other relationship books. Both of us had been really enjoying the ideas that the author, Harville Hendrix, had been putting forth. One of his strongest theories was that we choose our mate according to the negative qualities of our early childhood caretakers (usually parents or whoever was raising us). I was experiencing an example of this premise.

"I had paired up with a father figure – "Of course," say all the books…"

I can remember sitting at the table after dinner, listening to Dave's rationale as to his upset and watching his face as he explained, angrily, why he was upset. As I listened and watched, I could feel myself climb out of my own upset, and I could also feel a smile creeping slowly over my face. What I had noticed was that when angry, Dave very closely resembled my father - who, when cross, was always tight-lipped and would raise his voice to be louder than my own.

No wonder, I thought, that I felt a bit afraid of Dave - even powerless - when he was angry. It was as if I was back in a little girl's body, being taken to task by my father. I was experiencing having settled down with someone who was like one of my parents. At first, I was a bit taken aback by the powerfulness of my insight. A good thing was that even though I had found out that Dave's anger was just like my father's, I knew that Dave was a really good person…and that I enjoyed being with him.

There were just so many redeeming qualities about him that it was not difficult for me to get over my upset. Many people are really weirded out by the fact that they have chosen someone who has similar qualities to one of their parents. However, that didn't bother me. I understand the psychological dynamics and I don't find it to be that weird or confronting. After all, my parents did raise me and take care of me, and most importantly, they loved me. So maybe finding a person who is a bit like them isn't the worst thing - or so I tell myself!

"The analysis of our relationship..."

I could feel myself come back into my body, in that moment, and then the situation between Dave and I took on a whole different flavor. It seemed that as I had reframed my current upset by seeing the similarity with childhood upsets, the current one was totally diffused. I was, to borrow an expression from my Irish girlfriend, gobsmacked!

I shared my insight with Dave - and particularly about my upset disappearing when I saw how he reminded me of my Dad when he was upset. In light of the book he and I were reading together, it was gratifying to me to see how I was learning to apply my new knowledge in my life. However, it was mystifying (and not reassuring) to Dave, who didn't have as much experience as I did about what makes relationships tick.

I encouraged Dave to do some similar analysis of his side of the upset. To me, it seemed likely that if we had read this about upsets, and then I had experienced it, that he, too, had most likely experienced a similar basis for his own upset. It would be about something different, of course…Dave's upset was something about being asked for his opinion, and then having it ignored. He thought that I had turned it down because I didn't trust his judgment…that his idea or belief was not good enough. There was probably an even deeper cut than that one - and he did take a look - but seemed unable to get to the bottom of it. I conjectured that that might not matter. It might be enough to acknowledge that the upset was just part of a button pusher scenario… and that this knowledge, alone, might be enough to de-fuse the current upset for him.

I wondered if this scenario would ever be duplicated in the future, or if my insight was limited to this one incident. I didn't have long to wait as another one soon came on the tracks of the first one. This time, my insight came faster, and the upset, therefore, was quite a bit less and the third one weaker still. It didn't take much longer before I would feel it a little, but it was beginning to be no more than a little 'blip' before it was gone.

There are other sources, too, for my upsets than re-living my dad's displeasure with me. In all cases, I have been able to get back to a likely source and defuse them. The defusing is the main point, and I have found that if I am committed to being in the present and not run by my past, I don't even have to find the original incident. I just have to remember that the current upset is not about what I think it is about - but rather, it is about something that occurred long ago, when I was very young. For me, a theme of feeling powerless runs through most of them, and also the theme of not feeling good enough or even feeling stupid.

"Here we go again – or so I thought…"

Recently, an incident grew between Dave and I where I had a massive reaction. I was so quick to go out of control that, without warning, I burst into tears and dashed out of the room. A short while later, once I started feeling more like myself, I began to analyze the incident to see what I could learn from it. For one thing, I seemed to have this dragon inside that was on high alert to protect me from who knows what.

In addition, I knew what I felt on the outside was not feeling cared for or loved or valued. I also experienced, that bit by bit, I was being worked out of the relationship. Then the thought of being out of the relationship brought many other fears and feelings, including a groundless fear of not being able to afford to pay for all my needs if I were to live on my own. My mind started to go wild, and an even bigger fear sprang up at the thought of being out of the relationship - and that was the fear of being on my own again. At my age, companionship felt essential - even though I know, deep down, that of course, I'd be alright if I were on my own. But the fear that it could happen one day was still lingering.

However, the worst thing I was experiencing was the fear of failure. I had already put a great deal of time, thought, and consideration into creating this relationship as a winner. Therefore, much deeper was the worry about having to start all over again. When I calmed down and was back into a reasonable frame of mind, I realized that it was just the words I had heard – that meant to me that my partner was wanting out of our relationship, whereas my experience was the opposite…it was of being very connected.

"Is this just a set-up…?"

Before Dave and I met, I had declared my next relationship would be my final one and that I would be complete, and it would be a loving relationship that I would stay in. I was so committed to this idea that I had even thought I might get a marriage out of this, my final relationship. This is a bit of a set-up for failure and shame. How can one even think that they can promise to make something work that involves another person? There is a well-known truism, 'The only person's reaction you can control is your own.' That being said, it was foolish of me to think that I would be getting a marriage out of my next relationship when it involved another person.

A relationship isn't like a business, where it is up to you to make it successful. In a relationship, the other person has to be just as emotionally invested…and it has turned out that Dave is not. We have changed so much since we first got together that I can no longer feel confident in where we are going. However, up to that moment, I was still in the relationship, still growing up, still learning to love more deeply and to be non-judgmental - those being, primarily, the reasons for me to be in a relationship.

"How much should we have in common...?"

One of the trickiest aspects of a relationship is the sharing of interests. People talk about having interests in common as being high on the compatibility list. There is a lot of research to support the premise: the more interests there are in common, the higher the chances of longevity in the relationship. If that is the case, Dave and I have a very low chance of surviving. Rationally thinking about it, it could be true. However, having an interest that your partner doesn't share doesn't necessarily have to be a deal-breaker. You could survive that if there is an understanding between the two of you to indulge in that interest separately.

My challenge seems to be that I have been going along, based on an underlying assumption, that we would have this, whatever it may be, in common forever. Now, as I feel it ending (or if "it" isn't, something is changing, and it feels like it is the relationship that is coming to an end), I have been shocked. Dave is easy with the changes. My challenge seems to be to accept this new situation, make a new choice, a new plan...and get on with it. I thought I was a flexible person, but I was beginning to see that I have a huge difficulty moving forward into each new situation. However, I knew that I had to adjust graciously to my partner no longer dancing...or lose the relationship.

"A surprise discovery was how I didn't lose easily…"

The following are the "initially expressed interests-in-common" that fell away in our second year - dancing, traveling, making meals together, watching a TV movie or DVD every night we were both home, reading together, attending personal development courses, going to bed at the same time. We had all these things in common in the beginning, and then, one by one throughout our second and third years, Dave lost interest in them or stopped doing or talking about them. The first to go was the dancing. There were both physical as well as emotional reasons for this one –but I think that dancing together was the one that I had counted on the most – and therefore, Dave's quitting this activity affected me the most.

He had been getting quite good at swing dancing, but then he abruptly dropped it. At first, it was because his hip hurt. But when he recovered, he still wouldn't return to the dancing. I thought it might be because of the group we were attending and so I raised that to Dave…that perhaps we could find a different type of dance, which would mean a different group of people and perhaps closer to home.

He balked at the whole idea. So that was the end of our dancing. I was disappointed, upset, and sad. Nothing that I said - about new things we could perhaps try where dancing was concerned - mattered. Dave was done with it. It could have been that he was done with me, but at the time, I chose to think that it was just the dancing. The end of dancing did bring me emotional distress, however, that I had to get over. I could have gone alone, but then again, I had (mistakenly) thought that I might even be getting a marriage out of this relationship - and as Dave backed off, so did I.

Chapter 24
Losing a Dancing Partner Was
The Most Difficult Loss

In the beginning, when Dave quit, I didn't keep going. We spent our time watching movies instead because that was something that we liked doing together. It felt nice to snuggle with him and spend our evenings in front of the screen. However, after a few weeks or so, Dave protested the fact that I had stopped dancing. He said that he was not going to take responsibility for my quitting dancing. I never blamed him, though; it's just that I liked spending time with him, which was a higher priority than dancing. I had let Dave know that it was a higher priority for me to spend time with him, and at that moment, it was true and from the heart.

I was not just saying that to spare his feelings or hope he'd make some huge compromise... my intentions were pure and straightforward. However, feelings change as time passes. Sometimes it happens that you end up feeling different even after only a few days...or months... and that is what happened. I thought I could replace the love I had for dancing with watching movies with Dave, and I managed to do that for a short while. But after a bit of time passed, staying at home and missing the dancing didn't work for me either, so I decided to start dancing again.

The fact that I wanted something different from life soon caught up with me. First off, I found that going back to dancing brought several hardships with it. The trip to the dance hall was long and took even longer when returning late at night because of fewer buses. Moreover, I no longer had companionship at the dances. Though I loved dancing with young people, we shared minimal conversation in most cases. I was old enough to be their mother and, in some instances, even their grandmother. I hadn't particularly minded that; I even found it enjoyable to watch the dancers or just dance by myself at times.

I had done that for years, off and on. Prior to Dave, I used to drive five or six hours to a jazz festival - sleep in my car, eat out of my cooler, all of which was fine, but lonely. Mistakenly, I had thought I was done with that lifestyle. I understood why he wasn't dancing and accepted it, but I was not entirely over my loss. Since life goes on, I learned to make the best of it. It is better to accept things, rather than forcing your partner to do something they don't want to do.

That would eventually build up resentment and not be healthy or workable.

"Silently, things in common, slipped away – the dancing, the reading…"

Nothing much changed in the first year. Dancing was the first thing we had in common, and it was the first thing to go. This happened at the beginning of our second year together. Gradually, during that second year, other things followed until early in our third year, everything we loved doing together was gone.

Maybe Dave was doing those things at the start because he thought I'd want him more…and since the relationship was new, he was going along with them. Or maybe he was willing at first to try the new things with me - but soon learned, one by one, that he really wasn't interested in any of them.

One of those interests was to read a Relationship book together and to watch Relationship videos. Almost daily, we would read a few pages in the evening. I had thought that reading the book set us up beautifully to be equipped for all manner of emotional eruptions that we might experience - it could give us a perspective and tools to handle it all. While I still found the guidance in that book to be very useful, Dave seemed to have forgotten the lessons - or not value the insights. I treasured them because I have been at this personal development business for about thirty years and the ideas in the book were a refresher for concepts I had previously learned. Plus, a few years ago, I had already read this exact book, so I was enjoying the reread.

For Dave, this book was new, but the ideas weren't all new, so a lot of it made sense to him, and he seemed to like what we read. Still, it was new in some way. Whereas, I was able to more quickly apply the ideas from the book to our relationship in that they were not new to me. Dave took his time reading and understanding what Harville Hendrix was trying to teach.

Even if I was applying the ideas faster, I was applying them to my own emotional eruptions, not to his. I thought that that would make it tolerable and even enlightening to him as it gave Dave an example of how to put Hendrix's lessons into practice. However, now I'm not sure - maybe Dave felt I was trying to be superior - and if that was what he thought, I can understand if he didn't appreciate it. I'll never know because he always just said he didn't want to read it anymore.

"We had let other things get in the way…"

At some point during that first year, we got so busy with our dancing and our DVD watching that we let go of the reading. Then when the DVD store unexpectedly closed and we finally had more time for reading, Dave was no longer interested. He was beginning to resist many of my ideas by then. I guess you could call that the 'power struggle' phase of our relationship. In the beginning, perhaps he didn't feel safe enough to disclose his disinterest. The power struggle is something that couples go through…it was inevitable, especially since I could be very strong-minded – and he, also. However, I figured that it was just silly…going through that phase at our age. Anyway…we were!

"I guess he was lamenting the loss of meat more than I realized…"

Right about then, Dave's son got into a relationship with a woman who liked to cook. She would often make beef, pork, potatoes, pasta, or tomato sauce meals for Dave. He had stopped eating red meat when we got together…because

I ate only chicken and fish. Previously, the only times when Dave indulged was on special occasions when we were eating out. Therefore, he was naturally delighted every time his son's girlfriend brought over meat-based leftovers for him. Shortly after this, Dave met up with a woman friend who used to work with him. They began to meet up for coffee about once a week, and she started giving him a stash of soups plus mostly beef and pork meals The reason she had all this food was that her husband turned up his nose at her meals, and she would promptly freeze them. Giving them to Dave felt great to her…and just like that, our meal-making experiences stopped happening. That was just one more thing we didn't do any longer, and I must admit it caused me some grief.

It took me a while to realize what was happening - Dave had mouth-watering meals to eat, and I wasn't the one providing them. Previously, our way had been for one of us to raise the "what's for dinner" question late in the afternoon, and then together we would look in the fridge, talk out loud about what we were seeing and thinking, and put the meal together on the spot. But now, every time I raised the question, Dave would say he was thinking about one of his meals in the fridge, and I would look in the fridge for myself and see nothing much there. It wasn't a huge thing…but little things can turn into big things. That was one of those little things since the frequency soon increased until it was almost daily.

At this point, my need for "togetherness" became severely challenged. This happens a lot in relationships. Simple arguments turn into big fights. Dave had known what I liked and didn't like to eat, and for a while, he had tried to go along with me, doing things my way. But circumstances changed, and he stopped caring about my needs and eating preferences. However, there was no longer anything for me to eat in our fridge anymore (because he had also been the shopper). I wanted him to still take that into account when restocking the fridge. He didn't say 'no'…but he just didn't do it any longer.

"He had been lamenting no meat – I was now lamenting no meals…"

I would be typing away on my book, and I'd hear Dave open the fridge door and fix his dinner. The next thing I realized was that I found myself feeling uncared for, and this was upsetting for me. This scenario continued for a few more days, and I came to the conclusion that my time of enjoying cooking with Dave was over. Now, I had better get pro-active and start cooking for myself, or I would always feel like a victim. There was no use sitting around and wallowing in self-pity because he was now fixing dinner only for himself.

I took stock and came up with another approach...I decided to ask Dave the question about dinner wishes early in the afternoon, and depending on his answer, I would formulate a plan. Then I took over the planning of the whole dinner meal. That way, I figured I was in charge, whether Dave and I cooked different meals, or I prepared the entire meal for us both.

He's good at making sauces and gravies, leaving me to make the rice and veggies for us both. With me now being the coordinator, I had a better chance to ensure that we were both ready to sit down at the same time. That was still the hardest thing to coordinate though - since Dave was just reheating his meal, and always wanting to eat it hot. Therefore, he often got ahead of me while I was still cooking.

My next progression was that I started to care less about it all as I got used to doing things on my own and was practicing not taking any of it personally! So, in the end, the answer was just to get over it and move on. That seems to be the answer to a lot of things in relationships. Rather than forcing things to stay as they were, it is much better to accept the new "what's so" and create a new action plan. Forcing your partner to be as they had been, can only result in them feeling suffocated, resentful, and eventually, wanting out of the relationship. As difficult as I might find it, sometimes…communication and compromise are key to making any relationship work!

"Uh-oh! Upset again – and a new chance to 'grow up'…"

However, one day, I got caught again. This time, I thought I knew that there was no obvious meal for Dave, so I marched into the kitchen to check. I was right. I went into the living-room to let Dave know what I was planning…it turned out that I had guess wrong and he had dinner already prepared in his head, with leftovers that I had missed seeing.

I became agitated, only because I didn't feel like creating my elaborate meal plan all for myself, and I didn't have an alternative in mind. My ego was hurt because I was interested in doing this meal for the two of us and he wasn't thinking about me at all. It was like I was no longer a part of his daily schedule. I put the ingredients back in the fridge and went into my office to work through my emotions and create a new meal idea. In a couple of minutes, however, Dave, much to my surprise, came into my office to say he'd like me to go ahead with my idea and that he didn't have to eat what he'd had in mind.

That was a nice gesture; however, the fact that my needs were an afterthought for him still lingered. A lot of things flashed before me…I quickly reflected on my past, a place where I wasn't mature yet and realized I better give up feeling hurt, because old upsets and new incidents were colliding here. I also realized that if I could get over it, I would be a much better partner. This was more like the "me" I was used to – that ever since I was very young, has always wanted to better myself at every turn…and I was grateful to see that it still follows me, even to this day.

Another thought flashed before me…I concluded that eating separately would not be a good thing for the health of our relationship. Also, our relationship was not going to fall apart if we ate different foods at the same meal…the main idea was to sit down to eat together…it is a good chance to communicate and have an opportunity to negotiate and work things out that are bothering us. Moreover, no matter how things went, both of us had a constant opportunity to learn to be gracious and loving.

Not getting things my way isn't pleasant or fun – but is great for my spiritual and personal development. When this happens, I'm forced to learn to adapt and become better at dealing with the problems that life has brought my way. Life always has something to throw at you…and it's just an opportunity to become better…learn to be giving, forgiving, to communicate, and to compromise. It may seem like a lot to deal with…but having an open and positive outlook on it will make you appreciate it as an opportunity rather than being constantly upset or frustrated.

"I forgot to follow my dreams – as I was all wrapped up in the relationship…"

Another area that I needed to work on was on having the courage and commitment to follow my path and dreams and not giving them up in favor of the relationship. I have always had a tendency to allow my relationship to come first. It is easy to let yourself go when in love. After all, the feeling of being in a relationship is fantastic, and I didn't want to be the one sabotaging it. However, over the years, in looking back, I did grow to regret not looking after my own needs as I went through life. Usually, I would allow myself to be absorbed in a relationship to the point of letting myself be swallowed up by it…my own path and dreams disappearing. Some of us do this in the name of compromise and finding a new way together. However, too much of this - particularly if the giving up is too one-sided - can lead to resentment. The thing is, I deliberately allowed myself to be put in that situation (even if subconsciously), so I had no one to look to but myself. I was the one who decided that the relationship was more important than myself. So how could I blame my partner?

I believe in spending time together to create a connection. This caused me to have a strong tendency to choose spending time with Dave. For example, if I wanted us to go dancing and Dave didn't want to go, I would opt for staying home with him. Then he would point out that it wasn't right for me to choose him over dancing. Experiencing his nonpossessiveness was great. Here's the kicker; I wanted to be wanted more and found him to be non-possessive to a fault.

When you are in it for the long haul, there is a fine line between being non-possessive and making the other person feel unwanted. Treading that fine line needs a lot of consciousness, communication and trust. As our things-in-common disappeared at an alarming rate, it became difficult to maintain the connection and to develop and deepen our relationship. Dave seemed adamant about maintaining his autonomy, his space, his rights, and his power...so much so that he didn't have much time or attention to give me - and perhaps not enough desire any longer.

Looking back, I have an idea that his compromising and giving up his natural sexual expression played havoc with his feelings and desires. Perhaps without sexual expression - in a traditional way - there wasn't enough for him to maintain his initial closeness and care for me. Non-traditional sexual expression wasn't new for me, and moreover, it was enough - I am very sensual and therefore more satisfied by sensual expressions than sexual. However, for Dave, it was a new way of expressing his sexual feelings - and perhaps it wasn't enough. He seemed to enjoy what we had...but he possibly needed at least some traditional sexual expression added into the mix - to maintain his attachment to me and the "juice" and "spice."

Therefore, the task of maintaining this relationship seems to have fallen upon me alone. I laugh as I read this because it reminds me of a relationship course, Women Sex and Power, that I took many years ago. The male leader, Justin Sterling, asked a room of women, "Would you consider letting a dumb animal look after your relationship?" Because he was a man asking the questions, I didn't have to worry about it being "male bashing". On the contrary, I considered the question, thoughtfully - and where he was coming from. The obvious answer was, "No." So what was the alternative?

The leader suggested that the area of "relationship" was best left entirely to the woman. He said that it was the woman's job to enroll her man in activities and actions that would be healthy for the future of their relationship. That was about thirty years ago and two relationships of about six years each; four of two or three years each; and many short ones...and the answer is still the same - the responsibility for a relationship is entirely in my hands.

"For better or worse - as the woman - I, alone, am responsible for the relationship…"

Do I like that? Yes and no.

'Yes,' because I have control and the chance to create better, wiser, outcomes than the man perhaps would.

'No,' because it takes constant awareness. I can never let things slide…I have to be ever vigilant if I am committed to our longevity.

'No,' because I am faced with how self-absorbed I am and how I sometimes don't want to make an effort to be loving, kind, and generous…I don't always want to have to be the one to make Dave feel special. This all takes time as well as thoughtful and heartfelt output, and I am amazed how often I don't feel like it. I'd rather read - or watch a movie - or listen to one of the "Got Talent" re-runs - or just go to sleep!

Admitting all that about myself took a lot of guts. However, it's all part of making a relationship work. I always have a choice, and so far, I have mostly chosen the loving route because that is who I truly am, and anything else is just laziness or my ego. Easy to see and to say…but not so easy to do. The thing that keeps me going is what it feels like on the other side of the choice. I am grateful for my choices, because, in most cases, they are my opportunity to grow up.

Dancing was the first thing to drop away - what a disappointment that was. That was when I realized how much I had counted on Dave to choose to go dancing with me.

Travel was another one. I expressed an interest in traveling with him when we first got together. One of the ideas was to go to Halifax to see his daughter and future son-in-law; a second one was to travel to various jazz festivals. Also, I wanted to drive, fly, or go by train some Fall to the Kalispell Jazz Festival in Montana; or the one in San Diego, California that takes place over the American Thanksgiving weekend; or to Seaside, Oregon at the end of February. There are a couple of wonderful Festivals in the southern part of England, and because I am Irish, I wanted to go at least once in my lifetime to Ireland. I was also interested in traveling to Machu Picchu as well to volunteer at a Panda Reserve that I think is in South America.

We went on one trip to Halifax for his daughter and new son-in-law's wedding. The only redeeming factor about that trip (as a trip) was that we stayed in a cottage with Dave's new in-laws - and they were great - they bent over backwards to make Dave (and I) feel comfortable and make sure we enjoyed ourselves. If he had just been alone with me, he probably would have ditched the wedding and returned home by himself!

We tried one jazz festival in Penticton, and that was the end of jazz festivals. Dave didn't enjoy the crowds; I guess I should have known that, what with him being the strong, silent type. He didn't even like that amount of jazz…and missed the daily routines of home.

We went on one excursion to Victoria on Vancouver Island (a ferry trip away from Vancouver). I was free for a few days in between my very long stay with my grandson - near Victoria. Dave went to and from on the ferry by himself, and we met up for a rendezvous for a few days - it was inexpensive and sweet as we house-sat for a friend near the ocean in Victoria - we could walk to everything.

Other than a few short excursions near home, that was it for our traveling. I kept Tuesdays open for short excursions - particularly in the summer - and that was my attempt at doing something together. We both like to walk the beach - that was a common interest – but not regularly because Dave had other places that he enjoyed walking (which I did not) - so even that was short-lived.

In reality, Dave's and my relationship didn't turn out to be perfect...in fact, it was far from it. Even though it was love at first sight, both of us made some decisions during the early part of our relationship that caused hardships. However, from the beginning, I had always held firmly to the belief that this would be my last relationship. Therefore, I was doing everything I could do to make sure that it would last. That seemed to be the crux of it. Dave was doing what he would usually do, and I was attempting to make sure that things went according to what I thought was needed for a long-lasting relationship...but after a while, I could see that we weren't on the same wave-length as to what that was, and I was getting worn out, "swimming upstream."

However, after four years, I was called, unexpectedly, in a different direction - my son-in-law became terminally ill, and my daughter needed more support than I could give her, living so far away. Because Dave and I had become quite detached by then, I chose to leave him and move to Vancouver to support my daughter. On the one hand, I was surprised at the new direction of my life. On the other hand,

I realized it was probably inevitable, sooner than later, given the choices we were both making. After the first year, we hadn't been operating like a unit, but rather, each of us was making independent decisions and choices as if these didn't affect each other. We were beginning to operate like islands unto ourselves.

So…what I had perceived as magical and lasting, within four years had gone the way of all the many previous… and was turning out to be not "final" - any more than any of the others. There was a difference, though, with this separation. By the end, I was not longing for another relationship…I felt done…and still do, more than five years later. Dave was more emotional over my leaving than I had thought he would be. In his own way, he was attached - more than I had realized. However, at the same time, he was very gracious about my departure and understood my daughter's and my need to be closer and more accessible than we had been, with me out in White Rock and her in Vancouver. This was a pretty big turning point in my life as I could not reasonably leave my daughter to struggle alone in this tragic time of need…but it would take me giving up on my commitment to my relationship with Dave.

But, after a couple of months of me driving into Vancouver a few times a week - and staying overnight wherever I could find a bed to stay in - I decided to pack my bags and head into Vancouver for good in October of 2014 - exactly four years after I committed to living with Dave. Even though the move was primarily to be there for my daughter and even though my reason for spending more time with my daughter was not a happy one, nevertheless, the change turned out to be good for me. For some time, I had been floundering in the relationship I was in and was becoming more and more unhappy. Fortuitously, life had presented me with a reasonable opportunity to leave.

Chapter 25
Final Phase Of My Life:
ON MY OWN

I soon settled into my Vancouver life - I was now on my own for the first time, ever…and at long last…I was ready for that! What I appreciated most was the long hours alone where I could explore, uninterrupted, what was next for me. My main activities and deliberations were:

Dance a few evenings each week (there were many to choose from).

Reflect on and research how to take my health to new levels.

Long walks with my daughter when I could be my daughter's sounding board during this troubled time.

Walk her dog to give her freedom to be with her partner at the hospital - or after he had died, freedom to deal with bringing new order to her life.

Look after my friend's mother, who had dementia – (several times a week). That way Maharra could get back to doing her job more fully and easily than had been possible while her failing mother was living with her). Really, I was only a stop gap while she figured out the next stage for meeting the needs of her mother. In the end, it turned out that I was able to help her with that too. I got a list of nursing homes from Maharra and figured out which ones were within about a twenty-minute drive from her place. Then I visited each one, created a shorter list and assessed them for her. After paring it down to three, my friend went and visited those three. Three she could manage, but to deal with the whole process, along with doing her work and looking after her mom's needs had been daunting and impossible. She made the choice and proceeded with moving her mother.

Once her mom was settled in her new "home," Maharra and her son decided that they would take turns visiting her a few times a day (only 5 minutes' drive from their apartment). Soon they were satisfied that their mom/grandmother had settled in well enough to back off a little. Within a couple of weeks, they were going just twice a day for her noon and dinner meals. At that point, I began going about three times a week for the dinner meal and helping her get ready for bed. That relieved Maharra a bit…and we continued that routine for a year until her mom just quietly "slipped away."

I was happy to live a life of service - to have the time to help. I was particularly ready to experience a life with no one to answer to - no one to distract me - free to be of service, if and when I wished. I had spent a lifetime in relationships to prepare for this moment in my life!

I have had a lot of men in my life - I have a really strong attraction towards men (total - energetically, their minds, not just sexually - and in fact, very little in this way, any longer), and these feelings are reciprocated by them. This is demonstrated by the fact that in just this past month, I have had four men proposition me.

One - I met him on a bus, and as it happened, we both got off at the same stop. He then helped me with my grocery shopping and carried it home. A short while later, he made a pass at me at my place…and within a day or two, had proposed a sexual relationship (which, of course, I didn't take him up on). He kept trying to go in that direction, so I gave up on him.

Two - A former boyfriend called me and suggested a "romantic" trip together in the near future.

Three - A man met me online and kept in touch while he was away on a working trip, suggesting that we get into a relationship when he returned shortly.

Four - A man I have known for many years and who has always been somewhat amorous towards me…recently his ardor took an upswing, and he is more outspoken about his feelings towards me.

My way of being interested in men has changed over the years as my sexual drives have changed and matured. Therefore, what I get pleasure in…what I want from each relationship…has hugely changed. What has never changed is my attraction for and by men. A small anecdote demonstrates this: last May (six months away from my 80th birthday) at my monthly Sing-along, there were six women and twelve men present. That speaks volumes to me.

Chapter 26
Family – My Elders of Influence

"There were three - Aunt Lil, Mom, Dad…"
Aunt Lil

The relatives on my mother's side of the family impacted me the most. These people were my grandmother, step-grandfather, plus their five children, spouses, and children (my aunts, uncles and cousins). One of mom's siblings lived in eastern Canada, another one in the States, and one on the family farm in Saskatchewan for a few years until he joined his mom and dad in the Vancouver area.

We were the closest to Aunt Lil, Uncle Peter, and their three boys. We went on picnics, to the beach or Maple Grove Park, which was about a mile from our house, and in those days, a mile was considered an easy walk. Once, we even took their oldest boy with us when we went to visit my grandparents' farm in Saskatchewan. Dad stayed home and worked while my mother took us all by herself on the train. I was four, my sister was two years old, and I think my cousin was three. I marvel that my mom readily took all three of us on a train ride when we were so young. I mean, three young children are quite a handful. But I guess, being a schoolteacher, she was comfortable with children and completely capable of controlling us - or far greater numbers than the three of us!

As we grew older, our families didn't spend as much time together. But we stayed closely connected. That is what happens when you grow up. At first, you are too young to notice the change. Just like in most families, as we entered adulthood, we no longer saw each other except on very special occasions, like when an aunt got married – or on our annual summer picnics.

Our grandparents set the standard for regular family gatherings or reunions as we began to call them because family members would come from south and east and once in a while from the north and even other countries like England and Australia. Every time my Aunt Lil and I saw each other at the reunion, we would light up. But we wouldn't look each other up while away from each other, in-between times.

"Suddenly everything changed…"

It was 2005, and at the time, I think my aunt was eighty-nine. One day, she was walking by herself to the store using her husband's walker, and she tripped on the curb. She lost hold of the walker and tumbled face-first onto the sidewalk. Someone called 911, and an ambulance took her to the hospital. When I first saw her, I thought she was dying - she just lay there, not moving…it was really serious. It took her a few days to gain consciousness…and then she was extremely disoriented and terrified of what was happening and why. Her three sons, grand and great-grand-children, her youngest sister, brother-in-law, and friends all visited when they could.

As for me, it was my summer holidays from teaching piano, and therefore, I had quite a bit of free time on my hands. No one had nearly the kind of time I did - so I visited her daily, and soon became her anchor - the one she depended on. Everyone else continued to visit, but I was the one continuously supplying reassurance, encouragement and love in large doses. In addition, because I was always there, I could see things that even the health professionals hadn't noticed, and therefore, I could be her advocate because I was not afraid to raise issues and push for different care at times.

"Her life hung in a delicate balance…"

For a while, the doctors weren't sure of the extent of her injuries (particularly to her head) and, therefore, to what extent her recovery was apt to be. That went on for weeks, but meanwhile, she was getting stronger physically. One day, I was told she was being moved to another hospital because she was not in a critical condition any longer, and she needed rehab, which the other hospital offered. On the day that she was moved, I wasn't free till much later than usual. When I finally found her new hospital and poked my head in the doorway of her new room, Aunt Lil got all teary-eyed and said, "Oh Maren, I'm so glad you're here."

She shared with me her frustration at the strangeness of it all. She was still disoriented from her accident and didn't quite understand what had happened. They probably explained things to her, but she hadn't understood much of it. That and the fact that this was the first day I had been so late in visiting her just gave way towards more disorientation. Also, a granddaughter visiting from out of town didn't arrive till after me, so my aunt had been alone all day in this strange place with new staff, and with very little understanding of her situation. Until I arrived, she had felt lost and disconnected in every way possible. I regretted the misfortune that I had arrived so late to see her on her "moving" day. However, I saw even more clearly than I previously had, how critical my role was in her recovery, in that she needed someone with her as much as possible to help her to stay calm and oriented throughout each new turn in her days.

Hospital professionals carry out each job at hand very well - but that didn't seem to include explaining things or, particularly, reassuring her. Therefore, from that time on, I spent as much time as I could with my aunt, filling in the missing bits - which, I discovered, were many. It's funny how life works - how it comes back full circle. The important thing was that I was there to take care of her at this time in my aunt's life.

It took her a week before she finally started to figure things out. Before that, even simple things like knowing where she was and what year it was, were hard facts for her to recall. The hospital staff encouraged her to go for a walking tour of her floor. That helped her grow steadily stronger - however, she was never totally sure of herself. At that point, given everything that had happened, she had no confidence in herself. However, the hospital staff and doctors were pleased with her progress…that, at least, was good for me to know.

After a few weeks, they declared her ready for the next stage of rehabilitation…which meant changing to yet a third hospital. They were to take her in a transfer ambulance, again. This time around, however, I wasn't going to make the same mistake - I was determined to be part of her transfer. The day before her move, I got all the details and informed the hospital staff of the role I intended to play.

I arrived early in the morning before the move and connected with my aunt. I made sure she understood what was going to happen. When they came for her, I walked beside her, holding her hand. After she was whisked into the waiting ambulance, I hopped into my car and dashed over to her new hospital in order to get there before her arrival. When her ambulance drove up to the door of her rehab hospital, I was standing on the sidewalk, waiting for her.

They wheeled her out, and I held her hand while we entered the new hospital. Before the attendants left, they helped Aunt Lil into a wheelchair, and I wheeled her into the admitting office. She was an entirely different person this time. Her improved health was probably a part of it, but I had been nervous about the transfer and determined not to have a repeat performance of the earlier move - and it all went smoother than I had even hoped for.

This hospital was entirely different; they made her work hard, even when she didn't want to. It was plain luck that I lived just about a ten minutes' drive from this hospital, and I was able to visit her more than once, daily. I often visited her twice, and she flourished with the extra attention and love. I was able to nip things in the bud before she could get all wound up about something, or if she was about to get wrong or insufficient rehab.

I made sure she got to her appointments on time, that she understood what she was supposed to do, and, most of all, that she felt loved and cared for. The time she spent at the rehabilitation sessions was rough on her, so I needed to make sure that everything went as smoothly as possible. That was another thing that I took on. The rest of the family continued to supply all the love they could give, and she just lapped it up and steadily improved.

"The miraculous recovery, complete..."

When she was getting close to a clean bill of health and able to return home, she went on a little visit home to her husband. The first visit was very hard for her, and she slept through most of it. She didn't want to try it again, even though she really did want to be home and with her husband. She had just had a major accident and at her age, being around medical professionals was quite a bit more reassuring. Everyone just let her be...and eventually, she tried it again and did much better the second time around. The third time was even easier. One day her doctor said she was ready to leave the hospital and move home - just returning periodically for out-patient rehab sessions. I remember my aunt turning to me, full of wonder at the doctor's pronouncement.

"My uncle had his own quiet sort of miracle ..."

My uncle Peter was more than ready to have her come home again. She spent the better part of her first week sleeping on the couch. I think that was her way to adjust to being home. Uncle Peter looked after her at first, and this was a miracle in itself because Aunt Lil had been the primary caregiver for Uncle Peter before she fell. While she was in the hospital for a couple of months, Uncle Peter did all kinds of things he wasn't doing before; like going outside, going on car trips, going for walks, making meals, and many more things. The family was amazed and grateful, because they hadn't been sure how to meet his needs, with Aunt Lil gone.

At first, when Aunt Lil returned, she wasn't able to look after him (or herself), so she watched and let my uncle take on what had been her role previously. Later, as she found her strength, she resumed some of the tasks - but my uncle had become somewhat independent in her absence…and moreover, liked it. Therefore, he wanted to continue doing some things for himself (and now, for his wife).

I suppose there is a life lesson in there for people who think that they cannot be independent of their care givers or their parents. My aunt Lil used to do everything for Uncle Peter - and I do mean everything! However, when push came to shove, he just had to buckle down and take charge of his own life. You can apply the same mind-set to just about anything. When something that we depended on, is no longer possible, we might be worried about how we will manage…and then find out it's fine - we don't need the help after all - nice as it had been – and this was Uncle Peter!

"We did it – with love…"

Aunt Lil had become very reliant on me during these two months. However, after I delivered her home, I promptly developed a head cold. Looking back, this was a blessing in disguise as I had to reluctantly bow out, and they had to pick up the slack. My uncle was a shy, self-reliant person and I think he was delighted that it was just the two of them, left to their own devices to figure things out without my suggestions and perhaps my too easy readiness to help.

After a couple of weeks, I had stopped coughing and was feeling good enough to visit them. My aunt answered the door, which had meant that she walked across their living room, down the inside hallway, through their door, down another hallway, through a second door, and across the foyer to open the outside door for me. All of which was quite an accomplishment, given how unsteady she had been not long before. She was beside herself with excitement when she saw me. First, she threw her arms around my neck, and then she backed up against the wall and threw her arms out wide.

"Look at me, Maren, look at what you did!" she said. She looked vibrant, an incredible picture of health, compared with her sorry state when she arrived in the hospital a few months previously - and her unsure, timid state when she had arrived home just two weeks previously. At first, I was embarrassed that she attributed that outcome to me. However, upon reflection, I realized that she was at least partly correct and that I had been pivotal in her transformation. However, her gratitude was profoundly touching.

My aunt and uncle gratefully settled down into their lives once again, and I visited my aunt only about twice a month after that…which was the middle of September. They had each other for a couple more years when my uncle passed away. When my uncle was gone, Aunt Lil didn't feel comfortable living on her own and she asked one of her grandchildren and her six-year old great grandson to move in with her and help her with her needs. It was a wonderful set-up for all three of them while it lasted - for a couple of years.

By this time, I was living out of town and when I would come into Vancouver once a week, Aunt Lil was often my first stop until her passing, about a couple of years later!

Chapter 27
My Last Days With My Mother

About two months later, my mother, Aunt Lil's elder sister, made a big decision. Near the end of November 2005, my mother declared her intention to stop eating. What had led up to this decision was an invisible brain condition that caused Mom to feel like she was in a thick fog. This, in turn, made it difficult for her to be with people. She always felt like she was very far away, and it took a massive effort for her to be present with people - her family and friends. It was enervating, uncomfortable, and made her feel nervous. This went on for a few years, getting progressively worse, and she was going out in public less and less.

Going to church and family gatherings, attending her church's women's group, and being a part of her monthly educational sisterhood; these activities had been the highlight of her life. She had essentially built her life around these activities before. But now she was willingly giving up on them. That made me realize just how bad she must be feeling. She hung in there quite a while after she first gave up church. At first, she and dad listened to an evangelist's service every Sunday. Next she stopped going to family gatherings (and eventually even our family reunion picnics every summer.

"Mom's biggest fear…"

But what turned out to be the final straw for my mom was that she had started feeling like she was holding Dad back…which was probably somewhat true. Dad was in love with her, to her end and even to his own. He just couldn't bear leaving her alone while he was off and having fun. At first, he would try finding someone to stay with her even if he stepped out for only a short while. However, it seemed hard to find someone that Mom was also comfortable with. The obvious choices were my sister and me.

My sister travelled a lot and therefore was not often available. As for me, I was usually the designated driver to chauffeur Dad to his special occasions, so that made me unavailable, too. Then Dad just gave up the idea of going…and I could understand why mom felt terrible when that happened. For me, it was difficult to see the person who raised me, giving life up like that. But I guess old age happens, and people who once seemed invincible… they falter. When Mom made her announcement, Dad panicked and phoned my sister, who went right over. After talking with Mom, she realized that Mom was very lucid and had carefully thought this out. My sister, having been a doctor, knew that if Mom followed this through, that she would soon need nursing care. The next day, my sister went with our dad to his doctor to share this with him and to enlist his help in finding a place our mom could be cared for during this process. He soon found a senior care facility that had that service already in place…and it just happened to be in the building right next door to their condo!

My sister helped mom choose a couple of pieces of furniture for her room in this facility, plus some pictures and curios that had special meaning for mom. My brother-in-law put Christmas lights up on the patio railing of my Mom and Dad's condo so she could easily spot her home.

The doctor and my sister communicated mom's wishes with the care facility where she was going. Then they took her over to her new home where Mom and Dad did some paperwork that the care facility required. During all this, I stayed at home and tried to digest this news. It was a tough time for everyone involved.

I knew just how hard all of this was hitting me when I saw my mother going through it…so I can only imagine that the whole thing must have been very tough for her, also. She was leaving her lifelong partner - the love of her life - and moving to a senior's facility, with people she didn't know at all. Even though the condo was right there next to the facility, all she could do was stare out the window at the lights on her old balcony. As it turned out, however, because Dad was equally missing her, he spent a lot of time just sitting beside her in her new "home." That way, they had each other's company as much as possible.

But although that brought Dad some comfort, it also brought an equal amount of sorrow over his love's plight. When this became too much for him, he'd head home and work on finishing writing and mailing his Christmas cards that he and Mom had begun before she moved to the care facility - I think they had a Christmas list of about 60 friends and relatives from all over the world. That gave him something else to get absorbed in.

"Mom's final home…"

I went to visit her as soon as she was settled. By that time, I had somewhat come to terms with mom's decision. She was peaceful and expressed her gratitude that the staff was kind and thoughtful. Also, she said that she felt so at home in her room with the few personal possessions that were arranged around her. It particularly made her feel more "at home," being able to have tea with visitors. Therefore, whenever we visited her, we had tea together. I went to see her almost every day for the next seven weeks while she was alive.

During the first couple of weeks Mom spent a lot of time sitting near the window – and lying down for only a couple of naps during her day. At first, she had had a drink of tea twice a day. My sister had taken Mom her own teapot and her favorite teacups plus her electric kettle so she could make tea for herself and, in addition, could serve tea for her visitors. After a couple of weeks, she stopped getting up for anyone and just stayed lying in bed to visit. At some point, she stopped drinking tea, and drank hot water, as part of her transition. Eventually, this became just sips of water. The caregivers always asked her if she wanted anything to eat and she would always answer, "No thank you." They had never seen anyone so strong (or polite)!

One evening, I realized they were mashing her blood pressure medication into applesauce. I reminded them that she had requested no food, to which they were quick to say that it was a lot easier to swallow with the applesauce. However, I noticed that they discontinued the apple sauce right after that. It was her decision… it was her life, and I wanted to make sure that she had her wishes fulfilled. Now, as I write this, I realize I didn't at that time cop to the blood thinner medication - what a bizarre thing to be giving her, seeing she was doing everything she could legally think of…to end her life. Apparently, no one else copped to it either!

The staff got her up and dressed her every day. At first, she would mostly get up with her visitors. After a couple of weeks, she was staying in bed more, only getting up for the occasional guest, or some tea. By the third week, which was Christmas, Mom rarely got up any longer. She got up just to go to the bathroom. There was a Christmas party soon after she arrived. The facility invited all the families of the residents…all my children and a sister of Mom's and her husband plus my sister, brother-in-law and dad were all present - there were a couple of friends, too.

By that time, Mom wasn't getting up at all for visitors. She was dozing off most of the time, but that day she spoke to each family member. All of us took our turn being with her. Soon after that, Mom began to withdraw, more and more. It wasn't long before she had her eyes closed all the time. When that phase started, I suggested to the staff that they not dress mom up anymore for visitors as it was becoming more difficult to take her clothes on and off - I thought it best to think of her comfort as her visiting phase seemed done.

"Mom's completion..."

However, there was one important thing that seemed incomplete, and so I went to see mom's sister, my Aunt Lil. Having grown up together, she had been closest to Mom. These days, since her "falling" accident, Aunt Lil rarely went further than she could walk. This day, I told my aunt how Mom was...and wondered if she wanted to go to see her before Mom slipped further away. My aunt quickly answered, "Yes," so I drove her out to see mom.

When Mom heard her sister's voice, Mom opened her eyes and said, "Lily?" My aunt Lil sat on Mom's bed. They got their two heads together and chattered away happily, like two little girl sisters together. After aunt Lil left, no other visitors saw Mom's eyes again or heard her voice - the only exception was to whisper, "Water." I brought my daughter-in-law and my three grandchildren one day soon after that, but Mom was done with people. It wasn't long before she spent most of her time, rolled onto her other side, facing away from the room. After that, I rarely found her facing into the room and never saw her eyes open again. By now, she always seemed to be breathing deeply, as if she was asleep. She didn't seem to pay any more attention to life going on around her.

I drove to be with Mom most days and usually popped in to see my Dad. With mom being in the senior care facility, he busied himself doing his annual, mammoth Christmas card project. He and Mom had done their cards every year at the end of November. This year it was particularly satisfying to him, as it helped him cope with his stress. To handle my own stress, I had brought a huge stack of their photo albums to Mom's room and put them on a table for myself…and visitors…to browse while there. I enjoyed that little activity, reviewing our life together. However, going over the memories while looking at her withering away, was also haunting. Losing my mother was probably the hardest thing I have ever gone through, especially given it was her choice. However, I do know…and accept…that it was her decision… and she knew what was best for her. None of us could know what she was going through. It was out of our hands. She was completely lucid when she made her decision, and we had no other choice but to accept that.

"However, I didn't know the degree to which I was stressed out until…"

I may have been very accepting of her decision, but I misjudged how bothered I was by my mother's decision to choose death. One evening, after I tucked Mom in, as I was driving home, I didn't notice that the car ahead of me had stopped in the tunnel where I was driving. Seeing my mother in that state had taken a lot out of me, and I guess I was still in a daze as I rear-ended that car. To make matters worse, four cars were involved in this accident. Three of us had crashed into the fourth car in front.

About three minutes earlier, that same car had driven beside me on the icy loop of the on-ramp just before then entering the tunnel. It was a Porsche with two very young men driving it, laughing, screeching, and sliding. I didn't feel comfortable with that and put on my brakes and let it shoot ahead of me as I declared to myself that I would hang back and not meet up with it again. Well, the two young men entered the tunnel and about three-quarters of the way through they slammed on their brakes and spun their car sideways.

The car way in front of me braked but slammed into them. By this time, I had distractedly caught up to them, and at the last minute, realizing they were stopped, slammed on my brakes, but collided into them anyway. At the same time, a car drove along beside me on my right. He didn't notice that the rear of the Porsche was sticking out in his lane and slammed into its rear.

While we were all collecting our wits, the Porsche started up, righted itself, and drove away. The rest of us; all able to drive, then also drove out of the tunnel. At that particular place on the freeway, there's both off-and-on ramps, abutments for an overpass...and no legitimate shoulder.

Finally, I (and the other two) found a place to pull over. The car we all hit did not pull over there - and the driver who hit the Porsche in its rear said he saw it stopped back under the overpass.

The Porsche driver never did report his accident - and no one ever saw them again! With the agreement of the others, who had all jumped out of their cars by now, I phoned 911 and asked that they send a police officer to our accident site. The people in the car that I had hit said they were going to see if they could find the Porsche and they took off, saying they'd be back. A policeman then arrived. He asked a lot of questions of the man and me. Then the other car returned, and that driver joined the questioning.

We exchanged information, we all agreed we'd phone in, make police reports and go to ICBC (our B.C. mandatory insurance company). When I went to ICBC, I found out that the Porsche hadn't shown up, yet. Much later, I asked again, if it had ever come forward - but no.

I don't know what I learned from that experience besides that Porsches must be built from solid steel to have been able to be hit three times - and this was including the driver's door twice and also the rear - and be able to drive away with no one dead (though we'll never know if they were unhurt). When they passed me on that on-ramp, they were looking for trouble - and they succeeded big time! And they got off, scot-free. There's no obvious moral to this story…for me, at least.

But I do know that I usually am a pretty good driver. In hindsight, I can understand that it was mostly due to the emotional stress and being in a daze after being with my mother. I'd like to think that I could have avoided that, had it not been for the fact that I was on my way back from the hospice.

"I declare that Mom made a powerful choice…"

Out of the accident, I certainly learned how stressed out I was about Mom. Eventually, after many hours of sitting, thinking and feeling, I came to see something powerful about Mom's choice. She had started to feel powerless over the way her life was going…and she stopped eating as the only way she found to take her power back.

For the most part, her family felt stressed, upset, and sad, but at the same time, acknowledged that it was her choice - even if not ours! My mom has always been a very level-headed and stubborn woman. Huh, maybe that's where I got it from! And a great mother, always taking care of my dad and her family, even when we were being headstrong and doing the annoying things that children do. We could not see this as a crazy, spur-of-the-moment decision…but rather, clear, level-headed…and stubborn.

She died alone, in the early morning of January 6th, 2006, almost seven weeks after she entered the Care Facility. A caregiver had found her on their first morning rounds, and then they phoned my sister, who called our Dad and me. I am not an early morning person, usually…rather I'm a night owl. But on this particular morning, I was awake at about four or five o'clock, for no discernible reason…and because I was wide awake, I got up and began to do some reading online.

It was almost as if I was waiting for the phone call. Mom visited all her girls in some way or another, that morning. My daughter, her granddaughter, had a dream of her grandma. So did my daughter-in-law. Also, my granddaughter (Mom's "great") said she was dreaming of her great grandmother. My son said, with a laugh, "Grandma knew better than to try to wake me up at that time of day!"

"Mom's timing was impeccable."

My sister and husband were on their way on a boat trip that would have been difficult to cancel because of how much was involved. Whereas, with Mom giving us an early start to our day, they handled everything they needed to, for Dad's sake, regarding Mom. They emptied what had been her room, stayed with Dad while he processed paperwork with the care home, as well as a bit of government/bank stuff. Then they unloaded all the furniture at Dad's apartment, and I drove them to their ferry on time.

As for me, I was to join my family at Whistler resort that day; but just a day earlier I had wondered if I would be able to keep my plans. That would have meant both my sister and I would be gone at the same time, leaving the whole emotional load to Dad. However, as things turned out, I was still able to go as planned. Thank you, Mom.

Some of my kids would have felt bad for not being in town with us all, at that time. However, I was able to bring the news to them - and then we spent the weekend sharing beautiful memories of our mother...and grandmother...and great-grandmother.

Chapter 28
The Story of Dad - Post Mom

The love of his life – for over seventy years – gone

Dad mourned. It was a huge loss for him. At the time my mother passed, she was a month short of her ninety-fifth birthday, and Dad was just over his ninety-ninth. They had been together for a month short of seventy-one years. Their age was an amazing feat of its own, and the length of their marriage was a rare phenomenon, these days. No one voiced the question to Dad, of course, but we all wondered how he was going to make out with Mom gone. At first, he was pretty quiet. Fortunately, a fairly big project came due right at that time.

A widowed friend, who had turned one hundred years old the previous summer, had died in the fall. Dad had been the executor of her husband's estate for many years - part of which was being trustee of the Educational Trust Fund for his friend's nieces and nephews. As an aside, Dad, who was a chartered accountant, was often asked over the years to be the executor of people's estates - it was something that could replace his work and that he took great pride in doing well.

Now, the timing was fortuitous as it gave him something else to mull over which helped him to move on from the loss he had suffered. Dad had gratefully switched over from his Christmas card project to working on finalizing the Educational Trust Fund that had come due at that time. Even though my dad was 99 years old, he was still doing these kinds of things that he had taken on as a retired chartered accountant - and now, nearly forty years later, still enjoyed doing them for friends and relatives (although I think that was his last one - he had even begun letting my sister take over the doing of his own tax return)!

Surviving the passing of a loved one is a part of life. I have always noticed that when someone passes, it is hard on the ones who are left to live with the loss. It is often unbearably hard, knowing that someone who has been there for so long for you, is suddenly gone…and many elders don't survive long after losing their spouse of so many years. If it was hard for me to lose Mom, then I can only imagine how hard it must have been on dad. We got to see Mom a few times a year, but he had been with her every day for seventy years…waking up, and going to sleep with her, every single day.

Therefore, it was terrific timing for him to get his hands on such a project just then. Looking after the educational trust for all the young nephews and nieces of his friend and his friend's wife had kept going for another year at least, after her death. The tax ruling stated that Dad couldn't file the final tax papers on her estate's behalf until the last of them turned twenty-one and received their final inheritance. He also had a fair amount of paperwork to do in completing Mom's business, such as notification of her death or taking her name off all their joint affairs. I suppose it gave my father a purpose, something to get out of bed for, every day.

"His riding buddy, Sharon – a precious part of extending his riding years…"

Another thing that helped him was his weekly rides on his horse with his riding buddy, Sharon. He had been riding all his life and for the past ten or fifteen years he had had a riding companion. How Sharon got started was that she wanted to ride, but she didn't know that much about it. She didn't even really know where to ride and, quite understandably, was a little intimidated by it all. She had heard about Dad because he was a well-known figure amongst horse people in the area of Campbell Valley Park in Langley near the U.S. border. Someone at the stable recommended she speak with Dad and see if he would be okay with her tagging along on some of his rides, at least to get her started. He was willing, and so their riding relationship began.

When Sharon joined him, Dad was riding three times a week. However, after a few years, his heart wasn't in it anymore…he thought that it was too much time away from Mom in addition to not leaving him much time to do other things. In the beginning, the young lady found three times a week too much for her, so she didn't go every time. But by the time that Dad cut his rides down to once a week, Sharon sometimes went to the stable on her own for a second or third ride.

At some point, Sharon bought herself her own horse and would go to the stable much more often after that, just to work with her horse. Because hers was not leased as Dad's was, meant that she was responsible for all her horse's needs. By this time, she was a competent rider, and she felt confident riding by herself. Therefore, it wasn't a hardship to ride by herself, now…although, we knew that she loved best to go out with Dad. Lots of his friends teased him about it because she was about forty or fifty years younger than he was.

"A big moment…"

It was a tough moment for Dad when he chose to give up his Driver's License. It was in his hundredth year, a few months before he turned one hundred. He had broken his wrist earlier in the year when he had been wrestling with his horse, attempting to get the horse to go into its horse trailer. Dad was pulling pretty hard, and when his horse changed direction, causing there to be slack in the rope, he lost his balance - and down he went, taking the brunt of his weight on his wrist.

Dad was unable to drive for a month or two, and his doctor had rescinded his driver's license. This was no small matter for Dad who soon realized that he would have to take both a written exam as well as a driving exam - neither of which he had ever done in his life. When he was a young man, a few farmers were beginning to get cars - but only those who had a fair bit of money. My grandfather bought one of the first ones in his community, so Dad was initiated into the world of cars before he was old enough to drive or own one. In those days, if you could walk in the door of the license bureau, had enough money to pay for the license…and could sign your name…you could have it.

This being the case, Dad walked in, put down his money, signed his name…and got his first driver's license. However, on thinking about it now, Dad figured that he wasn't going to start all the licensing nonsense for the first time when he was almost one hundred years old. On top of that, he had always told himself that he would give up his license when he turned one hundred – and he was by then only a couple of months short of that.

"Now he had a big dilemma…"

However, now he was wondering how he was going to get to the stable to ride. He talked with me a couple of times about it, and how he was really against his riding friend, Sharon, driving him back and forth. He thought that really wouldn't be fair to her, even though she had already offered, long before it became a reality. She had said that if and when he gave up his license, she was fully prepared to transport him. I reminded dad of her offer and pointed out to him that maybe it wouldn't be fair to her if he turned down her offer.

I reasoned with him that she enjoyed her rides the most when Dad was with her (she had confided this to me). I think my sister also put the same bee in his bonnet.

We didn't want dad to give up riding just because he was unable to drive over to the stable. All of us had responsibilities of our own to take care of - so we didn't want to give these up when he had valid transportation to and from his hobby. It was up to him to work this out. As it turned out, when his arm was ready for riding and he had no license any longer, he graciously allowed Sharon to begin picking him up for their ride each Wednesday morning. Most of the time, she returned him about two or three hours later…and once in a while, they would stop at the little pub near the stable and have a bowl of soup.

She did this for about a year and a half, and altogether, she rode faithfully with him for ten to fifteen years; their friendship was mutual, each supplied something the other needed and valued…so it wasn't only a means to an end…it was a sweet friendship. People either forget - or don't know - that honest, real and deep friendships are possible…and sometimes between the most improbable of people!

"The moment came to recreate himself..."

When his Trust Fund paperwork was complete, he phoned me up and told me that he'd like me to take him shopping. He wanted to buy a new wardrobe though he didn't want to toss the old one because most of it didn't look old. That all made perfect sense to me - I knew that this was not about needing a new wardrobe, in the usual sense. This seemed to be dad's way of marking the moment when he decided his life was still worth living.

When I took him there, Dad had a blast. We went to a moderately high-end store that sold men's clothing - particularly dressy. He was an older gentleman, so naturally, we wouldn't be buying him jeans and those sorts of things. Dad had been there before and liked their clothing as well as their way of treating their clients.

From the moment that we entered the store, till we departed, they gave dad royal treatment; I am pretty sure that they were fighting behind the scenes to be one of the people serving him. In fact, there were far more clerks standing around, watching and listening, than were needed. Dad was in good form, telling stories and had them laughing...and ooh-ing and ah-ing. It was exactly what he needed. He left the store with a bounce in his step and feeling renewed.

Another thing he did around the same time - and for the same reason…to signal moving on…was to join a nearby Golf club. He wasn't a golfer, but they had a lovely dining room that gave members special discounts and very good service. That turned out to be a great move and he used it as an extension of his own dining-room. He invited a certain number of guests a month (it was a package I think for a monthly price). I don't remember the details - but I do remember that he was extremely pleased with himself for signing up.

Being around people and away from things that constantly reminded him of his love, was good for his soul. He needed to be with people. The most powerful thing that can be done to get over losing someone special is just to convince yourself to move on. If you don't take this step, eventually - albeit, a lot more slowly - you will move on. But if you do take it - not allowing yourself to wallow in self-pity, and, rather, just move ahead - that doesn't mean that you are, in any way, disrespecting the memory of your loved one. Instead, you are accepting that they have departed…and you are moving on.

"Dad was coming up to his one hundredth year mark…"

It wasn't long before Dad began to plan his one-hundredth birthday "bash," as I fondly called it. He thought of people close to him in his life, and he didn't see anyone leaping forward and offering to put on his party. He also voiced to me that he didn't see that any one of us was free enough to put it on. Well, this wasn't entirely true, because my sister, my aunt and I would have. On the other hand, we were thrilled just to be helping him, rather than doing all the thinking and the doing. It was much better that he was doing it by himself. That way he could have what he wanted, and of course, my sister, aunt and I were there to help him out. And additionally, that was just another way to keep himself happily busy, which he needed a lot.

In a way, though, Dad was correct. I was tied up a lot of the time with courses and study of my new-found diversion, which was real estate investment. In addition, my sister was going to be gone for the five summer months from May till about late September. She and her husband went out on the water every summer in their large boat (a reclaimed fishing boat). They did a lot of fishing - but it was with lines on poles (unlike when people fish for a living). Their boat design was a sophisticated design and had been adapted from what had originally been a fishing boat…therefore "fishing boat" does not give the right impression)!

Their trips took them up the coast to Alaska and the Queen Charlotte Islands (or its historic name, Haida Gwaii). They were either on the inside of Vancouver Island, which was sheltered by the Mainland, or on the outside, or western side of Vancouver Island. We all knew that nothing was going to change that plan. Therefore Dad, was probably right in concluding the party planning was up to him,

"Details details…"

I inherited my Dad's ability and love for details. Even approaching his one-hundredth birthday, his capacity to project and figure out details was amazing. I loved and appreciated this quality even more at this moment. It was so amazing to see that even at his advanced age he was still working in this high capacity.

He chose the venue first… "his" Golf Clubhouse turned out to have the most all round, appealing offer. Next he worked on the guest list, followed by the printed invitation. Once he knew the numbers, and the wording of his invitation, he asked me to walk over with him to the printers to place the order. While waiting for it to be ready for pick-up, Dad worked on things like choosing the menu, and the seating arrangement - he wanted to decide who he would place beside each guest. It took a lot of thought, but he wanted to do it.

When the printer phoned to say his invitations were ready, Dad went and picked them up by himself. Addressing them all kept him happily busy for quite a long while. He had sixty invites, and almost all of them accepted - even the ones who were out of town. At the end of each project, he would bring me into it to give him feedback. Sometimes he took my suggestions well and other times he didn't want to make the changes I suggested - and I didn't mind that in the slightest.

After the passing of my mother, I didn't know how much time I had left with him. Just being a part of the process was good enough for me. We worked very harmoniously, with give and take, as we proceeded along. This was not something we were able to do very well in my younger years, and I was interested to notice the change that had taken place between us.

"Little touches…"

The people in his closest circle added a few touches of their own. A granddaughter and her partner suggested we make buttons with the pictures of Dad, Mom, our family, and his relatives and friends. One of my sons and I went through Dad and Mom's albums, stacks of them. We then photocopied over a hundred pictures to be used for the buttons. We made duplicates and put these up on three large poster boards to be set on easels for viewing at the party. We took that upon ourselves as Dad didn't know any of these plans. I told him that a few things were being planned that he didn't know of. He said, "O….kay…." rather reluctantly. He was afraid we were going to blindside him and embarrass him; he didn't quite trust anyone on this, but I took his response as a "yes."

Dad didn't have anything to do with the decorations, and he was happy to leave that to my artist girlfriend and me. She had decorated Mom's 90th, so both dad and I were confident in her ability to do the job. Because Dad was a horseman, she worked horses heavily into the theme. She painted pictures of horses that she then stuck to the walls, added some balloons and colorful streamers, and the room was transformed and ready for a party.

Another nice touch was added when Dad's great-nephew offered to be the roving photographer, and that added a great deal of enjoyment long after the party. We assumed that we didn't have much time left with Dad, so having pictures taken of his special day was much appreciated.

I decided to get his approval of one thing that I added in, and that was a "Sing-along." He and I had a long history of singing together, so I thought he might like it...and he did. I got out some songbooks and helped him choose his favorites, like O Danny Boy, and some rousing Irish ones because that was his birth right. We had put our hearts and souls into making this a special day because it was an extraordinary moment for him.

"Everyone loved the buttons..."

When it came to the party time, the buttons were a huge success; Dad also seemed delighted. We had the buttons put into two or three baskets, and as people came in the door, they were asked if they would like to choose and wear one, or more. It's a good thing that we made lots of extras because most wanted more than one button. They kept them as souvenirs to take with them to remember and celebrate my father's life. There were squeals of delight as they'd spot pictures of various family members that were taken long ago - and many wanted a picture of both dad and mom as well. A couple of great-grandchildren circulated the room finding individuals who missed the baskets at the door when coming in.

Dad also didn't know about the poster boards with many of the same pictures as were on the buttons…plus there were many more pictures that covered Dad's one hundred years. After the party was over, I took the poster boards to Dad's suite and propped them up against the furniture for a few weeks so he could enjoy them for a while longer, until he felt ready to dismantle them.

"Dad was good-natured about the roasting his former partner gave..."

One surprise was the speech given by Dad's former partner from his chartered accountant firm. Dad had been a little afraid of asking him to say a few words, and Dad was right to be worried. It turned out to be more of a roast than a toast. Dad had tried to control the speech by giving his partner a few suggestions of things to cover. Well, Dad lost that one, and we all had good laughs. Though, in his favor, Dad was a good sport about it. The evening was a huge success - and dad was both happy and satisfied. I was thrilled with how smoothly it went and what a wonderful time we all had.

Dad and I were a good team now. But, during most of my life, that hadn't been the case. Dad had been very controlling, and most often I had felt left out of the picture when plans were being made. I didn't like hearing about things only after they were complete. However, I had experienced a considerable change in this, a few years before - while my mother was still alive. Mom asked me if I would consider driving them on a memory trip. To be specific, mom wanted me to drive them on a trip, east and north of Vancouver into the Caribou where dad had spent much time hunting and both mom and dad had rented cabins for holidays - usually beside lakes - where dad would go on "trail rides" while mom knitted or made dinner while waiting for dad to return. When mom was along, dad didn't usually go on a trail ride every day, but instead would take mom and go driving around, on some of his "free' days.

"I didn't have the heart to say 'no'…"

That was a hard decision for me to make. Driving isn't my favorite activity. In addition, I had a whole lot of projects on the go that I didn't want to give up. I don't remember how long the trip was going to be but maybe a couple of weeks. I hadn't spent more than a day at a time with them for many years, and the idea didn't thrill me to be honest. But…I couldn't say no to my mom. Even though I had grown up and grown apart from my parents, I still loved them a lot and decided to make a compromise…and that was for me to be able to camp on my own, at least a little bit apart from them. They intended to stay in motels and cabins, whereas I wanted to tent beside or near lakes or rivers. They agreed with my request and in a few days after mom asked me, I told her that I agreed to drive them.

I came over to their apartment early in the morning the day we were leaving. I was afraid my dad would freak out when he saw how much stuff I had brought. He let me in the garage area, and I parked behind his car. I told him that I would take everything out of my car and lay it first on the garage floor. Next, I would select and decide the best place for everything to go. I told him not to freak out by the size of the pile because I was willing to leave some things behind if it turned out to be too much in the end.

I asked dad to go upstairs and bring down his and mom's suitcases and bags so that I'd be sure to have enough space for their things. That didn't take him long, and I now had everything. In the end, I did leave a couple of unnecessary things behind, but it didn't take me long to pack all the rest in. I went upstairs to mom and dad's suite and told them that I was done. I invited dad to come down and pass inspection. Down we went, and when dad saw that there was nothing left on the garage floor, he slowly looked in the trunk and then in the car. He turned to me with a big smile on his face and said that he hadn't thought it was possible to get it all in and so neatly, with lots of room left inside the car for us to comfortably sit.

That was rare praise from my father because he and I would usually be at odds about this sort of thing. However, I was still thinking about him as if I was a little girl. Because I had limited knowledge as a young girl, he was usually right to point out my mistakes. However, since then I had matured and had become skilled at many things…one being, how to pack skillfully - learned from the best by guess who - so his praise needn't have shocked me.

Just the same, I could hardly believe what I was hearing because it was so far from my old memory of me and dad. When I was very young, dad would have already packed the car, and I'd come along with some more things. I could always get a few more things worked into nooks and crannies. However, when dad came along, he'd notice the newly packed items and promptly wipe me aside, and either finish it the way he wanted, or repack the car from scratch. That would make me upset because I thought things were fine the way I had fit them in…or at least I thought so when I was a kid. However, he would not relent.

"A corner had been turned in our relationship…"

This was a different dad - and most probably a different me as well. We both went upstairs to get mom - and on the way down, dad gave a rave review to my mom on my packing job. This was a good omen. However, dad and I had to work out the driving part. As far as I was concerned, I was along on this trip to do the driving; I hadn't thought I was a mere back-up. At first, dad wanted to drive and get us on our way...but then, it was hard to find the right moment when he would change over with me. I think I had a nap. I had been up late the night before at a dance, so this was welcome enough, even though my mood was one of exasperation.

Finally, dad gave the car over to me - and I drove the rest of that day. The next day, dad spelled me off when he noticed I was drowsy. After a couple of days, I was doing all the driving, and I realized that dad had just had to get used to the idea of not doing everything by himself. It was a big moment for him, letting go of control - particularly of driving which he had controlled his entire life. But he was a different person now, and it didn't take him long before he realized that it was very relaxing to be chauffeured!

"The trip was a huge success – all way around…"

Mom and dad both enjoyed the trip "down memory lane" as did I, having visited many of the same places during my lifetime. Some trips had been with mom and dad when I was young – they took my sister and me to various lakes or dude ranches for summer holidays; and others later on with my husband and children. In addition to revisiting old memories, I enjoyed the new memories created by this trip with mom and dad. In addition, it is one thing to go on a trip with your parents when you are a young child and another thing altogether to go with them as elders. It seemed that that trip changed the way we viewed one another. That parent-child one was finished and now we looked at each other more like equals.

Just as I had imagined I would, I thoroughly enjoyed the tenting beside or near lakes…and the swims. A bonus was that I completed a project that I had brought along…one that had been hanging around for a long time. However, it turned out to be very easy to complete it in the quiet focus that was possible when there was nothing else to distract me.

The following year, I took mom and dad on a simpler version of the trip we had taken a year earlier. Instead of pulling up stake almost every day like we had the previous year, we selected three favorite places and stayed a few days in each; it worked out great and was much more relaxing. Again, mom and dad gave me a lot of time on my own, so it was a great holiday for me too - whereas I was their "ticket" for the things that they weren't so able to manage anymore...a win-win. A few years went by before I made more trips because the following year, they flew to Haida Gwaii (the new name for the Queen Charlottes). My sister and husband picked them up and toured them on their boat, all around the islands.

During the following winter, mom and dad went on a Hawaiian cruise for a change. By the next year, my mother wasn't up to traveling any longer. In looking back, I was delighted that mom had asked me when she did - and that I had accepted her request to drive them on all those trips. I consider myself fortunate that I was able to spend that kind of quality time with her because soon, she left us.

"Bella Coola – what a trip that was…"

The summer after mom was gone, dad asked me if I would drive him to Bella Coola. This was another of Dad's ways of moving on. Bella Coola wasn't a place that was a big memory of mom. Rather, it was on his Bucket List…and what a trip it was! As usual we would often stop at lakes along the way for me to swim. By this time, dad was using a walker, and he would usually wheel his walker down near the water and sit on it while I swam. Then we would eat a picnic lunch before driving on. Often, we were able to find a place on a lake to stay overnight…and of course, I had to swim again! I've often told people that I'm a "fish" and that swimming is one of my greatest pleasures…so it wasn't surprising that on this trip, I took every chance I could to swim.

I remember that there was one rather uncomfortable one in a lake that was taken over by mosquitoes, and I had to flail my arms rapidly in every direction until I was in the water, swatting them out of my swimming path. Even then, they were following me as I swam, so I had to duck under water until I was quite a way out from the shore. Then to return, I had to swim underwater close to the beach and then run for it when I got out. Dad and I always had an enjoyable and fun time together and usually when I swam, he liked to sit at the lake's edge, watching me. This particular time, though, he was wise and watched the goings on from the safety of our cabin (the window had screens for a reason)! What a hoot!

To add to the "fun," in the morning, we woke up to float planes starting up their motors. They did that all morning long. We hadn't noticed the aircraft when we booked in. We were told that it happens on most of the lakes in the caribou - taking tourists to remote sports camps - and we thought we were quite isolated, ourselves, but apparently, the sports camps were even more so. What was happening was that the many planes moored outside our cabin would fly one group out and return over and over again until everyone was gone. Then the same thing would happen later, returning them at night. Dad and I acknowledged that it wasn't so great, being beside a lake with all that commotion. It seemed bizarre to us that such a remote, beautiful spot should be noisier than the cities we came from!

We drove to Bella Coola that day, stopping at more lakes, of course. The road trip on that day, alone, was memorable (and not in a particularly good way). I've forgotten what the locals called it, but it had "death" expressed in its name. That much I remember. Oh, now I remember...it was called, "Suicide Hill." The reason that it got its name was that it was full of switchbacks and wasn't wide enough for more than one car at a time. Therefore, when we met someone, we had to dive into a little pull-out that had been hollowed out of the cliff by previous drivers. Also, the hill was so steep that we had to use our brakes almost the whole time until we could smell the rubber burning - even using low gear.

It was scary. I was glad to arrive, safely, at the bottom. However, I knew that it was up to me to drive us back out of there because I certainly couldn't ask my dad to do it. By now, he had long since given up control in my favor, so I was the only one to drive us to safety. It was a quaint little town…very old and existed around the arrival and leaving of a ferry. We booked into the hotel and then made the rounds of the few stores that Bella Bella boasted: a little museum, a gift shop and a general store. We had a lovely "homemade" meal at our hotel and a great sleep in this sleepy little town that did not have any seaplanes!

Boy…did I ever heave a massive sigh of relief when I had gotten us back up Suicide Hill and safely on the highway again! That trip did take its toll on me and I was glad to arrive back home. After that, I decided that I shouldn't drive on any more trips. It was a little more than I felt good about any longer. Unlike my dad, I had never had a picture of myself driving until anywhere near one hundred – or even past eighty. Even though I was really glad to have done these trips, this was it… "finito". As it turned out, my sister agreed with me - and she asked me if I would be willing to take dad on an Alaska cruise instead. That sounded like an interesting alternative - although, all my life, I had become seasick whenever I was out on water. I wondered, though, if I would be affected in the same way on a large cruise ship as opposed to a smaller boat. I accepted!

"Alaska Cruise – the 100th-year gift from my sister and brother-in-law…"

The following summer, my sister and her husband bought two tickets for dad and myself to go on a cruise to Alaska as a gift for his one hundredth year birthday. They wanted him to go on a memorable trip, and they are never free at that time of year to take him anywhere, themselves. Dad and I were both thrilled about the Alaska cruise. Even though I had to contend with a tiny bit of seasickness, it wasn't anything I couldn't handle with a little bit of help from "seasick" medicine. This was far easier for me than taking dad touring all over western BC!

We soon found that dad's walker was okay for a few activities on board, but for the most part, the distances on the ship were too great for him, and we asked for a wheelchair. That made it very relaxing for dad as well as giving me more exercise because I could go as fast as I wanted to go and I didn't have to worry about dad falling behind. He and I marveled at the variety and quantity of food available to us at almost any time of day. I, for one, came off the cruise ship heavier than when I arrived on board. The entertainment was first class, the service was perfect, and we had a fabulous time.

Once we were back home, we carried right on with our regular visits. When mom was alive, I was regularly visiting her once a week, on dad's horseback riding day. She would still be in bed when he left for his morning ride, and I went in time to help her get up, dressed, fed, and out for a walk. I stayed with her until dad came home, which would usually be around lunchtime.

Or if he were staying for lunch with a riding friend, then I would stay till mom lay down for her nap. Dad felt a bit gypped if I didn't stay a while - so if he hadn't had lunch, I would stay through lunchtime. If he had, sometimes I stayed a little longer after mom had gone down for her nap. Often, I didn't feel like I could spare any more time from my studies and projects and would skedaddle off home once he arrived back at their apartment. Looking back, I realize that was such nonsense - not staying…what else could really have been more important!

"When Mom was gone, I carried right on with the visiting tradition…"

A weekly visit seemed to work - but obviously, I changed it to a day when he didn't ride his horse. I usually stayed much longer with dad than I had with mom. She had not been very communicative in those last months, whereas dad was very lively and into things right up to his last few days.

Dad always loved me to sit and listen to one of the oldies - Perry Como, Frank Sinatra, or a Lawrence Welk show. I still think back to those days that I spent, first with mom and dad, and then with dad, alone. How blessed I feel when I think of my relationship with them. Once dad was on his own, I became much closer to him than I had before because now he was the only one left - and my attention was undivided.

For me to have them that long, was precious in itself, but the quality of our relationship was rare. However, I only realized that, long after they were gone, as over the years I have shared my experiences with my friends. They have let me know just how precious our relationship was. People don't usually get that kind of longevity with their parents because people typically don't get to live as long as my folks did…it is amazing that we had as much time as we did. That was a blessing in and of itself because I got to learn so much from them and make their last days a lot better. I have always believed that I needed to better myself at every opportunity that I had…and that included having a good relationship with my folks. It hadn't always been so. I only began to take responsibility for how our relationships were (and weren't) back in 1981 after I had completed the first personal development course that I took (called EST).

That was when I first became aware of the importance of one's early relationships with both mother and father. That's also when I learned that I had control over how they were affecting my life presently. It was all news to me…I had no idea, really, how my relationships with my mom and dad had been, or how they were impacting my current life. I had never realized that there was any point to even thinking about that…it all just was how it was. I just had to put up with it – and how my relationships with them were. Well…what a big wake up that all was.

Since then ('81), I got to "work" on our relationships for the next 25 to 30 years while they were still alive. I was so fortunate to be able to do this "work" - and that they were alive to receive it (many of my course mates had already lost their parents) However, we learned that it didn't really matter if they weren't alive – we could still work on the relationships because the work was "inner" work. On the other hand, if they were alive, there could be "outer" work because then there was an opportunity to improve our current relationships with our loved ones). The biggest thing I got from that first course was that they loved me - and that nothing had to change…just know that they loved me - no matter what. That might seem simple and clear. However, I didn't always know that - and therein lay the only problem!

Chapter 29
How Soon 'Not Now'
Becomes 'Never'
Martin Luther (1483-1546)

Back to my story about dad. At the time, I thought it was the beginning of his memoirs, and it was…only he passed on before we got very far. In his last year, working on his memoirs was the thing that drew dad and me much closer. What happened was, I got this idea of getting out mom's and dad's albums and going through them with dad. I discovered that many of their albums were already marked with details like "Date Taken", "Names" of people and "Places", as mom had kept up with that quite well. Then I came across three really old ones.

These were the personal albums that mom and dad had each created before they got together. mom had one album of her childhood pictures, through to her teacher training year, called Normal School in those days. dad had two albums, one while he was in high school and the other while attending the University of Saskatchewan. At first, we poured over his two earliest albums as dad exclaimed over different scenes when he saw old friends again. Dad's albums were both unmarked and here he was, 85 years later, pouring out names and dates to match up with all the pictures.

Seeing him do this gave me the idea to document the pictures with names of people, places and years - dad would speak into a little recorder, and then I would type it at home and have the typed pages ready to bring back the following week. Each week, we'd proof it and then produce some new tapes for me to repeat the process the following week. It blew me away that eighty some years later dad could still name almost everyone he saw. By the time we had finished going through the albums, there were very few unnamed people. He even remembered most of the people in mom's collection.

It was an honor to be in his company, seeing him do that and getting to be a part of it. It showed me just how much he loved mom to be so deeply entrenched in her life as to not only remember everything about her, but also all the people who had been a part of her life…and were in her albums.

"We got rolling along with his memoirs…"

Every once in a while, he would break out with a story that one of the pictures reminded him of. Again, I used the little recorder and transcribed it in the following week in between our visits. When we were done with his two albums, then we tackled mom's early girlhood album. Sometimes, we'd be working on a certain part and dad would get a brainwave to go back and re-do someone's name. At one point, dad said to me, "I hope your mother forgives me for the mixed-up job I'm doing on her album!" By the time we had finished the three albums, more stories were beginning to pop. Dad and I had a lot of fun doing this project - I loved to hear the stories, and they gave us a lot of good laughs.

But we were only just getting going when dad developed a bad cold .He insisted that he felt well enough to celebrate his Hundred-and-First birthday with my sister and me, along with a niece and nephew and a sister- and bother-in-law (my aunt and uncle) - just a few very close relatives. For the next couple of weeks, he wasn't well enough to go on his usual horseback ride, on which he had gone nearly every Wednesday for years. Consequently, he had missed celebrating his birthday with his horsy friends in the usual pub near the stable where he leased his horse. He leased his horse, now, because he was getting sensitive to outliving his horses and having to put them down.

It was understandable. Being a hundred years old, he had lived for an entire century. You don't have much in common with anyone left...and forming attachments and then outliving them is just too much (even if it's your horse). This particular stable, leased him one of their horses with the understanding that he would get the same horse every Wednesday, and otherwise, the stable could rent "his" horse out on any other day - it suited him perfectly.

One day almost three weeks after his birthday, he phoned me up in early November. He told me that he had just returned from the pub where all his horse-loving friends had taken him out for a belated one hundred first birthday lunch. He said he had even felt ready to ride again, but the weather was atrocious, and his riding companion, Sharon, and dad both agreed that they wouldn't ride that day. I think that they popped in to check on their horses (she kept her own horse there too) but just stayed in the stable, brushing and cleaning and doing odds and ends until it was time for lunch.

"His final thrill…"

Back to dad's phone call. He was thrilled that his horse friends had thrown a lunch party for him at his favorite pub. My dad was a very upbeat man, but even so, I hadn't heard him that excited for a while. His cold and no riding had held him down. However, even though he had seemed on the mend that day as he shared with me about his birthday lunch…even so, he took a sudden, downward turn and was gone within the week. On looking back, it seemed that after that final "horsy" celebration, he was complete with his life. He had done everything that he wanted to do, with nothing left undone, unsaid, and even though he could keep on creating his future…he did not…it was time for him to let go.

We found out later that technically, he had had a small stroke. My sister found him struggling to do a few things that he usually had no trouble with. Because he couldn't navigate easily, she called for an ambulance and had him taken to the hospital for doctors to establish what was wrong. There were a couple of hilarious stories about his time in the hospital. It wasn't all doom and gloom for him by any means.

I was privy to one of them – my sister to another. When I arrived at the hospital, I went into Emergency and asked for Mr. Rudd. The woman didn't respond to Dad's name, so I added, "He's over one hundred and…" The woman cut me off. Oh! you mean the man who rides horses. Come right this way.

The next day, my sister was standing near dad's bed and was talking with the doctor on call. This doctor was telling her something about old cars. Dad (who, up until then had been having trouble articulating his words) broke into their conversation and with really clear enunciation, set the doctor straight on some piece of information about old cars, and very animatedly told him proudly about a car he had owned back in the mid 20's…an old 1928 Oldsmobile Cutlass (or some such name). My sister and the doctor didn't let on their surprise to Dad, but they were both flabbergasted at his "pick up."

However, even though he didn't seem to us to be close to his end, he was gone by the next morning. He just went to sleep that night and didn't wake up again…November 20, 2008. My sister and her husband had a trip planned to see their kids and granddaughter in the east. We all decided that they should continue with their plans – it would give us all more time to prepare for his final "party."

We held Dad's memorial on December tenth, after they returned. There were about one hundred and fifty people there - some had flown in, relatives, partners in his chartered accountant firm, former students who had articled with his firm before graduating, friends of my sister and I, relatives, his "horsy" friends. A few relatives stayed with me (the same ones who had stayed with me a bit more than one year earlier when visiting for his one-hundredth birthday 'bash.' Even his horse attended - this was the stable owner's idea - plus he included a sweet touch that the owner knew of (an old cowboy tradition) - hanging dad's boots in the stirrups - to infer he died in the saddle!

To reiterate a couple of dad's final stats:

Dad was driving until just before his one-hundredth birthday…

And horseback riding until just after his one hundred first birthday…

And he died at one hundred one, one month and one day **October 19, 1907 to November 20, 2008.**

Chapter 30
Business In My Life

"My Reflections On Death…"

Having just finished talking about my father's final moments, I will pause for a bit…and talk about death as it directly affected me throughout my life. I was in my late 40's when my husband, Robert Boese died in 1985. He was the first major death that I suffered. Even though we were no longer living together, we were both very young (late forties) and still very connected…so that his loss was quite difficult for me to accept.

Then there were no more until my friend, Jhake Stokink died in 1998 in his late 70's. He had health problems and so it was not entirely a surprise. We were not living together anymore, but he was still a very close friend and confidante so, it was a big hole in my life.

Next was my Mother, Rose Emily Rudd, who died in 2006 at almost 95. Two and three-quarter years later, my Father, Robert Frances Rudd, died in 2008 at 101 years old. In one way, neither of their deaths was a surprise, but the loss of one's parents is always a shock at any age. Technically, I became the matriarch of the family…I say "technically" because in "reality," I looked up to my sister who was a couple of years younger.

Then there was my Aunt Lil Reimer in 2011. She was in her mid-90's too and therefore her passing was not entirely unexpected. However, I missed her a lot, too.

My first relationship following my husband was Val Contini. A mutual friend bumped into me on the street and told me that he had just recently learned that Val had passed away in 2015. I had lost touch with Val and was so sad I hadn't been able to visit him before he passed and also that I had to learn of his passing through a friend.

Most recently, Des Pratt, a really good dancing friend, died from an accident when on a holiday in his beloved home of New Zealand in early 2020.

The passing of each of these important people in my life all have had an impact on me. With each one, their passing caused me to reflect on my own life, and on life, itself. The reflecting, of course, is good - but often a little tough, emotionally.

I just felt a need to pause, reflect, and say a little about the passing of all these people who have impacted me hugely, but are with me no longer. Now I can move on.

"Business in My Life…"

I have had only a little exposure to the world of business, during my life. My initial entry into working was briefly as a teacher. My next exposure was my own business - although my husband and my father had handled the business end of it, and I had only been involved with the production end as well as designs and recipes. My next exposure to business had been the running of other people's business offices, their bookkeeping etc. Then there was my piano teaching business - a very simple kind of business. Network Marketing businesses over the years were also simple kinds of businesses.

A Real Estate investment business is a very complex business to run – with many legalities to take care of. On top of it all, I was very slow to learn the concepts - particularly about how to borrow and invest large sums of money. My family - father, sister, three children - all voiced their various concerns about me investing in real estate. One son thought

I should fully retire - just relax and enjoy my life. What he didn't see was that I was enjoying my life, immensely…particularly when studying and learning (which was real estate investment at that time). That was what enjoyment in life was for me.

I was always studying or exploring unknown territories. In addition to being involved in volunteering for Landmark Education and taking a few courses with them, I also spent time with family. Time with friends was almost non-existent at the time, an area where my priorities seemed skewed. I think my health was reasonably good, though my stress level was high, and that always works against one's health eventually. I managed to dance most days of the weekend which was good because I never went for walks nor did I do workouts in the gym.

"How I got interested in REI…"

My interest in REI (Real Estate Investment) began in 2006 when I read a local advertisement by Robert Allen's company. He is a real estate investment "guru" based in Utah. Well, I say it started there, but, in reality, it was probably a culmination of reasons. For one, other involvements had all come to an end about that time - and I wasn't satisfied with my finances, so I was on the lookout for a new source of income - although, for me to be interested; there had to be a strong service-to-people component.

I got a card in the mail, announcing their introduction evening. After attending, I signed up for a weekend starter course. There I met up with a woman from Abbotsford. She was a natural at REI (Real Estate Investment) having been interested and dabbling in it for many years. At first, we hobnobbed a lot. She was younger and a go-getter. She knew a lot about real estate investing and had many ideas. I had more time than knowledge so we were hopeful that we would be a good combination.

Our original intention was to become partners in some way. However, no matter how much I tried, I found that I just didn't know enough to help her. My lack of experience was making me more of a hindrance than a help. After almost a year, in August of '07, we joined BREIN, Bellingham's REI (Real Estate Investment) network and began attending monthly meetings. Within a year or two, because she had very little time to spend with me as a friend, and because I was causing her more time than I was saving her in her REI business, eventually, we went our separate ways.

"I took a look at the U.S. REI market…"

In Feb of 2007, I went on a little REI-based trip for about three weeks. It was hard for me to leave my dad for that long…but he assured me that he was okay with me taking the trip. I did feel a bit guilty though, even though I arranged for other family members to drop in on him. I also phoned him quite often while I was gone. To begin with, I flew to Chicago for Robert Allen's EWI (Enlightened Wealth Institute) five-day Conference. By then, I had done a few courses with EWI, read many of his books, and had an REI coach out of his Institute.

By this time, I was also connected with another company besides Robert Allen's, namely, Kurt Mortensen's Persuasion Institute. After the conference was over in Chicago, I took a commuter train to a little town in Iowa, straight south of Chicago, called South Bend, Illinois and I switched gears to an REI field trip led by a leader from the Persuasion Institute. The U.S. mortgaging disaster had already begun, and we evidenced whole streets and neighborhoods that were deserted like ghost towns. It was scary for me. However, people who were veterans in REI knew enough to be able to take advantage of these times. Being a 'newbie,' I still didn't have the nerve to jump into Real Estate Investment. But the timing was critical. I just wasn't ready for it and it was a missed moment.

After that, the game of REI stayed mainly the same, but it became subtly different, and it was over that difference that I couldn't seem to overcome my nervousness and fears...or gain the necessary confidence I was lacking. In hindsight, what I needed was a partner. However, when the woman from Abbotsford didn't work out, no one else just naturally appeared to fill that role. Moreover, I didn't actively pursue that: my loss...or just karma!

"A couple more courses before I admitted that REI wasn't for me..."

Later that same year, I took REI courses from a couple of different teachers. In 2008, I took my final REI course. This time around, it was from a Canadian trainer - and my eldest son agreed to do it with me. Before the year was up, following this course, I finally admitted that I was clearly never going to invest in real estate. I loved to learn about it, and the whole thing was exciting. But I didn't trust myself when it came down to the moment for investing. This was an honest admission that took a lot of courage to admit. I felt very guilty and like a failure for a while. Gradually, however, I realized the truth about REI for me - that there was nothing bad or wrong about it - it just wasn't a natural fit for me.

"Making money online – not for me either…"

However, my interest in REI had primarily begun from my desire to expand my income. Therefore, when it became apparent that I was not going to use REI to do that, I resurrected a home-study course on Making Money Online. I had purchased it a few years previously, with the thought that there could be something to it for me. My rationale was that I already was spending a lot of time online and making no money, and I wondered if it was possible that I could learn how to make money this way.

However, I discovered that the thinking was too new for me and I couldn't seem to get the hang of it either. Over three or four years, I made a few attempts at it from different angles. However, after a couple of years - and trying many avenues of making money online - I realized that I wasn't going to do it this way either.

"Network Marketing was a possibility...

There was a growing tendency for me to be dissatisfied with the amount of my income. All around me, there was a wave of interest and advertisements for being one's boss. I was a piano teacher, so I had some familiarity with having a business of my own. However, one type of business that has continued to interest me for over thirty years is called Network Marketing. Over the years, I had dabbled in many different network marketing companies...but never made any serious money.

I loved the concept, though, so I kept trying yet another one. The outcome was usually the same - that I became a better customer than I did at selling to others - and I always loved the team aspect...the friendships. A new network marketing company that came along in about 2009 was a self-healing company called Amega Global. Again, I loved the experience - and to this day I am a good customer – and very comfortable with following the Amega lifestyle (self-healing through healing tools). I was fairly successful with the Amega business for about five months. Then something happened to the company, which changed my relationship with it. Now, I value the quality of many of their products - but I have never been able to regain my confidence and enthusiasm for it as a company for doing the business.

That experience led me to an alkaline-based company, Seven Point 2, and again, I became a good customer. Then a new company, Seacret came to my attention – they have a skin care line (using Dead Sea minerals). Once again, I became a very good customer. However, have I said it enough yet…I don't enjoy the selling side of things…and therefore I made very little money in that industry.

"Trading stocks? Definitely not...!"

In 2011, I ventured into the area of trading stocks - but it didn't take me long (less than six months), to see that this wasn't for me, either.

"Write my memoirs? Possibly…"

I didn't think that writing my memoirs would make me any money. However, I had been dabbling with writing my life stories since 2011 (nothing very strenuous). I was strongly drawn at times to write down my memories…but weeks (or even months) would go by with no writing. It took me until late 2012 - after I had pulled out of all other projects and ventures – before I got seriously into my writing. Then my writing grew in both time and amount. Writing turned out to be far more peaceful than any other activity I had explored previously. A quieter pace is both possible and natural as a writer; there's no study or research necessary (at least in my kind of writing) and no pressure. At first, writing was highly stressful because I would sit down all prepared to write - and nothing would come.

However, I was committed to making it work and eventually, I learned how to drop into my writing more quickly each time I came to it. Previously I had been wasting so much time trying to find where I had stopped (because I wasn't working in a continuous fashion…rather, I was jumping around). I noticed that it was easier to find my place next time, if I created a marker at the end of my work, writing down a unique phrase in my final sentence that I could record and then use the "find" function to quickly re-discover it the next time. Also, I found it helpful if I wrote down any ideas that were in my head about the direction I was heading just before I quit. Things radically improved after I used these simple techniques to get me started.

Since that time, I have explored many other Online Marketing models - usually beginning with a program that supposedly, if I followed it, I would then begin to make money from my new business (which has never happened until very recently). Meanwhile, I have immensely enjoyed the learning and exposure to new ways of doing business! At about the one-year mark after I had joined my "romantic" partner in White Rock, I found I had a lot of time on my hands and that was when I began seriously to explore Online Marketing.

This is such an enormous field that there is basically no end to its possibilities - except if you quit...which I have many times, only to find my interest piqued once more - and then wane. This has become an on-going pattern by now for the past ten or more years! Now, as I am nearing the end of my book writing, I am finding my interest is growing once again.

This is 2018…I'll see!

"Postscript…"

Moving right along…this is now October 2020…First, I got seriously slowed down in my writing until recently (in the past year and a half). I've done about three "edits" of my book in that time…with more writing jumping out at me with each edit. Now I've just completed a final edit during Covid-19 because I have had an unexpected amount of free time. I feel very compassionate towards all who are suffering during these months of lockdown (early March to June). People have lost loved ones, businesses, jobs so there is a lot of anguish over loss and change. In addition, a lot of people are very lonely in these times. So far, I have been blessed and things are comparatively easy.

My daughter shops for me which is extremely generous and gives me even more time. All my children, friends, and relatives phone a lot - cutting down on my chances to be lonely. Now, in western Canada, we are not in 100% lockdown…I can go out in the world a little, maintaining self-isolating practices using the 2 meter rule and a mask if I go into a store (but mostly I still take my daughter up on her standing offer to shop for me).

In these Covid-19 times and largely as my way to cope with all the extra time on my hands as well as to ward off boredom…I began to explore an online business that I had only just begun in early 2020. I was proceeding slowly, and rather skeptically, after all these years of trying to make money online and to no avail. As I'm completing this final editing, I have a partner for my/our online business. I met him because we were both in the same program, but more than that, we were in a weekly support group and developing our online businesses as part of this program…back prior to Covid-19.

We approached each other to see if the other would like to partner together. We were of like minds. We hadn't figured out all the details by any means…but we were mutually interested in partnering. Together, we opened a little online shop and made modest sales almost immediately, following this program that had been guiding both of us. Then Covid-19 happened and it wasn't long before our suppliers couldn't fulfill our orders as their supplies dried up, and our little shop went slowly downhill, and our sales profits went out the door in Refunds. The downside is we lost money, and the upside is that I know now that I can make money online.

In the past couple of months, we have started up two more ventures (neither of them have physical products or shipping which was the source of our downfall before). Both are almost ready to launch on-line. It has been a huge learning curve (which always seems to be the way with any of my projects) and is lots of fun (which I'll "blame" my partner for)! Because my book is complete (at least the writing is), it won't be possible to let you know if my/our latest online businesses succeeded. But I am now unstoppable, having gotten a taste of success at long last! So that you can assume I will win at my latest adventure, Online Marketing…and soon! I'm now 81 (almost 82) so I have no time to lose!

Oh oh…don't get me started. There are many more pages wanting to burst out of me on that topic…but I've got to draw the line somewhere!

Chapter 31
Another Look At My Health

Because my health, over the years, was both an interest as well as a concern, my on-going health saga has certainly been a testament to the adage that "without health, you have nothing!"

The years in between thirty-two and seventy-two, after my health had restored itself (which was a miracle), were largely uneventful years, health-wise, with only minor blips from time to time.

However, in order to maintain this level of good health over the years, I have followed a lot of strict guidelines to ensure my wellbeing. But when I hit seventy, I found it was taking even more diligence…and at about seventy-two, in spite of my care, my health took a nose-dive. I was hit at a muscular level (that was a new one for me - usually it has been a bad cold and cough).

This time, I couldn't stand up easily - or once standing, I had difficulty in getting my legs engaged. I would shuffle at first, and then take small steps until I got myself going. There was no kneeling, no playing on the floor with my young grandson, no dancing. This was when I discovered TCM (Traditional Chinese Medicine) and drank a Chinese herbal tea twice a day for a couple of years. In addition, I had a good dose of Physiotherapy. After some months of these two routines, this combo got me back dancing - and up and down easily off the floor again! This all took me the better part of a year.

Then my health was good for about four years until October of 2016 (just before my 78th birthday) when it plummeted again. This time was one of my worst - a very scary health crisis that was quite different from the previous one (which had been almost entirely a mobility crisis). First came a month of vertigo - the dizziness and ensuing nausea were both scary and hard to manage – it took a few days in the hospital to discover what it was and what to do to overcome it.

In a month or two, this passed…but soon it was followed by a bad cold that ended up with a choking, convulsive cough. I was afraid to go dancing. In addition, we had a lot of snow and cold weather for months which was too uncomfortable to be out in with my sensitive throat - and dangerous with my balance issues that remained from my earlier vertigo. Western doctors couldn't find anything wrong - they all had different suggestions - but no one gave me any drugs stronger than a cough medicine or lozenges (and that approach didn't stop anything)! I was scared and upset and seriously run-down. This lasted four or five months. By about the fifth month, I had improved - but not back to the level of good health that I was used to. I began to wonder if I would perhaps never get back to square one - and if maybe I was showing the signs of my age and re-setting at a lower health level.

About this time, a very good friend said she'd like to share something with me that she thought might possibly be my answer…and of course I was interested. For a few months, she had been doing her own researching and experiencing a new way of eating and was very pleased with the results she had already achieved with a couple of health complaints that she had been dealing with, unsuccessfully with other more traditional methods (and even some alternative health methods).

My friend told me that she was hopeful that this same approach would also be the answer I was looking for. She said it was called a "Lectin Free Diet," developed by Dr. Steven R. Gundry (formerly a heart surgeon and researcher). He had been looking for something to improve his own health (persistent weight gain had been the personal health issue that had sent him researching to find a solution). His resulting diet would help any health issue, proclaimed Dr. Gundry. My friend concurred - because she had found it helped an entirely different symptom for her. She loaned me Dr. Gundry's book, The Plant Paradox, which outlined all the ideas behind it, and included a detailed Diet Plan and Recipes to support the Lectin-Free way of eating.

Because I had grown up in a strong family, I had learned always to be a fighter and never let anything bring me down. I rarely let anything get to me - even the asthma I was born with. Asthma or not, this hadn't stopped me from much - nor knocked the bounce out of me. Even though I missed about 90 school days in my first year, I kept up with my year's work with the help of my mother (an ex-teacher) who went weekly to my schoolteacher to get the work I had missed! Thankfully, I missed fewer and fewer days each year - and had, fortunately, outgrown my asthma by my early twenties when I became pregnant with my first child. Moreover, this was not the only health challenge I had as a child. Other medical issues abounded, including a ridiculous number of allergies - although they cannot be called real allergies because those would have resulted in a severe reaction requiring me to go to the hospital to get a shot - or stabbing myself with an Epi-Pen. Rather, the sensitivities that I had, resulted in minor inconveniences like earaches, coughs, rashes, sore throats, wheezing and sneezing. These usually went away when I removed myself from the presence of the undesirable object - or stopped eating the bothersome food. Or they wore me down, resulting in a cold and lots of coughing.

Although the after-effects were not usually excessive and merely inconvenienced me, I suppose some of them could have been quite deadly if I had been overexposed. This was brought home to me about a year ago when I had a reaction that caused me to choke and not be able to get any air for about twenty seconds…that felt like an eternity. In that moment, I was afraid I was heading for an untimely death. Fortunately I did not die (as an aside, I doubt that I came even close to dying) but at that moment, I had a premonition of my end - unless I was able to improve my throat and lung condition that had led to these continuous, convulsive coughing fits.

These had been going on for a few months and I was feeling in despair - and very rundown. It was around this time that my close friend had put me in touch with the unusual (and strict) diet plan that I mentioned a bit ago - called the Lectin-free Diet - and she was very curious if it might be my answer. Initially, it was my memory of these months of the racking cough, plus my friend's belief…that inspired me to try and stick with this diet to see if it would eliminate the cough altogether. Yes, my coughing spasms were occurring less and less - but they were still happening - and still scary because of my inability, sometimes, to get my breath for a few seconds.

I was in this despondent frame of mind when my friend loaned me her book. Nothing that my doctors had suggested seemed able to take me beyond this state that I was now in. Feeling that I had nothing to lose - and possibly a lot to gain - I opened the pages of this book, the Plant Paradox by Dr. Steven R. Gundry. He called his diet a Lectin Free diet…and he recommended following a Stage One diet for three months. He further recommended doing a brief assessment after four weeks, and if some changes had occurred - but not as much as hoped for - then continue for sure until the eight-week mark and assess again. At this point, I was to consider keeping on going for twelve weeks before moving into a Stage Two diet selection.

I read quite a few pages, but soon became impatient and found myself jumping ahead to the practical diet and recipe pages. Eight weeks was the trial period recommended by the "Lectin-free" diet's creator, Dr. Steven Gundry. He said that eight weeks was long enough to give a person at least a sense of improvement from the diet. He had encouraged us in the beginning to make a list of our health issues and then to take stock each week to see where these issues stood. At the eight-week mark, we were to decide if there were improvements - and if the progress was sufficient to warrant keeping on going for another month or so.

Initially I had decided to rigorously follow the diet, because it seemed to me that if I didn't follow it exactly, I wouldn't know which was to blame: me for not being exact; or the diet not being right for me. I did well, following it for the 4 weeks and at that point was blown away by the fact that I was already feeling better in my throat. My coughing was also much improved. Therefore, it was easy for me to decide to continue to follow it for at least four weeks more…just as rigorously as before. However, even though my health was not perfect yet, I now had a much more powerful arsenal to use to inspire, empower and motivate me to both regain and retain my health:

One, my success - the already outstanding results in the eight short weeks' trial.

Two, my memory of the previous winter's horror.

Three, my commitment to my health and therefore to follow the diet.

Four, this new knowledge about an optimum way to eat, i.e. food free of the allegedly poisonous (for humans) substances called "lectins."

Any one of these four tools or qualities are powerful. Applying them all at once was more than I needed!

I have always been in tune with my body, being able to connect certain responses to certain causes. For example, within an hour of eating something that bothered me, I was often able to feel the reaction. This degree of sensitivity might seem to be a curse. However, on the contrary, it turns out to be very helpful - most people can't feel the effect of a food they have just eaten so they have to rely entirely on the scientific allergy test model (which does not happen to be 100% accurate) to discover their sensitivities. Or they can just follow the Lectin-free Diet 100% and get the success they get - but have no idea from which specific food(s). However, to my way of thinking, this is a huge success in itself.

At first, I wasn't always that aware, either, so that by the time I experienced the reaction, too many other foods or smells or pollens etc. had occurred in between. However, my awareness pinpointed the bothersome food often enough for me to be able to zero in on many of the culprits. Over the eight weeks, my awareness increased so that I was able to pinpoint more accurately - and sooner - exactly which food had bothered me - I was certainly quicker and more accurate than in the beginning.

In future, when I am willing, it could be helpful to put myself through a final test period with any suspect foods. Even though they are on Dr. Gundry's "YES" list, or his "Eat In Moderation" list, there are a few "YES" foods that I am suspicious of. I would add only one new test food at a time in a five-day period. This would help me isolate the personally bothersome foods that I am wondering about. At this point, I don't plan to test any of his "NO" list of foods to see if I can eat them without reaction - most of them make sense and I have little to no doubt about those not being good foods for me!

At the end of the 8th week, I concluded there had been enough progress to be satisfied, but also not quite as much as I hoped for yet, and so I decided to keep on going…and at the time of writing this, I have passed the two year, nine month mark…and still going strong! At the end of the eighth week, I was getting comfortable with the foods and the routines. After that, I explored the rest of the YES list, adding a few new things to my daily fare. But what I have found is that the initial Phase I diet is where my health is most free of health issues - and therefore, where I have happily settled. Any expansion of that is only for a bit of variety and more like a treat…and then I settle back again to my Phase 1 way of eating. I'm lucky, I guess, that I don't need much variety.

If I like a food, I don't get bored with it. But if you are someone who needs variety - and lots of it - Dr. Gundry has produced at least one recipe book that I think could keep you happy for a long time - The Plant Paradox Cookbook, for one. You might wonder why I am almost obsessively passionate about my health. I think it's simply because I love life - and my life in particular. I feel that I have a lot to lose… or gain and look forward to if I am in good health. One obvious example is that I have three children…a boy, a girl and a boy…plus I have two grandchildren. I love them all dearly and still have a great deal more to be there for in their lives.

I also have a tremendous curiosity and passion for knowing all there is to know about health (particularly how it relates to my own health) and life. The latter keeps me always interested in meeting new people, having deep conversations, researching new ideas (particularly related to my health) as well as being very open to service (though, not formally). For me, serving people is always spontaneous and varied - an attitude, a way of being, "where I come from" so to speak. It can happen anywhere and most often is complete in a single interaction. Sometimes these are offers such as to look up information that, during our conversation, I became aware would be useful.

Or to meet again at a dance lesson so I can introduce them to the instructor and make sure they have a smooth entry…and usually in these cases, join the lesson if the "leads" (usually men) and "follows" (most often women) are missing a partner. To complete the interaction/offer, I usually offer an exchange of cell phone numbers so that we can text later if other questions come up. The places I most commonly meet these people are in my swing dance clubs, on buses or in shops as I go about my daily business - and sometimes amongst family members.

Here are a few other examples to give you an idea what "service" means to me when it takes place over a bit more time. One example is my hairdresser who was expressing a problem she had with her approach to her painting - I have no idea how we got onto that. She shared that she would feel pretty good about the picture she had just painted…but at the same time she would think that it was a bit weak and that there was just one thing she should change - something she should add. But as soon as she took a few brush strokes, she could see that she had already done too much and she had ruined it - it no longer had the misty or whatever other pleasing look about it. She said that that same thing would happen again and again.

After hearing of her plight, I said that if she would like, I would get in touch with her the following Monday (her day off and therefore her painting day). I would text her and remind her to be careful not to overwork her painting that day. So that's what I did the following Monday. When she received my text, she took a picture of what she had done so far…and sent it to me. I texted her back, "I think your painting is beautiful and very peaceful. She thanked me for my feedback and confessed that she had just been about to take some more brushstrokes which would have ruined the pastoral feeling she was aiming to achieve. Every once in a-while I text her on a Monday to check in with her. She told me the other day that she is beginning to hear my voice in her head and is able to prevent herself from ruining what she had already successfully achieved! We had a good laugh over that.

Another was a young woman in her late 30's that I met on the bus. Somehow, we got around to talking about playing the piano and she confessed it was her dream - but she couldn't seem to get started. Her boyfriend even had a good piano and often urged her to sit down and play, but she felt too self- conscious to do that. Before I retired, I had been teaching piano and I had noticed how difficult it seemed for adults to follow and succeed at this particular dream.

I invited her to look me up and consider coming over to my place (we had discovered that we lived really close to each other) and get a little bit of a coaching session on my piano. It took a while - but finally she did, and we really had a lovely hour together. I looked her up the other day, not having heard from her for a while and learned that her circumstances had entirely changed: she had parted company from that boyfriend (who had the piano) so she doesn't have a piano to practice on any longer. Now she's thinking of learning to play a guitar – it's cheaper, needs little space and is more versatile. I will keep prodding her until she learns a musical instrument - or strikes it off her Wishlist and moves on to the next item!

There have been four Korean young men that I met, over time, on the dance floor at one of my three swing clubs. None knew the others - they were all here in Vancouver at different times to learn to speak English. Apparently, the Korean government has strong assistance programs for those wishing to use their English proficiency in business when they return. My offer was the same to each one - to meet at a coffee shop or before a dance (etc.) and just converse. Perhaps we'd look up the odd word or expression (idioms were the toughest to learn), but mostly just talk. Two of them enjoyed the "meet-ups" the most - and in the end, using my extra support, learned to speak English quite fluently before both had to return home to Korea. I still stay in touch with them. One phoned me the other day and we talked for a couple of hours (he is married and has a three-year old daughter by now).

My latest "service" project came upon me unexpectedly. She was a long-ago girlfriend of my youngest son. One day about a year or so ago, my son asked if I would be willing to give his friend my old phone - hers wasn't working and mine - although somewhat old - still worked. I agreed. When I met her soon after, I was overcome with sadness at how her health and life had sunk to such a low level. Over the following weeks, I found ways that I could help her. She had so many needs that I tended to stay too long and give more than was best for my health and energy...but because I could...I did! What is gratifying, is that I can see - and hear

- the difference I make for her so that by now, she is able (and motivated and inspired) to look after many more of her personal needs. She even has an improved health so that she is able to create dreams of her own and has energy to bring them about.

About my "step-son" as I call him (really, he is my husband's 4th child with a different mother) – I taught him to play the piano. He has been my star pupil - practiced about an hour, almost daily, for the better part of two years. He just "gobbled up" my support (one of my most gratifying "pupils").

Also, my granddaughter has often reached out for my musical support over the past seven or eight years…piano, theory, singing - and quite often we go walking and talking because I live close to a beach walk - and we return to my home-made dinner afterwards. Moreover, she is able to unload her troubles - and as a young woman, it is a time of life when there are many - and she trusts me to keep her sharing in confidence. We are both grateful for our times together!

Many have told me that I seem a lot younger than eighty. Part of it is because of my way of eating - but I'm sure it's more that I am an outward and forward-looking person. Whereas too many people my age have retired and are quietly waiting for their end to come! They don't realize that they are a goldmine of knowledge and that at this time in their life, they finally have the time to give themselves to others. It seems to be reciprocal - as I give time and energy to others, I receive it back in return - and then some. Moreover, I notice that I don't feel used up but rather, the opposite...filled up, fulfilled!

Appendix I - Alternative Medical Practices and Services

I have laid out, in a descending order of their importance for me (not necessarily the most effective for you - healing is very personal), medical practices and services that I experienced over the past 40 plus years. There are others that I have not tried at this time, but this will give you some idea - and you can research more deeply, any that interest you.

ALLOPATHIC MEDICINE - it is basically western medicine and because I had grown up with it, I was inclined toward that for my first 30 years - and now, only for emergencies, or lab analysis (I have to pay for medical coverage, therefore I can utilize this system, but I only do it when it is useful for my understanding of my health).

FITNESS PROGRAMS - I have a lot to say about this. I realize this category doesn't belong in a list of "alternative medicine." However, it is a method that people use to achieve, or maintain, their health. That's why there are so many to choose from: Gym based, (with or without a personal trainer); Jogging; Rowing club; Aquatic based; Yoga, on your own or in a class; Martial arts; and more).

Signing up for one of these types of fitness programs is the most common approach of people as an attempt to take care of their health. Over the years, I sank a lot of money into gym programs. They always seemed like a good idea, but I didn't ever get very far before I found myself not sticking with them. I've even tried having a personal fitness trainer but that also fizzled. I don't really know why they don't work for me - but I'm clear that they do not.

Dancing was another story - there was no problem remembering to go - or not having the energy. Sometimes it was even the other way around - I would be very tired...and go regardless. The moral of this story is, there is no best exercise except the one that you will stick with! Sometimes it just has to make sense...like my 20-minute walking rule. This came out of the osteoporosis clinic I attended monthly for 3 years. The doctor who ran the clinic said I had to exercise daily - that 3 hours of dancing once a week was not sufficient...it didn't need to be much - but 20 minutes was needed daily. For the first time, exercise made sense and I promised myself I'd walk for 20 minutes daily - but usually that expands to 30 or even 60 minutes. I don't mind walking per se - it's the idea of stopping what I'm doing that is the hardest part. On a dancing day, I don't usually walk - but on the other days, if I have not been out walking by evening, I go at least before bed - that's my personal rule…and I have followed this ever since (seven or eight years at this time).

Enough about Fitness.

CHIROPRACTIC MEDICINE - this focuses on the treatment of diseases and conditions by manipulation of the spine. Chiropractors train at special colleges and are subject to a regulatory body that has been set up by the government to ensure quality and public safety. Over the years I have experienced many of their different approaches with a lot of success.

TRADITIONAL CHINESE MEDICINE (TCM) - as its name implies, this, came out of China and has long traditions. It includes everything from herbal teas to herbs to various practices for treating health. There are many Herbal shops in Chinatown that sell herbs that, to this day, still come from China. There are a few new herb farms that are growing some of the main Chinese herbs, but it takes time for these new herbal farms to get established. Trained TCM practitioners prescribe herbal prescriptions that the Herb shops can fill for people - in much the same way that north

American Allopathic physicians prescribe and pharmacies fulfill. TCM includes many different physical practices such as Acupuncture that has been a part of Chinese tradition for at least 2,500 years. The practitioner uses special needles to achieve the desired result. Moxibustion and Cupping are also popular TCM practices. Chinese herbal teas and Moxibustion are the ones that have given me the most benefit.

NATUROPATHIC MEDICINE - it is an alternative health care system, emphasizing prevention of disease; and utilizing treatments and natural substances that encourage individuals' inherent self-healing process. The naturopathic physician acts to identify and remove obstacles to healing and recovery, and to facilitate the self-healing process. Since total health also includes spiritual health, many encourage individuals to pursue their personal spiritual development.

AYURVEDIC MEDICINE - this is an alternative health practice that came out of India where it has been around for thousands of years. It focuses on the mind-body connection, using natural healing methods and is based on the belief that health and wellness depend on a delicate balance between the mind, body and spirit. Its main goal is to promote good health, not fight disease.

REFLEXOLOGY - it is based on the theory that there are connecting points in the feet for the entire body and that the correct sort of massage of the feet can relieve a person from pain and improve health to specific areas of the body.

IRIDOLOGY - this is based on the theory that by studying the eyes of a person, it is possible to diagnose illness through them.

That was the bulk of the health practices that I have discovered and experienced over the past upwards of forty years. There are other health approaches and with the Internet, can be easily discovered and explored...as well as exploring many more details about the above health practices.

***********END OF APPENDIX I***********

Appendix II - Health Diets

This list is only a beginning - I gave each diet an over-simplified definition - and this is a mix of my experience and knowledge (or lack thereof)! I recommend you go searching for more diets and to verify details for any of the below-mentioned diets that interest you (I found Wikipedia's list of Healthy diets to be enlightening)!

VEGETARIAN - Fresh fruit, vegetables and nuts form most of this diet - plus eggs and milk products (everything except for meat, poultry, and fish).

VEGAN (they are purist and don't agree with the inclusion of eggs or milk). They eat only food that does not come from animals - therefore, largely fruit, vegetables and nuts.

GLUTEN-FREE - anything goes, content-wise. It means avoidance of gluten foodstuffs - but there's no agreed-upon list of the grains that are included (or not) in this category.

LECTIN-FREE - avoidance of lectin proteins that are in hulls, seeds, skins, and seeds of fruits, many nuts and seeds and some seedy veggies such as cucumbers and legumes. It is a diet that Dr. Steven R. Gundry, M.D. has formulated that avoids lectins because of their negative effect on human health.

PALEO - high meat and fat, plus vegetable and fruit diet (low carbohydrates, no sugar).

KETOGENIC - another name for the Paleo diet - when weight loss is the focus of the diet.

FRUITARIAN - only fruit is eaten.

BREATHARIAN - water only plus exercises that intensify deep breathing.

There are other diets that I haven't named - mostly out of ignorance, rather than of lack of importance. Most of these are specialty diets with specific practices involved, like the Atkins diet…and many more.

Rarely is one particular diet best for a person for all time. As I see it, our diet is in constant flux and is ever changing and evolving to keep up with our changing health and age and stage of life.

************ END OF APPENDIX II*********

www.ingramcontent.com/pod-product-compliance
Lightning Source LLC
Chambersburg PA
CBHW031040110426
42740CB00047B/746